Readings on Language and Literacy:
Essays in Honor of Jeanne S. Chall

Readings on Language and Literacy

Essays in Honor of Jeanne S. Chall

Edited by
LILLIAN R. PUTNAM, Ed.D.
Professor Emeritus, Kean College of New Jersey

BROOK
LINE
BOOKS

Brookline Books

ISBN 1-57129-039-7

Library of Congress Cataloging-in-Publication Data
Readings on language and literacy : essays in honor of Jeanne S. Chall / edited by Lillian R. Putnam.
    p.   cm.
    Includes bibliographical references and index.
    ISBN 1-57129-039-7 (pbk.)
    1. Reading–Congresses.   2. Language arts–Congresses.
3. Literacy–Congresses.   I. Putnam, Lillian R.   II. Chall, Jeanne
Sternlicht, 1921-   .
LB1050.R427   1997
428'.4–dc21   97-11360
                                      CIP

Interior design and typography by Erica L. Schultz.

Printed in Canada by Best Book Manufacturers, Louiseville, Quebec.

5 4 3 2 1

Published by
BROOKLINE BOOKS
P.O. Box 1047
Cambridge, Massachusetts 02238
Order toll-free: 1-800-666-BOOK

Contents

Editor's Preface

Dr. Jeanne S. Chall: Her Contribution to the Field of Reading Instruction

LILLIAN R. PUTNAM, Ed.D.
Professor Emeritus, Kean College of New Jersey

From her early research and publications on readability in 1958 to three papers on research currently in press (1996), Jeanne Chall has been a continuously prolific writer for 38 years. Her publications include 15 major books, 6 comprehensive research reports, 4 reading tests, and over 200 articles and papers.

But far beyond the impressive numerical count is the unusual, superior quality of all her work. Always acknowledging former research, always basing her work on sound theory, always penetrating to the core of a problem, she brings a unique blend of practical experience and intellectual acumen to her writing.

An appendix to this book (p. 306) contains a brief biographical sketch of her honors and appointments, and a selected sample of her copious list of publications.

Foreword

A Tribute To Jeanne Chall

FLORENCE G. ROSWELL

Professor Emeritus, City College, City University of New York

It is a privilege to contribute to this book honoring Jeanne Chall for her long and distinguished career.

Jeanne has been a very close friend and respected colleague for many, many years. I first met Jeanne when she joined the City College faculty as a young instructor. From the very beginning, it was apparent that Jeanne was a deeply committed young woman who had vision and a clear grasp of some of the pressing needs in the teaching field, and who was succeeding admirably in meeting those needs. Indeed, her imprint on education has been immeasurable and far-reaching, covering a broad spectrum. Her many roles have included:

- dedicated teacher
- caring mentor to graduate students
- innovative researcher
- valued consultant to school systems, government agencies, and educational groups
- author of scholarly books and other publications
- capable clinician
- engaging lecturer
- ready advisor to all who have sought her wise counsel

As an expression of their appreciation and in recognition of their devoted professor, Jeanne's former doctoral students (who are now making their own impressive mark in education) and Jeanne's other colleagues and friends wrote this book.

Throughout the years, Jeanne and I have maintained a warm, friendly relationship. We enjoyed collaborating on various projects at City College and then, later, on developing reading tests and co-authoring a book.

And so, dear Jeanne, I say "Thank you," as I voice the sentiments of all those on whom you have had such a profound, constructive influence: teachers, students, children, parents, colleagues, friends, administrators, and through them, the many connections to future generations.

Introduction

In Honor of Jeanne S. Chall

ROSELMINA INDRISANO, Ph.D.
Boston University

It is a privilege beyond my capacity for adequate expression to have been invited by my friend Dr. Jeanne S. Chall to introduce her on this auspicious occasion.*

For several months, I have been searching for the words that would do justice to our remarkable friend and colleague, beginning with the inscription on the plaque that will be given this evening, and concluding with this introduction. To aid my search, I reread Dr. Chall's major publications and her extraordinary curriculum vitae. And with each reading, one word, timely to this season, recurs — thanksgiving. This evening, we who are her family, friends, and colleagues, on behalf of countless children, students, teachers, researchers, scholars, policy makers, statesmen, television producers, journalists, publishers, readers, and parents, gather to offer thanks for the gift of the life and legacy of Dr. Jeanne S. Chall. And we also offer thanks for the intellectual energy and commitment that drive her present work on several publications, which will give us all additional reasons for thanksgiving, now and in the coming years.

We begin by expressing gratitude to Dr. Jeanne Chall, the teacher and scholar. For more than 50 years, she has taught at colleges and

---

* This speech was originally delivered on the occasion of the awarding of the Samuel T. Orton Award to Professor Jeanne S. Chall by the Orton Dyslexia Society, in Boston, on November 8, 1996.

universities throughout the United States; 25 of those years were spent at Harvard University, where she was also the director of a reading laboratory that served as a model for those that followed.

I am fortunate to be able to offer a first-person report of Dr. Chall, the gifted teacher. Following her appointment as professor emerita at Harvard, we at Boston University were grateful to have her join us as a visiting scholar to teach her legendary course on the history of reading research. During the first course session, the students learned that when Dr. Chall teaches, she is concerned with the nourishment of the body, as well as the mind and spirit. On the second session, and on other occasions when my schedule permitted me to join the group, I witnessed a feast for both the eye and the palate. One of the students quilted an elegant tablecloth to cover the conference table, and others took turns with food preparation in order to give a worthy presentation for their beloved teacher. In that seminar room, charged with the energy created by a rigorous teacher with encyclopedic knowledge and high standards, Dr. Chall made possible a weekly banquet for mind, spirit, and body.

When I think about Dr. Chall's legacy as a teacher, I think of lines from Robert Bolt's *A Man for All Seasons*. While guiding a young man to consider his future, Thomas More asks, "Why not be a teacher? You'd be a fine teacher. Perhaps even a great one." To this the young man responds, "And if I was, who would know it?" Thomas More responds, "You, your pupils, your friends, God. Not a bad public, that."

The public also thanks Dr. Jeanne Chall, the scholar. In a 14-page bibliography that accommodates only "selected" publications, there is an unprecedented number of books and reports that have had an influence as profound as any in the field. To name only a few: *Learning to Read: The Great Debate; Stages of Reading Development; Becoming a Nation of Readers; The Reading Crisis: Why Poor Children Fail in Reading; Readability Revisited: The New Dale-Chall Readability Formula;* and most recently, *Qualitative Assessment of Text Difficulty.*

Remarkably, Dr. Chall also found time to compile an equally rich record of leadership on academic and public service advisory boards, including membership on the board of advisors of the Orton Dyslexia Society and the boards of directors of the National Society for the Study of Education and the International Reading Association. She has been honored with election to fellowship status by the American Psychological Association and the National Conference on Research in English, and to the presidency of the Reading Hall of Fame. Dr. Chall has been called upon by a succession of presidents of the United States and secretaries of education to bring her wisdom to national literacy efforts. She has been an advisor to projects conducted under the auspices of the Office of Education, the National Institute of Education, the National Academy of Education, and Right to Read.

For these contributions and more, Dr. Chall is, by my estimate, the only person to be honored by every scholarly group in education in the nation, including the American Psychological Association, the American Educational Research Association, the International Reading Association, the National Conference on Research in English, the National Reading Conference, and, this evening, the Orton Dyslexia Society.

This record of accomplishment has been made possible by a unique blending of the finest qualities of the teacher and the scholar, qualities that reach their perfection in Dr. Chall. I recall the words of Frank G. Jennings, which might have been written just for her.

> Learning and teaching and study are the triple strands of the examined life. They are secure against accidental privilege. They shield solitude against loneliness. They enhance our uniqueness, defend our differences and place the power of equality at the service of the individual.

Let us now turn to Dr. Jeanne Chall, the visionary and the researcher. In reviewing her legacy to this date, we celebrate not only the range of topics that have engaged Dr. Chall, but also her capacity to identify these issues decades before others, and more importantly, her tenacity in pursuing more than a few of these long after louder, if less thoughtful, voices have proclaimed them unworthy. Consider this partial listing: the importance of phonics in learning to read; the plight of readers who through poverty or disability have yet to claim their right to literacy; and interdisciplinary insights into the processes by which we acquire the ultimate human achievement, the ability to read and write.

In one of the finest articles ever written about Dr. Chall, the distinguished journalist Muriel Cohen wrote in the Boston Globe on June 23, 1996, that Chall has:

> encyclopedic knowledge of a whole range of disciplines, having done research in psychology, sociology, linguistics, pedagogy, and history of education, all of which she regards as important to the understanding of how and why children learn to read.

I was fortunate to be among those interviewed for this article. When I was asked by Ms. Cohen how it is that Dr. Chall has been able to hold steadfastly and silently to her principles through times of appreciation and times of criticism, I suggested that it is due to Dr. Chall's unfailing courtesy and courage. She is the noble visionary, the meticulous researcher, whose regard for truth and those who depend upon truth is an unfailing guide to all who join her in the noble mission of education.

Listen to her own words written in the preface to *The Reading Crisis:*

> It is common today, as in the past, to look elsewhere than to educational research for an understanding of the literacy problems of low-income children and for ways of solving these problems. Currently, cultural and political theories are offered as reasons for the low achievement of poor children and for the lag between mainstream and at-risk children. Although cultural and political explanations may help us understand the broader picture, in the end they must be translated, in practical terms, into what can be done in

schools and in homes. Such translation ought to consider the historical findings of educational research — that good teaching improves achievement and thereby can empower all children and especially those at risk.

Now, I turn to Dr. Jeanne Chall, the sage and the friend. Saul Bellow has spoken and written of the wisdom of knowing which ideas are worthy of our attention, and which are mere distractions. Throughout her remarkable life and career, and to this day, Jeanne Chall knows what is worthy of attention and what are mere distractions. She attends tenaciously and courageously to important matters. In this achievement, she has no peer, but she is to all of us the model we emulate. And she demands of her friends the same high standard.

Let me offer an anecdote: When Boston University joined the Chelsea Public Schools in a partnership on behalf of teachers, children, and parents, I searched the literature for insights into the ways I might be helpful. There was only one person whose advice I sought: Jeanne Chall, who cares enough about children and truth to be able to criticize the plan of a friend of many decades. During one of our regular dinners at a restaurant in Cambridge where members of the Harvard faculty are often present, I presented my plan to my friend. When she began to question me in her direct, penetrating way, the people at the adjoining tables — obviously scholars themselves — stopped eating and leaned toward us as if observing a doctoral candidate at a final oral exam. After close listening and more questioning, she paused, thought, and finally declared the plan promising. Whereupon our neighbors nodded in satisfaction, smiled, and turned again to their dinners. Not surprisingly, the plan, characterized by serious teaching of critical skills and abilities, is working very well in the hands of our dedicated teachers.

As I am certain you understand, my challenge this evening was not to decide what I might say about the remarkable life and legacy of this extraordinary woman, but rather, what I might not say. And alas, there is too much still left unsaid. So I leave to each of you the joy of recalling your own abundant reasons for thanksgiving.

I am grateful for the privilege of sharing some of my own reasons for thanksgiving to Dr. Jeanne S. Chall, teacher and scholar, visionary and researcher, sage and friend. And, on behalf of all who are here this evening, and of the countless others who have been blessed by Dr. Chall's contributions, I quote the words of the bard of Stratford-on-Avon: "I can no other answer make but thanks, and thanks, and ever thanks."

1

The Legacy of the Dartmouth Seminar

JAMES R. SQUIRE, Ph.D.

Senior Vice President, Silver Burdett & Ginn

The Anglo-American Conference on the teaching of the English Language Arts held at Dartmouth College during August of 1966 was a watershed event that defined for years to come the nature and direction of professional dialogue on teaching and learning in the English language arts. Sponsored by the Modern Language Association, the National Council of Teachers of English, and the National Association for Teaching English in the United Kingdom, and supported by the Carnegie Corporation of New York, the Seminar brought together for four weeks some sixty scholars in English and English Education (literary scholars, linguists, rhetoricians, and psychologists); specialists in teacher education and curriculum development; and school supervisors and teachers.

Half the participants came from the United States, and half came from the United Kingdom. The Americans were flush with recent research and development funded by Project English of the United States Office of Education (Shugrue, 1968; Steinberg, 1963) and proud of the efforts to promote curricular change by the Commission on English of the College Entrance Examination Board (Commission on English, 1965). The British were excited about plans for their Schools Council and other national efforts to reform traditional schooling. The deliberations of the 60 permanent participants were supplemented by a dozen or so visiting consultants and speakers.

Through preliminary papers written to identify issues, plenary sessions (often debates), permanent task forces addressing specific topics, ad hoc committees, and reviews of recently developed curricula, the conferees debated the ends and means of curriculum and instruction.

Two specially prepared volumes officially reported on deliberations and recommendations. One was an account by an American historian of what happened at the conference (Muller, 1967); the other was a creative and personal construct of what it meant, prepared by a British specialist in English education (Dixon, 1967). Views on specialized topics were also published in a series of monographs issued by the National Council of Teachers of English (Squire, 1967; Olson, 1967). In addition, the Seminar strongly influenced the subsequent writing and speaking of many who attended.

To a large extent, the Dartmouth Seminar marked the end of the influence of many curricula developed at Project English centers, as conferees generally rejected the direction taken by Americans as a result of work sponsored by the U.S. Office of Education. But more important were the efforts that the Seminar either set in motion or prepared American specialists to consider. Five will be discussed here.

1. The Dartmouth Seminar established the importance of maintaining a continuing dialogue among professionals in English-speaking countries.

Prior to the 1966 conference, opportunities for American and British professionals to confer on the teaching of the English language arts were sporadic and unlikely to lead anywhere. To be sure, an Anglo-American conference was called during the NCTE's Boston convention in 1964 (Squire, 1965), but that event was part of the preliminary efforts that led to Dartmouth. Important results of the productiveness of the Dartmouth discussions were the subsequent efforts to engage British specialists in North American programs — in Connecticut; in

Calgary; in Tallahassee, Florida; at the Ontario Institute for the Study of Education in Toronto; and at the Bread Loaf English Conference in Vermont. In addition, Americans were involved in programs at universities in England. Thus, the work of James Britton, Nancy Martin, Harold Rosen, and the London Institute of Education came in time to influence teachers in North America almost as extensively as in England.

In time, too, teachers in other English-speaking countries became engaged in the international dialogue; this happened first in Canada as the result of the participation of three Canadians at Dartmouth, and then in Australia, New Zealand, the Caribbean, and South Africa. Formal international conferences were subsequently called in York (1971), Melbourne (1975), Ottawa (1980), Ann Arbor (1984), Auckland (1989), and New York City (1995).

The international discussions have opened teachers of the English language arts everywhere to considering new research and developments in various countries. Marie Clay's Reading Recovery Program (Clay, 1979; Pinnell, in press), for example, began in New Zealand but, as a result of the increased sensitivity to foreign models, found its way to Ohio State University and subsequently into many American schools.

In the aftermath of Dartmouth, Americans also were more ready to consider the implications of comparative school studies such as Squire and Applebee's analysis of outstanding British high schools (1969), Thorndike's comparison of reading achievement (1974), and Purves's comparative studies of response to literature (1974) and of writing (Purves & Takala, 1982). Whether these studies would have found so ready an audience in the United States without the precedent of Dartmouth is highly questionable.

2. The Dartmouth Seminar promoted curricular programs that focused on student growth and development.

In rejecting a curriculum based primarily on subject content, and in stressing student-centered growth and development, the Seminar promoted a view of curriculum that remains powerful to this day. John

Dixon's report on the conference, *Growth Through English* (1967), saw student development as central to school programs. James Moffett, a participant on leave from Exeter preparatory school, rewrote his book *An Integrated Curriculum in the Language Arts* (1969) as a result of his experiences at Hanover. These two books helped to define the concept of growth in English. Equally important was the understanding that began to emerge at the Conference that the theory of transformational grammar was less a subject matter to be imparted to students than an explanation of how children — particularly young children — began to develop competence in using language. This concept, furthered by other specialists' work on process, has led to the development of preschool and early school programs, particularly those focusing on the developmental stages of early literacy and language acquisition (Cazden, 1991). It has also fostered acceptance of the concept of stages of growth in writing abilities, as reported in the work of Britton, Martin, McLeod, and Rosen (1975).

3. The Dartmouth Seminar prepared Americans for the overt concern with the writing process that began during the early seventies.

In focusing on the integration of the language arts (reading, writing, speaking, listening, and responding to literature), conferees at Dartmouth paid unusual attention to the writing of children and young people. Those wishing to promote creativity in personal expression stressed the cruciality of personal writing.

The processes of composing had been a special concern of the Curriculum Study Center at Northwestern University, and its director, Wallace Douglas, formed at Dartmouth a quick alliance with British participants also alert to the writing process. The independent publication of Janet Emig's analysis of the composing processes of twelfth-graders (1971) occurred almost simultaneously with the publications from the conference and helped to define the view of the writing process that emerged from Dartmouth. Shortly thereafter, a conference at the State University of New York at Buffalo focused on writing and involved both Emig and several who were at Dartmouth. These speakers strongly influenced graduate student Donald Graves, whose subsequent work did more to promote initial concern with the "process of writing" than any other body of research (Graves, 1978; Calkins, 1983). The Dartmouth Seminar did not originate the concept of writing process, but its concern with student-centered activity, creativity, and growth prepared the way for the major curricular effort to follow.

4. The Dartmouth Seminar focused attention on the extent to which the teacher should "interfere" in language learning.

Perhaps the chief bone of contention between American and British conferees was the extent to which children should be allowed to engage in extensive reading, writing, and speaking experiences without instruction on skills and processes. Many of the British felt that if children were engaged in expression, they would develop their own insights and correct their own errors. Such views were particularly strongly expressed by Jimmy Britton (1970). Many Americans, on the other hand, felt that children would learn best with some teaching or coaching.

The differences were never fully resolved at Dartmouth, and the views expressed there presaged the argument during the next decade over the British infant school movement, and anticipated the bitter battles between skill-centered advocates and whole-language partisans that have enlivened American curriculum debates since the late '80s. Today the issue remains unresolved and is still the center of much attention.

5. The Dartmouth Seminar shifted the focus in curriculum development from literature to response to literature.

Prior to the Seminar, the teaching of literature had focused on the canon of great works that comprised the Anglo-American tradition (Commission on English, 1965), and on the critical and analytical skills through which young readers gained access to the works. Again, conferees at Dartmouth were more concerned about the student reader and his reaction to the work. "We need to reexamine the traditional canon to find those works which speak to young people today," asserted Harold Rosen, and most conferees agreed.

Examining how to help young people to respond with increasing sensitivity and depth became a major concern — especially given the participation of Denis Harding, Walter Loban, and James R. Squire, all of whom had been studying the responses of children to literature (Harding, 1968; Loban, 1952; :Squire, 1964).

Professional and scholarly interest in response, which continues to this day, was heightened by the publication of two important works: Purves and Rippere's (1968) studies of response (Rippere had been a consultant visiting the seminar), and Rosenblatt's seminal work on the transactions between reader and writer (1978).

Some of the developments described above would certainly have occurred without the Dartmouth Seminar, perhaps somewhat later or in a different form. But all of them were anticipated or influenced by the Anglo-American deliberations.

Dartmouth did not cover every important topic relevant to English language arts. Chief among the issues ignored at the conference — surprisingly, given the predilections of some of the conferees — were the social dimensions of teaching language and literature, the urban educational reform movement already underway in the United States, and the "Back-to-Basics" teaching movement that would soon become so pronounced in America during the early seventies. Nor did conferees at Dartmouth debate the need for multicultural, multilinguistic curricula in the English Language Arts; this was an issue to emerge later.

But let us focus on what was accomplished there. The participants at Dartmouth changed the direction of American curricular reform efforts in the language arts and created a direction that continues to animate those seeking reform. Theirs is a legacy of which the profession can well be proud.

References

Britton, J. (1970). *Language and learning*. Portsmouth, NH: Heinemann.

Britton, J., Martin, N., McLeod, A., & Rosen, H. (1975). *The development of writing abilities*. London: Macmillan.

Calkins, L. (1983). *Lessons from a child*. Portsmouth, NH: Heinemann.

Cazden, C. (1991). *Whole language plus*. New York: Teachers College Press.

Clay, M.M. (1979). *Reading: The patterning of complex behavior*. Auckland: Heinemann.

Commission on English. (1965). *Freedom and discipline in English*. New York: College Entrance Examination Board.

Dixon, J. (1967). *Growth through English*. London: Oxford University.

Emig, J. (1971). *The composing processes of twelfth graders*. Urbana, IL: National Council of Teachers of English.

Graves, D.L. (1978). *Balance the basics and let them write*. New York: Ford Foundation.

Harding, D.W. (1968). Response to literature: The report of the study group. In J.R. Squire (Ed.), *Response to literature* (pp. 11-27). Champaign, IL: National Council of Teachers of English.

Loban, W. (1952). *Literature and social sensitivity*. Urbana, IL: National Council of Teachers of English.

Moffett, J. (1969). *An integrated curriculum in the language arts*. Boston: Houghton Mifflin.

Muller, H. (1967). *The uses of English*. New York: Holt, Rinehart & Winston.

Olson, P. (1967). *The uses of mythology*. Urbana, IL: National Council of Teachers of English.

Pinnell, G.S. (in press). *Reading recovery*. In J. Flood, D. Lapp, & S.B. Heath (Eds.), *Handbook for literacy educators*.

Purves, A.C. (1974). *Literature education in ten countries*. New York: John Wiley.

Purves, A.C., & Rippere, A. (1968). *Elements of writing about a literary work*. Urbana, IL: National Council of Teachers of English.

Purves, A.C., & Takala, S. (1982). An international perspective on the evaluation of written composition. In A.C. Purves & S. Takala (Eds.), *Evaluation in education: An international review series* (pp. 207-290). New York: Harper & Row.

Rosenblatt, L.M. (1978). *The reader, the text, the poem: The transactional theory of the literary work*. Carbondale, IL: Southern Illinois University Press.

Shugrue, M.F. (1968). *English in a decade of change*. New York: Pegasus.

Squire, J.R. (1964). *The responses of adolescents while reading four short stories*. Urbana, IL: National Council of Teachers of English.

Squire, J.R. (1965). *A common purpose*. Urbana, IL: National Council of Teachers of English.

Squire, J.R. (1967). *Response to literature*. Urbana, IL: National Council of Teachers of English.

Squire, J.R., & Applebee, A. (1969). *Teaching English in the United Kingdom*. Urbana, IL: National Council of Teachers of English.

Steinberg, E.R. (Ed.). (1963). *Needed research in the teaching of English: Proceedings of a Project English research conference*. Washington, DC: Government Printing Office.

Thorndike, R. (1974). *Reading education in ten countries*. New York: John Wiley.

2

A Co-Teaching Model for Literacy Education

ROSELMINA INDRISANO, Ph.D.
Boston University

NANCY BIRMINGHAM, SHEILA GARNICK,
& DENISE KEEFE MARESCO
Chelsea Public Schools

In 1989, Boston University and the Chelsea Public Schools formed a partnership to join the resources of a large urban university with those of a small urban school district. The partnership was created when officials from Chelsea, Massachusetts, invited Boston University President John Silber to enter into a 10-year agreement to assist the school system in providing high-quality education for all students. This multifaceted project has been the topic of a themed issue of the *Journal of Education* (Indrisano & Paratore, 1994), a reference for the reader who is interested in learning about the partnership and its effect on teaching and learning in Chelsea.

This chapter is presented in four parts, beginning with an introduction to the Chelsea Public Schools and the partnership. The second section describes the collaborative efforts of university faculty (Roselmina Indrisano) and school faculty (Nancy Birmingham, Sheila Garnick, and Denise Keefe Maresco) that resulted in a co-teaching model designed to eliminate the separation between classroom instruction and Title I services. In the third part, the classroom teacher (Denise Keefe Maresco) and the Title I teacher (Nancy Birmingham) describe the way the co-teaching model is implemented in one first-grade classroom. Lastly, the Title I director (Sheila Garnick) describes the ways in which she assisted other teachers in implementing a model for literacy instruction and assessment in their classrooms.

The Chelsea Public Schools

Chelsea is an economically depressed, ethnically diverse community connected to the City of Boston by a bridge that intersects the metropolitan area. Less than two square miles in area, it is home to 26,000 people, 70 percent of whom are members of a minority group, primarily Latino and Southeast Asian. The majority of the students in the public schools speak English as a second language. Chelsea has a long history of providing a home for newly arrived immigrants whose hopes for their children begin with education.

When the partnership began, the students were attending school in century-old buildings, with the newest built in 1909. Books and materials were in short supply and were supplemented by purchases from teachers' own salaries. During these difficult years, decisions were made to sacrifice professional development opportunities so that the limited available funds could be allocated to the needs of students. As a result of the partnership, teachers and university faculty members now join in ongoing staff development activities, including topical seminars and classes, graduate courses, classroom demonstrations, and professional conference attendance and presentations.

---

* New schools were opened in September 1996.

The Partnership

As would be expected, the first consideration in planning professional development activities was to establish ways of working together. The university faculty members decided that the goals of the partnership would best be served by adopting a cooperative approach to professional development, so that each school and university faculty member could contribute her unique knowledge and experience. The rationale for this approach is described by Luis C. Moll (1992):

> ... no innovation has a realistic chance of succeeding unless teachers are able to express, define, and address problems as they see them, unless teachers come to see the innovation and change as theirs. The ultimate outcome of the innovation (or replication, we should add) depends on when and how teachers become part of the decision to initiate change. (p. 229)

Consistent with this decision, university faculty promised teachers that the goals for professional development would be set collaboratively, that their commitment would be constant for the full duration of the 10-year contract, and that designing innovations would involve constant "interplay between research knowledge and local knowledge" (Goldenberg and Gallimore, 1991, p. 2). For the teachers, the professional development activities offered opportunities to acquire or extend their understanding of the relevant classic and contemporary research in instruction and assessment. A second critical purpose of these activities was to build teachers' trust in the promise that the relationship between school and university faculty would be cooperative and equal. It was evident that the majority of teachers wanted change, but they needed to be involved in designing the changes and, ultimately, to determine which innovations they would adopt in their classrooms.

The first professional development activity was a series of 2-week institutes offered during the first summer of the partnership. Among the offerings was a literacy seminar taught by Roselmina Indrisano and attended by Sheila Garnick. It became obvious that each discussion, regardless of topic, returned to a single issue: the need to improve the coordination between classroom and Title I instruction in a school system where four of the five elementary schools are identified as Title I eligible. At the end of the seminar it was agreed that in the next academic year Indrisano would meet in weekly seminars with the Title I and the first- and second-grade teachers to develop a plan for integrating regular education and Title I services. A proposal to free Title I teachers for the professional development seminars was funded by the school system.

Although the initial plan for the seminars was limited to one academic year, at the end of that period the participants decided to continue the seminars for 2 more years. This change had two advantages: (1) given the goals that had been set, a 3-year time frame was more realistic; and (2) in accordance with the promised teacher involvement in planning and decision-making, more teachers would be able to participate during the next 2 years. In year 2, newly appointed first-, second-, and third-grade teachers joined the group, and in year 3 kindergarten and preschool teachers participated in the seminars. Denise Keefe Maresco and Sheila Garnick joined the group in year 1 and Nancy Birmingham joined in year 3. At the beginning of the seminars, three questions were adopted as a constant guide to decision making.

- Each person would ask, "Is this plan based on valid theory and research and appropriate for the students in Chelsea?"
- Teachers would ask, "Does this work in my classroom for the benefit of the students I teach?"
- University professors would ask, "If I were teaching in a classroom, could I make this plan work for the benefit of the students?"

The Collaboration

To develop a cooperative model for integrating regular education and Title I services, seminar participants selected three topics for study and development: literacy instruction, classroom organization, and literacy assessment. For each of the topics the sequence of activities was the same. First, the university faculty member reviewed the classic and contemporary literature for insights that would inform the work in Chelsea. Next, the information was translated into principles that link theory and research to practice, and these principles were discussed by the seminar participants with particular emphasis on the implications for classroom practice.

Informed by these principles, seminar participants developed plans that were "written in pencil" until teachers could subject the designs to the test of classroom effectiveness. As these trials were conducted in the classrooms, teachers noted their strengths and weaknesses and returned to the next seminar session to discuss their reflections. Based on the results of the trials, plans were adopted or revised; if revised, the new designs were subjected to classroom trials until the plans were deemed to be effective. As each aspect of the plan was completed, that part of the model was incorporated into the classroom programs, and the seminar group turned to the next topic.

When the model was completed, the seminar participants described their creation as a "co-teaching model" that eliminates the separation between regular education and Title I instruction. At the present time, the classroom teacher and the Title I specialist are co-teachers, equally responsible for planning, instruction, and assessment in the classroom setting. The elements of the co-teaching model designed in the seminar series are described in the order of their development.

Literacy Instruction

The instructional plan combines three elements validated by theory and research and deemed appropriate for the students in Chelsea. The elements are: explicit instruction (Rosenshine & Stevens, 1984), strategic teaching and learning (Paris, Wasik, & Turner, 1991), and the gradual release of responsibility (Pearson & Gallagher, 1983). Based on these elements, the instructional planning guide shown in Figure 2-1 (opposite) was designed.

The first element of the plan, *explicit instruction* (Rosenshine & Stevens, 1984), includes four processes:

- demonstration/modeling,
- guided practice,
- independent practice, and
- application.

At the beginning of the cycle of instruction, the teacher demonstrates or models a strategy — for example, how to determine the setting of a story. Using a think-aloud approach, the teacher introduces the definition of "setting," reads the appropriate section of the story aloud, and identifies the setting. Then the teacher invites the children to ask questions about the definition and the example she has given. Their questions and the teacher's observations suggest the next steps in the instructional sequence; for example, the teacher may repeat the demonstration using other examples.

When the children's responses indicate that they understand the concept of setting and are familiar with the strategy for identifying the setting, the teacher provides guided practice — in this case, asking children to read a familiar text and describe the setting. As students practice, the teacher observes their progress and provides appropriate guidance. When observations of students' progress suggest that they are prepared to practice independently, the students use the strategy without preparation or intervention by the teacher. Finally, to give students an opportunity to apply the strategy, the teacher discusses the appropriateness of using the strategy in a particular situation. For example, students are asked whether and why it is a good idea to describe the setting when they discuss books with their peers.

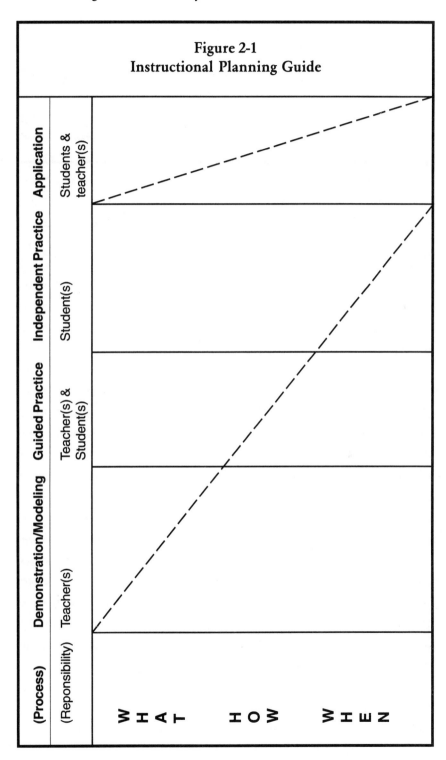

Figure 2-1
Instructional Planning Guide

While this description of explicit instruction may suggest that the procedure is sequential, it is actually recursive. The teacher's observations of children's progress in learning determine the order and duration of each step.

A second dimension of the plan is *strategic teaching and learning,* which emphasizes three types of knowledge: *declarative, procedural,* and *conditional* (Paris et al., 1991). Declarative knowledge ("what?") is definitional and requires an understanding of the elements of the strategy. Procedural knowledge ("how?") requires an understanding of the procedures required for the strategy. These two types of knowledge are emphasized most frequently during the teacher's demonstration and modeling and while students engage in guided practice. Conditional knowledge ("when and how?") requires an understanding of the circumstances that call for the use of the strategy. This type of knowledge is emphasized most often as students engage in independent practice and application of the strategy.

The third dimension of the plan is the *gradual release of responsibility* from teacher to learners. The success of this process, as with the others that have been described, is dependent upon the teachers' monitoring student progress and designing instruction based on the observed needs of learners and the goal of the lesson.

As the planning guide illustrates, explicit instruction and the gradual release of responsibility are interdependent. When the strategy is demonstrated or modeled, the teacher assumes major responsibility for student learning. During guided practice, the teacher and students assume equal responsibility for learning; and during independent practice, the major responsibility shifts to the learners. In the application phase, when students use the strategy in a different context, the teacher may need to assume major responsibility again. For some students, applying a strategy in a different context is as challenging a task as learning the strategy initially.

Classroom Organization

While the seminars were in progress, a university faculty member who was working with the teachers in Chelsea developed a flexible grouping model for classroom organization. Paratore (1991) describes her plan as an alternative to fixed ability grouping for literacy instruction.

> It integrates whole class instruction, smaller needs-based groups, cooperative groups, and peer tutoring. Each of these organizational options is selected at various points in the instructional plan in order to enable the teacher to address specific needs. (p. 3)

Teachers adapted the flexible grouping plan to meet the needs of their students and their own preferences. Most of the co-teaching teams discovered that the plan was particularly effective in easing the transition for classroom teachers — who were accustomed to having sole responsibility in the classroom — and for Title I teachers, who had formerly been responsible for providing services to small groups of children in a separate resource room setting.

Classroom Assessment

The final topic, classroom assessment, was the most complex, but a critical initial decision was made with little discussion. The seminar participants agreed that the primary purpose for assessment would be to inform instruction. Thus, the plan would need to accommodate the realities of the classroom.

The classroom assessment plan was based on intervention assessment (Paratore & Indrisano, 1987), a process that focuses on the progress of the student when effective instruction is provided, thus emphasizing the responsibility of the teacher and the promise of the learner.

The assessment focuses on the strategies for reading, writing, and learning that have been taught to students. Although periodic running records (Clay, 1993) are taken, the primary mode of classroom assessment is monitoring students' progress while they use and apply strategies for reading and writing. One of the advantages of the co-teaching model is that it affords time and opportunity for each of the two teachers to bring her unique insights to student assessment.

Assessment forms were devised and revised several times. One of the most effective editions is reproduced here — although it should be noted that individual teachers have adapted the form to accommodate their needs and those of their students. Common to all the forms is a list of students' names and the target strategies for the instructional cycle. As the teacher observes the student, one of three descriptors is used to indicate the level of intervention the student required for successful use of the strategy: no help, also described as independent; some help/minimum intervention; and substantial help/maximum intervention. Two sample assessment forms are provided here: the first form (Figure 2-2) is used to monitor comprehension strategies, and the second (Figure 2-3) is used to assess fluency in reading.

These forms serve two purposes: (1) to guide classroom management by providing the co-teachers with critical information for setting and revising instructional goals, and (2) to enrich student portfolios and thus to inform discussions of student progress by co-teachers and with parents.

Consistent with contemporary research that validates the importance of student involvement in the assessment process (Valencia & Calfee, 1991), a series of forms for student self-assessment were developed. The forms vary according to the level of the learners, from the simplest reading and response logs for beginning readers and writers, as illustrated here (Figure 2-4), to the more complex learning logs that are used by mature learners.

Figure 2-2
Assessment Form — Comprehension Strategies

Name	Characters	When/Where		Problem	Solution
Jessica	✓	✓+	--	✓	✓+
Robert	✓+	✓+	--	✓++	✓++
Ken	✓+	✓+	--	✓	✓
Brian	✓+	✓+	--	✓	✓
Denice	✓	✓+	--	✓+	✓+
Stephanie	✓+	✓++	--	✓++	✓++
Danny	✓	✓+	--	✓+	✓
Lauren	✓	✓++	--	✓++	✓+
Carl	✓+	✓++	--	✓+	✓+

✓ = no help or observed ✓+ = some help or prompt ✓++ = substantial help -- = N/A

Figure 2-3
Assessment Form — Reading Fluency

Name	Fluency	Uses illustrations	Reads ahead	Sounds out words	Uses spelling patterns	Self-corrects	Ignores errors	Asks for help	No response
Jessica	90			✓		✓			
Robert	80	✓		✓+	✓+		✓	✓	
Ken	83		✓+	✓		✓	✓		
Brian	94		✓+	✓		✓			
Denice	93		✓+	✓				✓	
Stephanie	65	✓+			✓++	✓	✓		✓
Danny	90		✓+	✓					
Lauren	70	✓	✓+		✓++		✓		✓
Carol	82	✓	✓+		✓++				✓

✓ = no help or observed   ✓+ = some help or prompt   ✓++ = substantial help

Figure 2-4
Student Self-Assessment Form

NAME _____

This is my best work because _____

_____

_____

_____

_____

_____

_____

_____

What would you like to do better in reading?

_____

_____

_____

_____

_____

_____

_____

_____

_____

_____

_____

The Classroom Implementation

In the Beginning

The first step for the co-teachers was to acknowledge and deal with the challenges that confronted them as two professionals with substantial classroom experience. The classroom teacher was accustomed to working independently in a self-contained classroom with one large group of children with a wide range of backgrounds and abilities. The Title I teacher, with a particular area of expertise, was experienced in working with individual children or small needs-based groups in a resource room. How did two teachers reconcile different philosophical, pedagogical, and personal views regarding the education of children? Above all, how did they capitalize on their individual strengths in this cooperative endeavor?

In the beginning, the co-teachers had an open and honest discussion of relevant issues, from the most basic — classroom routines — to the most profound — ways to educate children with limited English proficiency while acknowledging that limitations in language do not suggest limitations in promise. As the actual work began, the value of this initial investment in time and effort became evident. It was also apparent that participation in the seminars, where specific plans were developed collaboratively, resulted in a sense of ownership and preparedness.

Classroom management issues were anticipated and subsequently resolved by mutual agreement. Each teacher promised to support the full participation of her colleague, avoiding the temptation to allocate responsibilities in the mode of master-teacher and assistant. The co-teachers also agreed to exert all reasonable efforts to maximize the benefits of two equally able and responsible professionals working together on behalf of the children.

As the "incoming teacher," the Title I teacher agreed to abide by the established guidelines for classroom routines and behaviors in all matters from the trivial (sharpening pencils) to the critical (expectations for teachers and children). The co-teachers attempted to avoid conflict by agreeing to delay discussions of unanticipated problems until the children were not present and to hold these discussions in private rather than in the presence of their colleagues. It was also agreed that the Title I teacher would be allocated working and storage space in the classroom and given access to all materials and supplies. Underlying all these negotiations was an attitude of respect for the children and for each other, a primary and enduring criterion for successful co-teaching.

Classroom Organization

Having resolved issues of classroom management, the team turned next to responsibility for instruction and assessment. The teachers agreed to adapt the flexible grouping plan (Paratore, 1991) to accommodate the needs of the children and the goals of the curriculum.

In this classroom, grade-level texts are used for instruction, and fixed-ability groups are replaced with whole-class groups or small groups determined by the goals of the activity and the strengths and needs of the learners. The co-teachers attribute their comfort with flexible grouping to several factors:

- their common goals for the children they teach,
- their participation in professional development activities that allowed them to become familiar with the research that informs instruction and assessment,
- their adoption of a common design for instruction and assessment,
- their confidence in their ability to implement this design in the classroom, and
- their daily use of classroom assessment procedures that yield information on students' learning strengths and needs.

Whole-group instruction is used when students will benefit from the variety of experience and knowledge that resides in a large, diverse group of students. For example, the whole group may gather when the teacher introduces the text and students recall or generate relevant background knowledge. Small groups, including pairs of learners, may be needs-based or heterogeneous, determined by the observed needs of the learners and the goals of the lesson.

Literacy Instruction and Assessment

Literacy instruction and assessment will be described in terms of the three components of the classroom program: the literacy workshop, explicit instruction, and applied literacy. These components are also the focus of initial cooperative planning by co-teachers and the special education teacher at the beginning of each week. Following this planning session, which results in a master plan for the class, each teacher makes specific accommodations for the children she will teach that week. These plans are revised, as appropriate, at the end of each day. The instruction is characterized by three guidelines:

- Literacy instruction is the central focus of the first-grade curriculum.
- Emphasis is given to a limited number of critical reading and writing strategies.
- Literacy strategies are practiced and applied in all curriculum areas throughout the day.

The Literacy Workshop. Each school day begins with a literacy workshop, a time for children to concentrate on work in progress and to apply the strategies they have learned. The goal of the co-teachers is to increase the time devoted to the literacy workshop as the children's competence and confidence develops, and as they are able to work independently. This goal is typically achieved by early winter, at which time the children are ready to benefit from an hour-long literacy workshop. The books, materials, and interest centers for the workshop are all related to the theme the students are studying. The children, the classroom teacher, and the Title I teacher have specific responsibilities during the literacy workshop; these tasks are listed on the chart in Figure 2-5 (below).

Children spend their time rereading and writing reflections on the core text; forming literature circles to discuss favorite books; reading materials that extend their knowledge of the theme; rereading, mapping, and responding to narrative texts; adding information to their reading logs; editing or revising a piece of writing; adding new vocabulary to personal dictionaries/thesauruses; and working in creative arts centers.

The classroom teacher uses this time to help students prepare for the day; to monitor and assess reading, writing, and learning strategies; to demonstrate fix-up strategies; to help students solve the problems they encounter; to guide pacing, particularly for students who need to be challenged to move beyond their present level of activity; and to record notes regarding teacher intervention and student progress.

The Title I teacher spends her time with the students she and the

---

Figure 2-5
A Literacy Workshop

Classroom teacher	Children	Title I teacher
morning business	reread and reflect on core text	explicit instruction to flexible skills group and/or individuals
monitor reading	literature circles	
monitor writing	extended reading	assess
model fix-up strategies	story mapping	intervene
assess and record	respond	guide responses and retellings
individual instruction	dictionary/thesaurus	
guide pacing	keep reading logs	
	revise and edit writing	
	creative projects	

classroom teacher have determined to be in need of extra help. Because their decisions are based on daily informal assessments and periodic running records, these groups change according to the progress of the children. Title I instruction is provided to individuals or to small groups, for a period ranging from five to sixty minutes, for up to one week. This instruction focuses primarily on decoding words in context, comprehending and responding to ideas in text, and achieving fluency in reading connected discourse.

Explicit Instruction. Following the literacy workshop, the class is divided into two heterogeneous groups for a half-hour block devoted to explicit instruction; each teacher works with one of these groups. Using a core grade appropriate text or a theme-related trade book, the teacher begins by developing the language and concepts that are critical to text comprehension. Then the teacher reads the title of the text and calls attention to the illustrations. The children set a purpose for listening or reading and use the title and the illustrations to predict the content. As preparation for reading, students may first listen as the teacher reads the text aloud. This additional step helps learners, the majority of whom speak English as a second language, to become better acquainted with the sounds, concepts, language, and structure of the text. For the same reason, the concept-bearing vocabulary may be taught explicitly before the children begin to read the text. Finally the students read the text, guided by the teacher.

In subsequent days the children practice reading the text to achieve a gradual release of responsibility from teacher to learner. For example, children join in choral reading or echo reading; they read with a partner; and they read and respond to the text independently. During this time, the teachers work with individuals and small groups to provide differentiated instruction or practice on reading and writing strategies related to the text. The focus may be decoding, language use, conventions of written text, story elements, or response to literature. While both teachers work with the children during the literacy workshop, the classroom teacher often reinforces these lessons when the Title I teacher leaves the room.

Texts that have been introduced during the period of explicit instruction are used later for literary workshop activities. For example, children may reread and reflect on the core text, join in literature circles, or write entries in their reading or response logs.

Teachers also provide explicit instruction in strategies for reading, writing, and learning. The strategies are taught, practiced, and applied according to the instructional model described earlier in this chapter. The questions posed most frequently to the co-teachers relate to "phonics." Following a review of several approaches to teaching decoding, these first-grade teachers have incorporated elements from three approaches: the Benchmark Word Identification Program (Gaskins, Gaskins, & Gaskins, 1991), Cunningham's (1991) words for reading and writing, and Clay's (1991) construction of inner control. The decoding program focuses on explicit teaching of phonemic segmentation, sound/symbol correspondences, and word elements (Chall, 1996). Children are taught to apply these strategies to reading and writing words, phrases, sentences, and texts. Activities planned for the remainder of the instructional period are designed to review and extend the concepts and strategies that have been taught to the children.

The period of explicit instruction concludes with children writing a response to the text they have read that day. Because the goal of this activity is to help students apply the strategies and skills used by effective readers and writers, this process may take several days. Sometimes children work in pairs to reflect on their reading and decide upon their favorite part of the story, then discuss their decisions with the whole group. To prepare to write their responses, children draw pictures of a simple response, or complete story maps to organize a more elaborate response. As students write, teachers move about the room, offering assistance as needed. For example, during the editing phase, teachers may remind children to consult their dictionaries or the "word wall," which is an integral part of the word identification program. Teachers also use this time to observe and record notes of children's strengths and needs.

Samples of two children's writing, taken over the period of an academic year (Figures 2-6 and 2-7, a-c), illustrate their progress in reading and writing. It is obvious that the children began their first-grade year with different strengths and needs and that each child made progress during the year.

Applied Literacy. At the conclusion of the period of explicit instruction, the Title I teacher leaves this classroom and goes to another classroom where the co-teaching model is implemented. The classroom teacher turns to other curriculum areas, but applies literacy learning throughout the school day.

In this first grade, beavers — the topic of texts used for instruction and practice — become the focus of a science lesson. The teacher reads an expository text that describes the characteristics of beavers and of their homes. Following the reading, children discuss the traits of beavers and record the information in their journals. Consistent with the theme, during a social studies lesson students discuss the characteristics of beavers' homes and locate on a map areas of the country where beavers live. During a mathematics lesson children solve problems re-

Figure 2-6

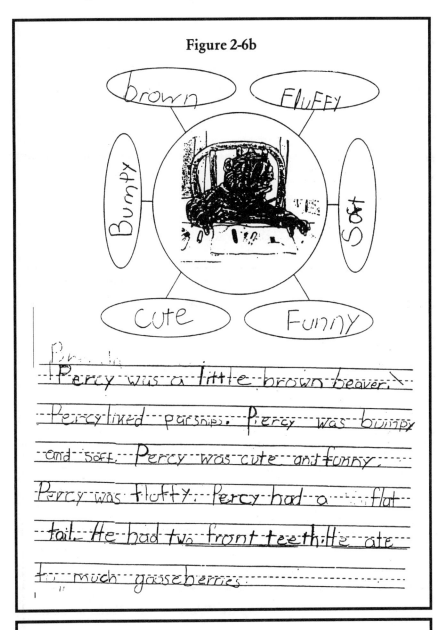

Figure 2-6b

brown
FluFFy
Bumpy
Soft
cute
Funny

Percy was a little brown beaver. Percy liked parsnips. Percy was bumpy and soft. Percy was cute and funny. Percy was fluffy. Percy had a flat tail. He had two front teeth. He ate too much gooseberries.

Figure 2-6c

I liked this writing the best because it tells me real things about beavers

Figure 2-7a

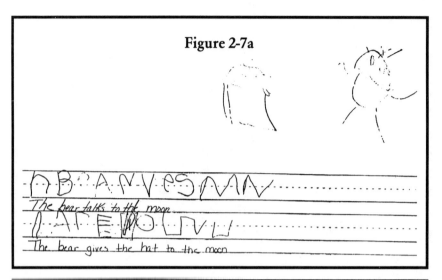

ΛB·ΑΛΥΕSΛΛΥ

The bear talks to the moon

ΛΤΕΙΛΟΛΥ

The bear gives the hat to the moon

Figure 2-7b

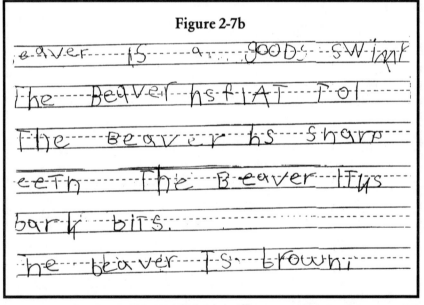

eaver — is — a — goods — swim
the — Beaver — hsflAT — Tol
The — Beaver — hs — sharp
eeth — The — Beaver — ITus
bark — bits.
he — beaver — Is — brown.

Figure 2-7c

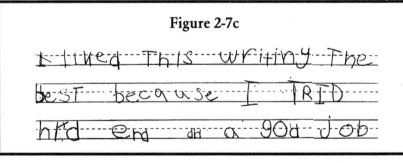

I liked This writing The
best because I TRID
hrd em an a god Job

lated to the numbers of beavers in a certain locale.

To make connections across the curriculum, students listen to and read other books on a single theme. Later they write imaginative stories or informational texts to teach others what they have learned. After revision and editing, these books are added to the collection of materials available for the children to read.

The school day concludes with book selection and discussion, as children gather on the rug that is used for group meetings. Each child selects a book from a thematically clustered collection that has been organized by color-coding. Following silent reading, children may take turns introducing their books to the other children, who ask questions of the reader. Or they may discuss their books in groups of two or three children who have selected the same text. Each of these activities is effective preparation for conducting literature circles.

Reflections on Co-teaching

Recently, at the conclusion of a presentation at a professional conference, the teachers reflected on their co-teaching experience. They described the benefits to children as:

- increased opportunities for teacher time and attention;
- elimination of the stigma associated with fixed-ability groups;
- provision for all children to learn to read grade-appropriate texts with differentiated instruction designed to meet their needs; and
- opportunities for all children to learn the strategies used by effective readers, writers, and learners.

The benefits to teachers were described as increased creativity and decreased stress resulting from eliminating the isolation that is too frequently the teacher's lot. When two teachers work together, the classroom teacher can spend time challenging able students, confident that the Title I teacher will provide the extra help needed by other children. With increased opportunities for monitoring and assessing student progress, interventions are more precise and more frequent. Most importantly, the co-teaching team has a common vision, a common core of knowledge, and a common approach to instruction and assessment based on the application of theory and research to practice. Each voice is heard, and each voice is valued.

Co-Teaching in Professional Development

The early years of the partnership have brought many changes to teachers and students. As has been described, new models for co-teaching and for classroom organization, literacy instruction, and literacy assessment had been developed and implemented in the early years of the partnership. The Title I lead teachers decided to adapt these same models to professional development, rather than to create new ways of working. The director of Title I, formerly a Title I teacher herself, describes these efforts in the final section of the chapter. (In the text that follows, she will be referred to as the lead teacher.)

After considerable discussion, the lead teacher selected demonstration teaching as the most promising way to assist classroom teachers in implementing the new changes in the literacy curriculum. A major factor in this decision was the opportunity for a classroom teacher and a lead teacher to work as co-teachers. Beyond the immediate benefits of introducing change in the classroom, this plan prepares teachers for other innovations that depend on co-teaching (for example, the integration of classroom and Title I instruction).

For purposes of professional development, the co-teaching model is implemented when the classroom teacher invites the lead teacher to work in the classroom to demonstrate a particular innovation. For example, the classroom teacher may wish to learn how to provide explicit instruction for a particular reading or writing strategy, how to implement the flexible grouping model, or how to monitor and assess students. Consistent with the models that were adopted for instruction and the gradual release of responsibility, the lead teacher begins the cycle by demonstrating or modeling the target strategy. The lead teacher continues to assume the primary responsibility until the classroom teacher is ready to become an active participant. At that point the co-teachers plan together, and the lead teacher guides the classroom teacher in implementing the change. When the classroom teacher is ready to function independently, the lead teacher becomes a consultant. The application phase occurs when the classroom teacher implements the innovation in a different context without the intervention or support of the lead teacher. During any phase of the cycle the responsibilities may change as the progress of the classroom teacher requires.

A description of an innovation in one fifth-grade classroom provides an example of the co-teaching approach to professional development.

Preparation

The classroom teacher asked the lead teacher to help her to incorporate literature circles into the classroom literacy program. At their first meeting, the lead teacher demonstrated for the classroom teacher the process of reviewing instructional texts and trade books to identify a promising theme for literature circles and for thematic teaching across the curriculum. After they reviewed the most promising selections in the literature anthology, the content texts, and the trade books, *conflict* was selected as the theme. The lead teacher then helped the classroom teacher choose materials representing a variety of genres and a progression of difficulty, from picture books to chapter books, to accommodate the wide range of abilities in the classroom.

In reviewing their collection, the teachers determined that the topics of the books could form a historical time line, from the early years of United States history up to the Holocaust. To bring focus to their teaching and to the children's learning, they selected books that represent a variety of genres including fiction, poetry, and informational texts. Having selected their materials, the co-teachers turned next to

the processes that would prepare the children to participate in literature circles. They set the objectives, selected the texts, and planned the
lessons for the instructional cycle.

Implementation

The lead teacher began by introducing literature circles to the children
and describing the steps they would take to prepare for this activity —
from learning to generate topics for discussion to understanding how
to be considerate of others while listening, taking turns, and responding.

To prepare the children for the first discussion, the lead teacher
selected a book to read to them. As a group, the children set a purpose
for reading: to listen for situations and events that would be good topics for discussion within the theme. As the lead teacher read the story
to them, students took notes on promising topics for discussion at the
end of the reading. After the discussion, the lead teacher taught them
to refine or revise their topics to encourage more thoughtful discussion
in the future. The classroom teacher observed the lead teacher and
assisted her in working with children as they generated and refined
their topics.

The next activity provided opportunities for guided practice. The
classroom teacher took responsibility for the lesson and began by
reminding the children of the guidelines for discussion. She invited
them to read a familiar text with a partner and write topics for discussion that related to the theme of conflict. After the children had completed these tasks, the co-teachers worked with them to help them
refine and revise their topics. Then, using their revised topics, the
partners discussed their books, attending to the ways their notes helped
them focus on the particular writer's interpretation of the theme.

Similar procedures were followed to help children refine their responses to each other. They learned how to become involved in the
discussion of the theme and how to join in the conversation by para-
phrasing the text or offering responses that relate to the ideas in the

text. Finally, they learned to elaborate on the author's ideas and to make intertextual connections among the stories, poems, and information sources they had read.

The children were then ready to begin to participate in literature circles. The co-teachers selected eight children who had read the same book and invited them to sit together. The other children sat at the outer rim of the circle and observed their classmates. The lead teacher assumed responsibility for the activity and began by reviewing the guidelines for literature circles. At first the children used the topics they had written, but as the discussion progressed they were able to generate new topics for discussion. When the activity ended, the participants and the observers, guided by the co-teachers, critiqued the literature circles and set goals for the next time.

In succeeding weeks, all the children had opportunities to become an observer or participant until each child had learned to function independently in a literature circle. During this time the emphasis shifted from refining topics to refining responses, as determined by the children's enhanced abilities and evident needs.

As the classroom teacher's competence and confidence grew, she assumed increasing responsibility for the literature circles until she could function independently. The final step in the cycle for the teacher and the children was to apply what had been learned during discussions of a literary theme to researching and discussing works with scientific themes.

Teacher Monitoring and Student Reflection

As we noted earlier, one of the goals of the partnership is to improve classroom assessment and to use teacher assessment and self-assessment to improve teaching and learning. In working with the classroom teacher to help her add literature circles to her fifth-grade literacy program, the lead teacher also introduced her to approaches for monitoring student progress and student self-assessment.

Consistent with their goal to teach children how to participate effectively in the literature circles, the co-teachers created a form for monitoring students' participation (Figure 2-8). The top of the form lists the goals for literature circles. To monitor student progress, the co-teachers use the system described earlier; the teacher marks the form to indicate whether the child is effective with no help, some help/minimum intervention, or substantial help/maximum intervention.

The children reflect on their progress by answering these questions: What did I do well? What do I need to improve? What are my goals for the next literature circle? (The student self-assessment form appears in Figure 2-9.) The co-teachers discuss the students' reflections with them, comparing their own observations with those of the students. In individual and group conversations, they assist the children in refining their self-assessments and their goals for the future.

An entry written by one of the students in a self-reflection journal captures her response to the literature circle experience.

> I learned a lot from the literature circle and things I did not understand were discussed in a small group. Many of the books I read I did not know about. I really enjoyed them. If I could I would absolutely do it again.

The classroom teacher's response reflects on her experience as a co-teacher in the literature circle.

> Teaching literature circles ... was great. The students were as excited as I to be working in groups. The class [members] cooperated with each other and respected each other's opinions. I am looking forward to beginning literature circles again this school year.

Conclusion

Recently the writers were among a number of participants in the Boston University/Chelsea Public Schools partnership who gathered to reflect on their experience at the end of six years (Indrisano & Paratore,

Figure 2-8							
Name	Becomes involved in discussion	Participates effectively	Asks thoughtful questions	Ideas paraphrase the text	Ideas relate to the text	Ideas elaborate on the text	Makes intertextual connections
Julia							
Arnoldo							
Jose							
Tany Ban							
Hiew							
Elissa							
Takara							
Christopher							
Richard							
Nicole							
Elaina							

Figure 2-9
Student Self-Assessment Form — Literature Circles

Name _____ **Date** _____

What did you do well? _____

_____

_____

What would you like to improve? _____

_____

_____

What are your goals for the next literature circles?

_____

_____

_____

_____

_____

_____

1994). In her concluding remarks, one of the writers offered advice to those who work in behalf of children and their education, an appropriate way to end this story.

> I think when you want to change something, you really don't want to change it, but you want to make it grow. And, instead of change, we should talk more about growth and start from what really exists and make that better... A good leader I think empowers the people, and then guides the growth... It's not just a professor or a superintendent, but a good teacher who's a leader in the classroom who empowers the children and guides their growth... I was thinking that Boston University faculty have brought me information, inspiration and support. I started to think that's really what we want to bring to our children, information, inspiration and support. So, it's really much more basic than people think. It's more empowering to guide growth rather than enforce change. (p. 133)

References

Birmingham, N., Garnick, S., Mauro, A., Maresco, D.K., Quinn, K., & Indrisano, R. (1994) Teachers' voices: Reflections on the Boston University/Chelsea Public Schools Partnership and its effect on the literacy initiatives. *Journal of Education, 176,* 127-133.

Chall, J. (1996). *Learning to read: The great debate* (2nd ed.). New York: Mc-Graw Hill.

Clay, M.M. (1991). *Becoming literate: The construction of inner control.* Portsmouth, NH: Heinemann.

Clay, M.M. (1993). *An observation survey of early literacy achievment.* Portsmouth, NH: Heinemann.

Cunningham, P.M. (1991). *Phonics they use: Words for reading and writing.* New York: HarperCollins.

Gaskins, R.W., Gaskins, J.C., & Gaskins, I.W. (1991). A decoding program for poor readers — and the rest of the class, too! *Language Arts, 68,* 213-225.

Goldenberg, C., & Gallimore, R. (1991). Local knowledge, research knowledge, and educational change: A case study of early Spanish reading improvement. *Educational Researcher, 20,* 2-14.

Indrisano, R., & Paratore, J.R. (1991). Classroom contexts for literacy learning. In J. Flood, J.M. Jensen, D. Lapp, & J. R. Squire. (Eds.). *Handbook of research in teaching the English language arts,* pp. 477-488. New York: Macmillan.

Indrisano, R., & Paratore, J.R. (Eds.) (1994). The Boston University/Chelsea Public Schools Partnership 1986-1994. *Journal of Education, 176.*

Moll, L.C. (1992). Literacy research in community and classroom: A sociocultural approach. In R. Beach, J. Green, M.L. Kamil, & T. Shanahan (Eds.), *Multidisciplinary perspectives on literacy research* (pp. 211-244). Urbana, IL: National Conference on Research in English and National Council of Teachers of English.

Paratore, J.R. (1991). *Flexible grouping: Why and how.* Needham, MA: Silver, Burdett and Ginn.

Paratore, J.R., & Indrisano, R. (1987). Intervention assessment of reading comprehension. *The Reading Teacher, 40,* 778-783.

Paris, S.G., Wasik, B.A., & Turner, J.C. (1991). The development of strategic readers. In R. Barr, M.L. Kamil, P.B. Mosenthal, & P.D. Pearson (Eds.), *Handbook of reading research: Vol. II* (pp. 609-640). New York: Longman.

Pearson, P.D., & Gallagher, M.C. (1983). The instruction of reading comprehension. *Contemporary Educational Psychology, 8,* 317-344.

Rosenshine, B., & Stevens, R. (1984). Classroom instruction in reading. In P.D. Pearson, R. Barr, & M. Kamil (Eds.), *Handbook of reading research: Vol. 1* (pp. 745-798). New York: Longman.

Valencia, S.W., & Calfee, R. (1991). The development and use of literacy portfolios for students, classes and teachers. *Applied Measurement in Education, 4,* 333-346.

3

Academic Success, Failure to Thrive, and a Safety-Net School

WOOD SMETHURST, Ed.D.
Ben Franklin Academy, Atlanta, Georgia

There is no shortage of critics of America's schools. Commissions are appointed, they meet, report, and fill the media with discussions of what to do about our schools. While recommendations for solutions vary widely, at least one theme seems common to all. Virtually all analyses of America's schools agree that (a) too many students fail to reach their educational potential, and (b) this waste of human resources constitutes a national problem.

My concern in this article is that, for those students who have failed to learn as well or as much as we or their parents would hope, catching up is often difficult and occasionally nearly impossible within the graded structure of conventional high schools. Once students fail or miss a significant amount of school, it can become a major challenge for them to turn matters around and repair the damage. It is not the purpose of this article to lay blame for school failure and serious underachievement (or *failure to thrive,* as I prefer to call it) on any particular school practice. It seems to occur across the spectrum of school curricula, organizational schemes, and educational philosophies.

As a way of addressing the problem of school failure and catch-up, I will briefly discuss work that my colleagues Martha Burdette and others at Ben Franklin Academy are carrying out to explore a promising solution to a small part of this very large problem: We want to help those kids who have fallen behind or gotten out of step with high school and who want to get caught up, get a good education, get a high school diploma, and get on with their lives. We think the beginnings of an answer, at least for those students who want to catch up, lies in the idea of a safety-net school. (For those who don't really want to do schoolwork or get a diploma, there may be other answers in community, military, and motivational programs, but ours is only intended to work for kids who want to learn, catch up, and graduate. Willingness is the indispensable ingredient.)

The problem becomes more immediate once we begin to talk about individual students who have fallen out of sync with school. In human terms, each child who does not seem to fit the system is a one-person tragedy that impacts on family, friends, community, and finally society itself.

Diane is now 15, but dressed up she looks more like 22; she is beautiful, with classic features and an attractive figure. Diane matured at 12 and began attracting boys' attention. Pregnant at 13, she had her first abortion in the eighth grade. She was hospitalized for drugs and depression later that year, had another abortion on her fifteenth birthday, and was hospitalized again for depression and attempted suicide. She still has not completed the ninth grade in the suburban high school she attends, and has very little in common with other ninth-graders. She has begun to skip school several days each week, and is now barely passing the courses in which she once excelled.

James is 17, nearly old enough to drop out and get a GED, but he wants a diploma and would like somehow to go to college. He has been in three schools in three years. He has attentional and auditory problems, and he struggles with lectures and directions. He ran into trouble in his first public school, then was sent to boarding school in an attempt to straighten him out. He ran away from the boarding school and wound up in a large public high school's open campus program, but lacked the self-management skills required to succeed in such a program and ended up failing out of school one more time. He has a job delivering pizza, and plans to take the GED when he turns 18.

Billy is a nice, dreamy kid, who dazzles his parents with his intelligence but does poorly at school. He just somehow doesn't fit. He says of himself, "I guess I'm a nerd." Good with computers, he pursues that interest at home. His parents are baffled by his inability to get interested in school. He doesn't seem to know what his teachers want, his parents say. He likes to skateboard, do computers, and hang out with his friends. He denies using drugs, but his friends say he uses "now and then."

These problems are pervasive. Every high school teacher knows students like these youngsters who are failing or struggling not to fail, but all of us who teach also know many students with "A" brains who muddle along with C's, and who do not really thrive in school or come close to reaching their academic potentials. Possible causes include lack of motivation, home and family problems, drugs, romantic distractions, peer pressure, and lack of adult leadership or role models, among others. It is true that some high school dropouts are among the school's most gifted pupils, but it is also true that many graduating C students might well have been more successful if circumstances had been different.

At Ben Franklin Academy, we have chosen to work on an individual basis with the problem of school failure and underachievement, and we believe that we can suggest a solution for a part of the problem. We seek students who have somehow fallen out of step with their conventional schools, but who want to learn, graduate, and get on with their lives. Not all are failing in the sense of receiving F's on their report cards, though many are. Some students simply feel out of place in ordinary schools, or they begin to fall behind, or they feel lost in the bigness and impersonality of their high school. There are, as it turns out, many ways for students to fall out of step, and getting back into step is tough in even the most caring of conventional schools.

When they try to catch up, students who fall behind have to make up the work they missed, and they must also keep up with their ongoing schoolwork. In the conventional system, it is very difficult for teachers to stop everything to let one child catch up. America's standard Carnegie-unit-based system is keyed to time in class, and time truly waits for no one. (Time has waited for no one in our schools since at least 1893, when the system was proposed by the Committee of Ten.)

We suggest a different approach to catching up that does not set such a premium on time in class. Instead, we prefer to base our unit of instruction on mastery of school subjects. This mastery learning is common practice in our society, and hardly revolutionary if you think about it. Consider correspondence courses, merit badge work by Boy Scouts and Girl Scouts, Junior and Senior Red Cross Lifesaving Certificates, and even drivers' licensing. In mastery learning, the student must demonstrate knowledge of the subject to be learned before credit can be given. Each mastery unit is roughly equivalent to a Carnegie unit in terms of subject matter and amount of material covered.

Generally speaking, in mastery learning there is some predetermined, understood, and agreed-upon level of knowledge or skill that must be attained, and gaining this mastery becomes the goal of student effort. We have attempted to translate conventional Carnegie units into mastery terms, and have produced a series of interdisciplinary humanities and other units on which we base our instruction.

The great advantage to using a mastery approach in catch-up work is that teachers can start by finding out what their students know, then help them learn those things they will need to know in order to demonstrate mastery of the subject. Using an individually planned mastery approach also provides flexibility for accommodating instruction to individual learning styles, needs, and interests. Students who work slowly can be waited out, or occasionally speeded up, but in each case they get the time they need to complete the necessary readings and assignments. This is also true for students with reading and writing difficulties, who naturally require more time and assistance for the completion of their work. Youngsters who need a lot of encouragement can get it, and students who work quickly can go ahead and finish without being held up by their slower classmates.

But using mastery learning by itself is not enough. The context of school learning is more important than we had thought: Bruner (1996), Chall and Carroll (1976), Rogoff (1990), and Cole (1971), among others, speak to this issue in recent publications, and Montessori (1995), Neill (1995), and Quintilian (A.D. 96) also spoke to it in their writings. Modifying the learning environment itself can be enormously helpful to youngsters desiring to catch up and succeed academically. For this purpose, we have devised what we call a "family school" approach, a school based on the idea of an extended family or intentional community. Caring and respect for others and for the school environment are essential to the success of this sort of arrangement. The school's size is a critical factor in encouraging a caring and respectful community. Small is beautiful to us for several reasons. We want every teacher to know every student, and we want all the students to know one another. We try to keep the size of the student body between 50 and 65 students; since we have rolling admissions and graduation, the size of the school fluctuates.

We are a work-study program. This means that the school day is 3½ hours long, and students work at paying or volunteer jobs from 10 to 20 hours weekly. This draws from Franklin's ideas of the usefulness of work and knowledge in the development of maturity and judgment as well as character. All students are required to work and to complete assignments related to their work. We believe that honest work pursued thoughtfully can contribute much to self-esteem and awareness, so work-study is an essential element of our program.

We believe that a relaxed, homelike environment can reduce stress for students who have encountered failure or threat of failure in schools. Our teachers agree that an informal, low-stress environment makes their teaching easier and more comfortable. This general ease and comfort of surroundings contributes to the shared sense that "this is a different kind of school." We treasure that attitude and seek to encourage it because we want the results our students get and the experiences they have to differ from those they had in previous schools.

The school itself is in a converted house near a major university. A family once lived here, and we try to keep it as homelike as possible. Two cats roam about the house, and students are free to move around at will. The kitchen is open for snacks and drinks at all times, and students are encouraged to use it. Smoking is not permitted in the house, but is allowed in the garden. The gardens are elaborate, actively maintained, and very popular. For those who may be interested, pictures of our gardens, students, teachers and cats are also available at our web site. Our home page address is

http://www.rnindspring.com/~benfrank

We have reasons for trying to keep formalities to a minimum, while working to maximize attractiveness and comfort. The easygoing environment encourages students to make their own choices about their time and their work. Many of them struggle in the beginning with the freedom, since our students often come to us lacking in self-management skills or in self-awareness and the understanding of boundaries. They work with their advisors to learn how to monitor and direct their own time and schoolwork; we consider these essential skills. We encourage our students to become aware of themselves as thinkers and learners who manage and evaluate their own thinking and learning.

The school runs on four rules, which we try to live by. I quote our four rules here, and hope that the reader will be able to see how following them helps encourage individual students to take ownership of their own learning and to respect the work of others.

Rule 1. Do your own work and avoid interfering with the work of others; be gentle with the equipment, furnishings, and animals; insofar as possible, be sensitive to the needs, feelings, and concerns of the rest of us.

Rule 2. Do what teachers tell you.

Rule 3. No fighting. No alcoholic beverages, illegal drugs, or weapons.

Rule 4. Don't let the cats out.

These rules, and our adherence to them, bind the community. We enforce the rules mostly by example and clear expectations. Advisors and other students *expect* a new student to get his or her work done, and to avoid distracting others. When there is a lapse, faculty members and the headmaster speak with the student, calling attention to his or her prior agreement to follow these rules. Since abiding by the four rules is a precondition to enrollment, students must choose either to obey the community's rules or to leave. Since we only accept students who want to come here and who agree in advance to follow these rules, discipline is seldom a problem. In our daily discussions of community matters like clean-up, parking, sign-out, kitchen use, etc., occasions arise for students to observe how each student's self-management can make the community work better and thus enhance the learning of all.

As I indicated earlier, our work is in its tenth year. In terms of developing a prototype safety-net school for failing and underachieving students, we are just beginning to get the kinds of results we seek. Several more years of work and research will be needed before we can make confident recommendations and conclusions. Nonetheless, some observations are in order, based on our own and others' work.

1. Failure in American high schools takes many forms, and is a grave and costly problem for our society.
2. Many youngsters who fail can be taught effectively in the Ben Franklin program, and can go on to lead productive lives.
3. Learning how to lead students from failure to academic success and self-awareness is a task that will occupy us at Ben Franklin for many years.
4. At least part of the problem of failure in high schools is soluble. Classically, in problem-solving one is taught to break off a small part of a complex, intimidating problem and solve the smaller part, then break off another small problem and solve that one, and so on until the larger problem is solved, In terms of school failure, we hope to be

able to devise reliable ways to turn students around, and to communicate those ways to other educators.

We would like to see safety-net schools established in communities across America. In the near future we will be offering a collection of suggestions and materials for parents, students, educators, community leaders, and others interested in starting such a school. In time, we hope to develop the understandings, materials, and strategies to make this approach to catch-up schooling widely applicable.

References

Bruner, J. (1996). *The culture of education*. Cambridge, MA: Harvard University Press.

Chall, J., & Carroll, J. (1976). *Toward a literate society*. New York: McGraw-Hill.

Cole, M. (1971). *The cultural context of learning and thinking: An exploration in experimental anthropology*. New York: Basic Books.

Montessori, M. (1995). *The absorbent mind*. New York: Henry Holt.

Neill, A.S. (1995). *Summerhill*. New York: St. Martin's Press.

Quintilian (Marcus Fabius Quintillianus, about AD 96). *Institutio Oratorio*. Rome.

Rogoff, B. (1990). *Apprenticeship in thinking: Cognitive development in social context*. New York: Oxford University Press.

4

The Great Debate

MARILYN JAGER ADAMS, Ph.D.
Bolt, Beranek & Newman, Cambridge, Massachusetts

Over the centuries and around the world, many different proposals have been offered regarding how best to teach people to read. While these proposals differ in countless details, the differences that have been most significant in theory and most divisive in practice — especially in the alphabetic languages — have centered on the size of the written units on which instruction ought to be based. Should beginning reading instruction be centered on letters, on words, or on the meaningfulness of text? In its various forms and reincarnations, this question has smoldered at the core of what Jeanne Chall (1967) so aptly termed "The Great Debate." In this chapter, the debate is reviewed historically. The goal is to give the reader some perspective on how our instructional discourse came to be so strongly dominated by this fundamental issue and why, at long last, we may consider it resolved.

Alphabetic Approaches

Although a language may express a limitless number of ideas and embrace thousands upon thousands of words, no language admits more than a few dozen phonemes. Thus, the alphabetic system of writing — one symbol for each elementary speech sound or phoneme in the language — has been hailed as the most important invention in the social history of the world. Historian David Diringer describes it as "the creation of a 'revolutionary writing,' a script which we can perhaps term 'democratic' (or rather, a 'people's script'), as against the 'theocratic' scripts that preceded it" (1968, p 161). In principle, the symbols in an alphabetic system, which tend to range in number between 20 and 35, are few enough to be memorized by almost anyone and, once memorized, are adequate for the purposes of reading and writing any speakable expression in the language.

In deference to this logic, the majority of methods for teaching children to read in the alphabetic languages have begun by teaching them the letters. Evidently, the alphabet was hard for many to learn, and in response it was variously set to music so children could sing it, or made out of gingerbread to excite their interest. Nevertheless, for the first 3000 years or so of the alphabet's existence, this practice prevailed without notable challenge or lamentations of its ineffectiveness (Mathews, 1966).

Of course, there was not much for people to read. Beyond the alphabet, the materials that were to be learned generally came to include the Lord's Prayer, the Creed, the Ten Commandments, a few Psalms — "all that was necessary for one's spiritual existence" (Smith, 1974, p. 8). For reasons of economy, these basics were often fixed to a piece of wood and laminated with horn (the hornbook). As partial credit was conferred in proportion to the task, it became acceptable practice for literacy initiates to sign their names with an X ("Christ's Cross," or "criss-cross"), showing that whether or not they knew how to use it, they had at least learned that the letters of the alphabet were generally arrayed in the shape of the Latin cross in these materials (Mathews, 1966).

Beginning in the fifteenth century A.D., and increasingly as technology made paper and print more available, all of this began to change. The instructional strategies of old were suddenly woefully inadequate, for now the reader was faced with so many words! Even having learned the letters and their sounds, many students found it insuperably difficult to use that knowledge to induce the words.

Lists of simple syllables — such as *ba, be, bi, bo, bu* and *ab, eb, ib, ob, ub* — were added to the hornbooks to illustrate and exercise the alphabetic principle. As the hornbooks gave way to folios, these lists were extended, first to tables and then to pages and pages of syllables and words, organized by their lengths and phonetic similarities. As a best-selling case in point, Noah Webster's famous Blue-back speller, first published in 1783, devoted 74 of its 158 pages to these lists, typically with hundreds of words or syllables per page (Smith, 1974). The student was to learn to spell and pronounce all of these before moving into connected text.

Such attention to phonetics was compatible with not only the methods but also the prevailing goals of reading instruction. In colonial America, reading instruction was initially legislated so that people could read (and better yet, memorize) the Bible. Further, because Bibles were still scarce and literacy even scarcer, the premium was on learning to read aloud for the benefit of others. After the Revolutionary War, as America's educational imperative shifted from one of ensuring spiritual independence to one of building the qualities of character and citizenship upon which the new democracy depended, the religious texts were generally displaced by nationalistic and moralistic material. But still, the emphasis was on reading aloud. Well-developed elocutionary skills were deemed critical to participatory government, and assiduous attention to pronunciation was further endorsed as a means "to diffuse a uniformity and purity of language in America — to destroy the provincial prejudices that originate in the trifling differences of dialect, and produce reciprocal ridicule" (Webster, 1798, p. x; cited in Smith, 1974, p. 38).

Even so, the extensive phonetic work was reportedly distasteful to many students, and certainly so to many critics. In Europe, Samuel Heinecke (1727-1790) derided it as a "senseless playing with sounds," a "babble-factory," a "pim-pel-pam-pel" (cited in Mathews, 1966, p. 35). In America, the method was condemned as "irksome and vexatious to both teacher and scholar" (Bumstead, 1840, cited in Smith, 1974, p. 87). It was objected that "for months, nay, in many instances, for years [the student] is occupied by barren sounds alone. He is taught to connect them, it is true, with certain characters; but of their use, viz. to convey the ideas of others to his mind, he as yet knows nothing" (Palmer, 1838, cited in Mathews, 1966, p. 68). "If the child is bright," argued Horace Mann, "the time which passes during the lesson is the only part of the day in which he does not think. Not a single faculty of the mind is exercised excepting that of imitating sounds.... A parrot or an idiot could do the same thing" (1844, p. 117; cited in Smith, 1974, p. 78).

Words

Eventually, the spellers fell of their own weight. This was not only because their synthetic, item-by-item approach to spelling and reading was adjudged too onerous and time-consuming, but also because new ideas about how to instill this knowledge were gaining precedence.

The shared conviction behind these new reading methods was that the introduction to letters ought to be mediated by whole, familiar written words, each tied in presentation to the action or object to which it referred, so as to ensure the salience of its meaningfulness to the children. As the children were then led to examine the spellings of the words, they would learn — and learn to appreciate — the letters in terms of their linguistic functions.

Within this movement, some argued that the earlier emphasis on teaching children the names of the letters was misguided. Instead of the letters' names, they argued, what children need to master is the letters' *powers,* or in today's terms, their phonemic significance. In support of this idea, the recommendation was to begin with regular, short-voweled words, two or three letters in length, and better yet to introduce only a few letters at first, thoroughly exercising those in a variety of words before moving on. Some authors recommended that the children be simultaneously challenged to write, augmenting their compositions with drawings and inventive spellings (see Smith, 1974, p. 100). More generally, the powers of the letters were to be developed through activities that included carefully pronouncing each instructional word, exploring the sound and articulation of its phonemes in isolation and combination, writing the words, and — as soon as possible — reading and writing short sentences (Mathews, 1966; Smith, 1974).

At least in the United States, however, the dominant realization of this approach consisted in moving from the words to the names of the letters and then, only after the names were secure, to the letters' sounds. Moreover, opinions quickly diverged as to when, in the course of instruction, children's attention should be turned from the words as wholes to their component letters. At one end of the spectrum were those who advocated teaching the letters as soon as each word was presented so that, by being presented with just a few short, well-chosen words each day, the children might be familiarized with the whole alphabet within a period of a week or so. Others, extolling the relative ease and pleasure with which children responded to whole meaningful words, felt that the essential power of the method would be strengthened if the children were variously engaged with some larger corpus of words before their attention was turned to the letters. In this spirit, their recommendations as to the specific number of words that ought to be taught prior to mentioning the letters ranged from a bare dozen to hundreds.

Similarly influenced were the criteria by which the first-taught words were selected. As Bumstead explained of the word choice in his reader,

> No regard whatever has been paid to length, or to the popular opinion that a word is easy because it is short. This is a great error. A word is not easy to read and spell simply because it is short; nor difficult, because it is long; it is easy or difficult, chiefly, as it expresses an idea easy or difficult of comprehension.
>
> (1844, p. 3, cited in Smith, 1974, p. 88)

Meaning

It was during the Age of Enlightenment that the words-first methods were introduced. At some overarching level, a theoretical justification for this shift was built from the era's philosophical transfixion with the marvel of the human mind and the wonders it might achieve by pursuing the laws of nature. As Gedicke explained, for instruction to proceed "from the Whole to the parts, from the results to the causes, is incontestably the natural way of the human mind and especially of the mind as it is first stirred into action" (1791, p. 7, cited in Mathews, 1966, p. 40).

Even accepting this perspective, however, there remained the question of whether words — or some more encompassing level of language or thought — represented the most natural and useful whole for purposes of reading instruction. Thus, several influential pedagogues, such as the French scholar Jean Joseph Jacacot (1790-1840), suggested that learning to read should begin with memorization, through repeated readings, of whole books or stories (see Mathews, 1966). In contrast, George Farnham, a New York educator, adduced that "thoughts complete in their relations are the materials in the mind out of which complex relations are constructed." That being the case, he continued, "it necessarily follows that the sentence is the unit of expression" (1887, p. 11, cited in Mathews, 1966, p. 118). With this in mind, he proposed that reading instruction proceed by inviting the children to dictate their thoughts to the teacher, resulting in written sentences that they could read naturally and with expression even before knowing the place of a single word. As particular words were brought to attention through their repeated occurrence, the sentence-wholes were to be gradually analyzed into their parts: the words and, in turn, the words' sounds and letters (Huey, 1908).

Beyond the quest for the proper whole, the more powerful factor behind the shift toward new methods of reading instruction was surely the pressure of print itself. Across the nineteenth century, as the number of available books, periodicals, and pamphlets rapidly increased (Kaestle, 1991), so did the scholarship and literary enrichment they collectively offered. The cultural response to this situation was clearly reflected in both the stated objectives and the content of reading instruction. Now, in place of refining one's elocutionary powers and moral fiber, the primary purposes of reading were held to be those of acquiring knowledge both for its own sake and for its uses, of improving the intellectual powers, and of expanding one's personal capacity for practical and intellectual flexibility and fulfillment. By this point, the religious and patriotic materials were all but wholly displaced by texts on science, history, art, philosophy, economics, and — last in time but hardly least in ultimate emphasis — by literature for the sake of literature. Charles W. Eliot, then President of Harvard University, wrote,

> It would be for the advancement of the whole public school system if every reader were hereafter to be absolutely excluded from the school. I object to them because they are not real literature; they are but mere scraps of literature, even when the single lessons or materials of which they are composed are taken from literature. But there are a great many readers that seem to have been composed especially for the use of children. They are not made up of selections from recognized literature, and as a rule this class is simply ineffable trash.... I believe that we should substitute in all our schools real literature for readers.
>
> (Eliot, 1891, p. 497, cited in Smith, 1974, p. 120)

At the same time, educators were questioning whether didacticism might disrupt the very goal of the endeavor. "The intent to teach," wrote Herbart, "spoils children's books at once; it is forgotten that everyone, the child included, selects what suits him from what he reads" (1895, p. 73, cited in Smith, 1974, p. 118). In complement, the view was emerging that if properly motivated and freed to think, children would "learn to read as they learn to talk [...] and we know they talk when they have something to say" (Parker, 1900, p. 13; cited in Mathews, 1966, p. 130).

Meanwhile, the preponderance of reading in which the literate population engaged was now silent rather than oral. This was appropriate, it was argued, because oral reading diverted attention from thought to pronunciations and expression, whereas true reading should be a process of thought-getting. Around the beginning of the twentieth century, however, even as this sentiment was growing, it was abruptly changed in force by the weight of evidence from early psychological experiments on reading. This evidence suggested — or so it seemed — that skillful silent reading involved qualitatively different processes from oral reading. At least within then-existing psychological models, the speed and efficiency of silent reading could not be explained by any underlying process of letter-to-phoneme translation, whether overt or covert. More plausibly, some suggested, skillful readers might recognize the words as wholes, like pictures (Woodworth, 1938).

The Contemporary Debate

Well through the 1940s, reading instruction was firmly focused on silent reading comprehension. Words were introduced through meanings first — to be recognized holistically by sight. When straight recognition failed, the children were encouraged to rely on context and pictures, to narrow in on the word's identity through meaning-based inference. Letter-sound instruction was relegated to the position of an ancillary tool, a back-up strategy; it was to be introduced gradually, invoked sparingly, and exercised only in coordination with the meaning-bearing dimensions of text (Chall, 1967). Psychologists, meanwhile, were preoccupied with their own science which, throughout this period, was firmly dominated by stimulus-response theories of behavior.

Then, in the 1950s, spearheaded by a best-selling book addressed to the mothers and fathers of America (Flesch, 1955), this practice was vehemently challenged. Flesch argued that too many children were not learning to read for the simple reason that the logic and use of the alphabetic principle was not being taught. Methodically built on the bottom-up stimulus-response frameworks of the psychologists, alphabetic instruction — a.k.a. phonics — regained a core position in the curriculum. But not for long.

In the 1960s, the psycholinguistic community produced a series of compelling arguments that human language acquisition defied explanation by stimulus-response theories of learning. Quickly thereafter, Frank Smith (1971) published an extremely influential book arguing that the same was true of reading. Drawing on reaction time data, Smith argued that skillful readers could not process the sequential letters or words of text, or their progress would be far too slow. Drawing on information theory, he argued that skillful readers need not process more than a scant fraction of the visual information on the page anyhow. Drawing on attention theory, he argued that if the mind can work with only one level of interpretation at a time, then reading must be focused, in process as in outcome, on the meaning and message of the text.

Smith's conclusion was that becoming a skillful reader must involve learning to sample the minimum necessary amount of visual information from several lines of text at once, and mapping that information directly to idea units. By implication, teaching children to attend to individual letters and words was misguided at best. Further, given the complexity and profusion of the functional features he had proposed, he recognized that they could not even be taught. The solution, he concluded, was that children must learn to read by applying their innately given language acquisition powers to text. Given ample, positively supported experience with meaningful text, they should find learning to read as natural and easy as learning to talk. Over the next two decades, Smith's theory blossomed into an elaborate instructional philosophy, known as the Whole Language Movement, under the auspices of which nearly every meaning-driven stance and approach of the previous decade was reinvented and brought to the classroom anew.

It was just at the outset of this era that Jeanne Chall published her seminal book, *Learning to Read: The Great Debate* (1967). In the effort to responsibly inform the then-raging debate over reading instruction, Chall interviewed leading educators and program authors, analyzed the objectives and methods of the instructional alternatives, and observed the materials at use in classrooms. In addition, she carefully reviewed the existing research on the instructional effects of the competing approaches. The results were clear and stunning. Relative to those programs that were built around whole-word instruction or that relied on teaching phonics in context, those that included systematic phonics instruction resulted in significantly better word recognition, better spelling, better vocabulary, and better reading comprehension. Moreover, the advantage of having been taught systematic phonics seemed to increase across the primary grades, and it was at least as great — though a bit slower to kick in — with children of lower entry abilities or socio-economic backgrounds as with readier and more privileged children.

Thus, across all these eras (at least in the background), despite the high profile of the competing beliefs, a number of educators held fast to the notions that working knowledge of the alphabet is indeed essential to proficient reading and is significantly fostered by teaching phonics. For just as long, however, and despite myriad proposals to make it easier (see Aukerman, 1971, 1984), alphabetic instruction has been dogged by one problem: Many students find it extremely difficult to induce the words from the code, no matter how they are drilled on the individual letters and their sounds.

In the last two decades, thanks largely to technology, research has finally delivered on these issues. Briefly, it turns out that authors' words and wordings constitute the indispensable raw data of their meanings. Consistent with this, skillful readers actually do fixate on virtually each and every word of text, quite meticulously processing the letters and translating the print to speech as they proceed (see Rayner & Pollatsek, 1989). Moreover, it is because this word- and letterwise processing is so fast, so automatic and effortless, that it is relatively invisible to introspection. And it is because it is rooted in remarkably rich and over-learned knowledge of the language's spellings and spelling-speech mappings, that it is so fast and effortless. Whether performed silently or aloud, reading an alphabetic script with fluency and reflective comprehension incontrovertibly depends on such knowledge.

Of equal importance, research has finally yielded an answer to the question of why learning to use the alphabetic principle is difficult for so many. The impasse lies in the perceptual and conceptual elusiveness of the phonemes (Liberman & Liberman, 1990). In fact, speech scientists surmise, humans are biologically predisposed to learn the phonemes of their native language and to perceive and distinguish them effortlessly, subattentionally, in service of language comprehension. For this same reason, however, they are ill prepared to access the phonemes consciously, as is required for understanding the alphabetic principle. If children can be persuaded to attend to the *sound* as opposed to the *meaning* of language, if they can be induced to conceive of language as a sequence of such phoneme-sized sounds, if they can be led to understand that the letters represent the sounds of their own speech, then much of the difficulty is lifted away. Moreover, researchers have demonstrated a variety of games and activities that effectively develop such phonemic awareness and that in turn produce significant acceleration in children's reading and writing growth (e.g., Lundberg, Frost, & Peterson, 1988)

More recently, and only through a convergence of much research along with significant advances in logical, mathematical, and computational sciences, theorists have begun to produce models that appear capable of mimicking the processes of reading and learning to read. For these models, whether they portray beginners or experts, the key is that they are *neither top-down nor bottom-up in nature.* Instead, all of the processes involved are simultaneously active and interactive, with every awakened cluster of knowledge and understanding at once both issuing and accommodating information, both passing and receiving guidance, to and from every other. The key to these models is not the dominance of one form of knowledge over the others, but the coordination and cooperation of all with each other. (See Adams, 1990.)

If, in reading and learning to read, the mind works interactively and in parallel with as many cues as it can recognize as relevant, then the purpose of instruction should be to help students assimilate the relevant cues in proper relation. In keeping with the spirit of the meaning-first curricula, then, these models emphatically reassert that literacy development depends critically and at every level upon the child's interest in and understanding of what is to be learned. With equal emphasis, however, they assert that children should be led to learn the letters and to appreciate their phonemic significance.

In short, due in part to the accumulation of trials and errors over

time but even more so to the research progress that the present times
have afforded, reading education is now supported with theory that, in
its very structure, reconciles the goals that once rent it apart. Again,
given an alphabetic system of writing, reading with fluency and comprehension depends critically on deep and detailed knowledge of the
the spelling-to-speech correspondences of its words. For many — if not
most — children, however, the insights and observations on which this
knowledge depends are not forthcoming without special guidance. By
implication, as Chall (1967) advised us thirty years ago, phonics does
indeed warrant explicit, systematic, and sensitive support in the classroom. Yet, as she also argued throughout her career (Chall, 1967, 1983,
1990), phonics is only a piece of the puzzle. Literacy growth depends on
the basics. Beyond that, however, it is best fostered through reading,
writing, spelling, language development, conceptual exploration, and
all manner of engagement with text, in relentlessly enlightened balance.

References

Adams, M.J. (1990). *Beginning to read: Thinking and learning about print.* Cambridge,
   MA: The MIT Press.

Aukerman, R.C. (1971). *Approaches to beginning reading.* New York: Wiley.

Aukerman, R.C. (1984). *Approaches to beginning reading* (2nd ed.). New York: Wiley.

Bumstead, J.F. (1840). *My little primer.* Boston: Perkins and Marwin.

Bumstead, J.F. (1844). *My first school book.* Boston: Perkins and Marwin.

Chall, J.S. (1967). *Learning to read: The great debate.* New York: McGraw-Hill.

Chall, J.S. (1983). *Stages of reading development.* New York: McGraw-Hill.

Chall, J.S. (1990). *The reading crisis: Why poor children fall behind.* Cambridge, MA:
   Harvard University Press.

Diringer, D. (1968). *The alphabet.* London: Hutchinson.

Eliot, C.W. (1891). Literature in the school. *Educational Review, 2.*

Farnham, G.L. (1887). *The sentence-method of teaching reading.* Syracuse, NY: C. W.
   Bardeen.

Flesch, R. (1955). *Why Johnny can't read.* New York: Harper & Row.

Gedicke, F. (1791). *Einige Gedanken über die Ordnung und Folge der Gegenstände des
   jugendlichen Unterrichts.* Berlin.

Herbart, J.F. (1895). *Science of education and aesthetic revelation of the world.* Boston: D.C. Heath.

Huey, E.B. (1908). *The psychology and pedagogy of reading.* Cambridge, MA: MIT Press.

Kaestle, C.F. (1991). *Literacy in the United States.* New Haven, CT: Yale University Press.

Liberman, I.Y., & Liberman, A.M. (1990). Whole language vs. code emphasis: Underlying assumptions and their implications for reading instruction. *Annals of Dyslexia, 40,* 51-76.

Lundberg, I., Frost, J., & Petersen, O.P. (1988). Effects of an extensive program for stimulating phonological awareness in preschool children. *Reading Research Quarterly, 23,* 263-284.

Mann, H. (1844). Method of teaching young children on their first entering school. *The Common School Journal, 6.* Boston: W.B. Fowle and N. Capen.

Mathews, M.M. (1966). *Teaching to read: Historically considered.* Chicago: University of Chicago.

Palmer, T.H. (1838). On the evils of the present system of primary instruction. *American Institute of Instruction, 8,* 211-239.

Parker, F.W. (1900). *Course of study, 1.* Chicago: University of Chicago.

Rayner, K., & Pollatsek, A. (1989). *The psychology of reading.* Englewood Cliffs, NJ: Prentice-Hall.

Smith, F. (1971). *Understanding reading.* New York: Holt, Rinehart, and Winston.

Smith, N.B. (1974). *American reading instruction.* Newark, DE.: International Reading Association.

Webster, N. (1798). *The American spelling book.* Boston: Isaiah Thomas and Ebenezer Andrews.

Woodworth, R.A. (1938). *Experimental psychology.* New York: Henry Holt and Company.

5

Implementing a Flexible Grouping Model in the First Grade

Meeting the Needs of the Lowest-Performing Readers

JEANNE R. PARATORE, Ed.D.
Boston University

JOY TURPIE, Ed.D.
Hingham Public Schools, Hingham, Massachusetts

In classrooms everywhere, teachers strive to meet the individual needs of every child they teach. For many years, they attempted to meet this goal by organizing students into reading groups based on text difficulty. Use of easier texts for children with lower reading ability was generally accompanied by slower-paced teaching and a focus on concrete, and often discrete, skills. Evidence from several studies suggests that children who participated in these groups failed to make the progress their teachers hoped they would make (Allington, 1980, 1984). In fact, the children with the most serious instructional needs often benefited least from the practice of grouping by ability or reading proficiency.

Other evidence, however, suggests that children do best in reading when they are taught with materials at their "instructional level," and do poorly when materials are at their "frustration level." Juel (1990), for example, reported that first-grade children's learning of basal words needs to be carefully monitored and remain high in order for them to achieve reading success.

In many cases, teachers are understandably confused and frustrated by these two seemingly conflicting points of view. How are they to reconcile the apparent push to "keep them all together" with the need to instruct students with materials at different levels of difficulty? Does heterogeneous instruction mean that during all reading activities, all children share the same book? How can a teacher move away from ability grouping and still provide every child access to literacy on an appropriate level?

In this chapter, we present one model for making difficult text easier in a first-grade classroom. It is based on a flexible grouping model (Paratore, 1991) in which teachers modify instruction by differentiating the types of experiences children have with text, rather than by changing the text itself. To illustrate the effects of the flexible grouping model, we focus on four first-grade children who were identified as at-risk readers early in the first grade. The teacher in the focal classroom, Joy Turpie, is one of the authors of this chapter.

Classroom Context

Joy's heterogeneous first-grade classroom consisted of 25 children. All children in the classroom were instructed using a combination of first-grade texts of a basal reading program and trade-book literature. The basal program, used system-wide, was an anthology of children's literature judged to be of high literary quality — characterized at the first-grade level by predictable and patterned language including rhythm, rhyme, and repetition. The supplementary trade books met the same criteria and were chosen by Joy for their compelling story lines, first-grade readability, and compatibility with the reading themes emphasized in the basal program.

As shown in Table 5-1 below, literacy experiences were organized around four components: (1) reading, rereading, and responding to shared text; (2) sustained silent reading; (3) phonemic awareness training; and (4) spelling-sound instruction.

Reading, Rereading, and Responding to Shared Text

All children in the class were instructed using a flexible grouping model (Paratore, 1991). This model was designed to meet individual needs through differentiated teaching, while eliminating the negative effects associated with ability grouping. The flexible grouping model utilized a variety of instructional practices, including whole-class instruction, needs-based small groups, and cooperative pairs. Whole-class instruction was employed for teacher modeling, guided practice, presenting new material, teaching specific strategies and skills, reviewing previously

Table 5-1
Schedule of Literacy Activities

Component	Approximate Time	Activities
Reading core text	1 hour and 15 minutes/day	Instruction in grade-appropriate text Reading and rereading grade-appropriate text Written response to selection read
Sustained silent reading	15 minutes/day	Reading easy text
Phonemic awareness training (Sept.-Jan.)	15 minutes, 1-2 days/week	Rhyming and alliteration activities
Spelling-sound instruction	30 minutes/day	Listening for, reading, and writing target sound

taught material, and providing feedback and correction. Small-group instruction might include any of these components except presentation of new material. In addition, the small groups provided a setting for independent practice and for additional review to meet the specific needs of the children in the group. Finally, cooperative pairs were used to reread a selection, to complete writing tasks, and to share written responses.

Each reading session started with whole-class instruction and discussion. In preparation for reading, the teacher instructed the whole class by accessing and developing background knowledge, often through the use of a semantic map. The children made predictions about the content of the selection and set a purpose for reading. The teacher read the selection aloud in order to familiarize the children with the concepts and language of the text. A whole-class discussion followed the initial read-aloud in order to facilitate understanding of the selection. Following the discussion, children read the selection as a chorus, while the teacher assisted any children who were having difficulty by pointing to the words as they read.

At this point the children were divided into a challenge group and an extra-help group. Children in the challenge group worked with a partner to read the selection, formulate a written response, and practice reading part of the selection until they could read it fluently. Children in the extra-help group worked with the teacher to review vocabulary and phonics skills and to read the selection as a chorus or with a partner. Toward the end of the extra-help session, the focus shifted from reading to writing and the teacher helped the students formulate written responses to the selection. Written responses were intended to elicit personal reactions, story summaries, or students' variations on the story. The students in the extra-help group then worked alone, finishing their written responses and reading or rereading easy text. During this time the teacher worked with the students in the challenge group to help them revise and edit their writing and reread the passage they had practiced. Finally, the extra-help and challenge groups reconvened to share their written responses. Sharing occurred either in a teacher-led group, in a peer-led group, or in cooperative pairs.

Children in the extra-help group received the following types of teacher scaffolding: (a) rereading the text with teacher and peers, (b) reinforcement of phonics instruction, (c) vocabulary development, and (d) practice on phonemes through writing. Children who were experiencing substantial difficulty had opportunities to reread each selection a minimum of four times at various times throughout the school day. The first and second rereadings occurred with the teacher or with a more able peer. The third and fourth rereadings occurred with any peer.

Sustained silent reading. In addition to the instructional reading time, children read for 15–20 minutes daily during Sustained Silent Reading. Children chose what they wanted to read from classroom texts, trade books, informational texts related to science and social studies themes, and books they brought from home. During this time, children who found the instructional text difficult to read chose easy text in order to gain fluency, automaticity, and independence in reading.

Phonemic awareness training. Once or twice a week for a 15-minute period, all children in the class participated in phonemic awareness training. Training included two kinds of activities: (a) categorizing pictures by rhyme or alliteration, and (b) letter-name and letter-sound training (Ball & Blachman, 1991; Chall, Roswell, & Blumenthal, 1963). In the first type of activity, children were given pictures and asked to choose one that rhymed with a given word or picture name, or to choose one that began like a given word or picture name. In the letter-name and letter-sound training, children played games such as bingo in which they had to match letter sounds and letter names.

Spelling-sound instruction. Each day the whole class was involved in 10–15 minutes of spelling-sound instruction that correlated to the vocabulary in the selection being read (Juel & Roper/Schneider, 1985). During a typical lesson, sentences from the selection were read aloud, while the children listened for a target sound. As they identified words with the target sound, the teacher wrote them on the chalkboard. The children examined the words and identified the spelling pattern that represented the target sound. Words with the target sound were then dictated for them to record in journals or on individual chalkboards.

The children also engaged once a week in Making Words (Hall & Cunningham, 1992). During this 15-minute activity, each child was given a limited number of letters to use to form words. After the teacher said each word, the children manipulated the letters to form the words at their desks. The activity began with two-letter words and progressed to words that used all the letters the children had been given.

Monitoring Children's Progress

In order to make certain that all children were succeeding in the instructional model, Joy incorporated two assessment routines: running records (Clay, 1979) and story retellings (Morrow, 1988). Running records were taken from individual children during the period when their classmates were engaged in Sustained Silent Reading. Based on the running record performance, word reading accuracy, self-correction rate, and reading fluency were calculated. Accuracy was calculated by dividing the number of words read correctly by the number of total words read (Clay, 1979). Self-correction rate was calculated by deriving a ratio of the number of self-corrections to the total number of errors (Clay, 1979). Fluency was calculated in words read per minute by dividing the number of words read correctly by the total reading time expressed in minutes.

Story retelling assessments were taken in two ways. Sometimes they were recorded while children retold a selection as part of the instructional routine. For example, as part of the daily instructional activity, one child might be asked to retell the story while the rest of the children listened and monitored their own recall. At other times, a retelling was elicited from an individual child immediately following the administration of a running record. During story retelling, Joy noted students' recall of each of the important story parts and the sequence in which ideas were recalled. Recall was recorded on a prepared observation form (Morrow, 1988).

Joy monitored the performance of her lowest-performing readers weekly, and evaluated other students approximately once a month. Both running records and oral retellings were conducted on the selections children read in class.

To examine the effectiveness of the instructional model, we focused our attention on the performance of four of Joy's lowest-performing learners. The section that follows describes the progress made by each of these children.

Adam

Adam was a motivated young reader. He was generally enthusiastic about learning and focused on the task at hand. However, at the beginning of first grade, he scored at the 35th percentile on a reading achievement test. He had difficulty fingerpointing to text even while reading along with the teacher or a more able peer. He had no sight vocabulary and was unable to use any cues to adjust his fingerpointing while reading chorally.

At the start of the study, Adam read grade-level text with 83% accuracy, averaged one self-correction in every 13 errors, and demonstrated a fluency rate of 15 words per minute. At the end of the school year, Adam was routinely achieving 99% accuracy when rereading instructional text. His self-correction rate had increased to one self-correction in every two errors, and his fluency rate had increased to 50 words per minute.

Adam also made impressive progress in story comprehension. At the start of the study, on the story retelling measure, Adam averaged 6.8 points out of a possible 10 points for recall of major story elements. At the end of the school year, he consistently recalled all story elements, achieving an average score of 9.9 across stories read.

Joy observed that throughout the school year, Adam maintained his high level of enthusiasm and demonstrated increased confidence in reading. He often brought books from home and sought opportunities to read these books to the class, with his friends, and on his own during Sustained Silent Reading.

Teddy

Teddy was a cautious learner. He had a hearing impairment which required that he wear hearing aids and lip-read to improve his understanding. His mother reported that he seemed to lack confidence since he wasn't sure how much of a conversation or instruction he had heard. At the beginning of first grade, he scored at the 33rd percentile on a reading achievement test. He never volunteered any information during instruction in a whole group, but was more willing to participate in a small group.

The instructional model had a strong effect on Teddy's reading performance. At the start of the study, Teddy read grade-appropriate text with 72% accuracy, averaged one self-correction in every eight errors, and averaged a fluency rate of 13 words per minute. At the end of first grade, Teddy was consistently averaging 97% accuracy when rereading instructional text. His self-correction rate had increased to one self-correction in every two errors, and his fluency rate had increased to 49 words per minute.

In retelling the major story elements at the beginning of the school year, Teddy averaged 7.1 points out of a possible 10 points. At the end of the school year, his recall had increased to an average of 9.5 points.

Joy observed that Teddy became more engaged and self-confident with each reading. He was more willing to read with peers after he had practiced a selection four times or more.

Mark

At the beginning of first grade, Mark scored at the 12th percentile on a reading achievement test. He was apathetic about reading, but he enjoyed adult interaction and became involved in reading when Joy guided him individually or in a small group.

At the start of the study, Mark read grade-appropriate text with 71% accuracy, averaged one self-correction in 10 errors, and demonstrated a fluency rate of 15 words per minute. At the end of the school year, Mark was consistently achieving 97% accuracy when rereading instructional text. His self-correction rate had increased to one self-correction in every two errors, and his fluency rate had increased to 39 words per minute.

Mark also improved in comprehension. At the beginning of the school year, he averaged 5.5 points out of a possible 10 points on a story retelling. By the end of the school year he had increased his average to 9.5 points.

Joy observed that throughout the year Mark remained minimally involved in his learning. He read carefully only when he was closely monitored by the teacher. His ability to read independently and with a peer increased with practice, but his desire to read remained static. He would not independently choose to read.

David

David was a motivated learner. He was interested in animals and their habitats and other topics related to science and social studies. His mother read to him extensively and he retained information and contributed enthusiastically to class discussions.

However, David was extremely distractible. He was interested in all that was going on around him. His attention continually shifted during a lesson or while working on an assigned task. He worked best in a small group or individually with the teacher nearby to refocus his attention. He had difficulty working independently.

At the start of the study, David's average reading accuracy was 65%, his self-correction rate was one word in every 12 errors, and his fluency rate was 14 words per minute. At the end of the year David achieved 96% accuracy when rereading instructional text. His self-correction rate had increased to one word in every two errors, and his fluency rate had increased to 46 words per minute.

David also made strong progress in his ability to comprehend. At the beginning of the school year, he averaged 5.5 points out of a possible 10 points for story retelling. By the end of the school year he attained an average of 9 points.

Throughout the school year Joy observed that David maintained a high level of enthusiasm and engagement in reading. He often brought informational books from home which related to the science, social studies, and reading curricula. He shared them with the class along with his knowledge of the topic.

What Did We Learn?

Our experiences in this classroom indicated that the level of text difficulty was an important factor in children's successful word reading and comprehension. However, consistent with earlier research, we found clear evidence that text difficulty is influenced not just by the words on the page, but also by the instructional actions the teacher initiates. In this classroom, when the teacher provided differentiated learning experiences for struggling readers — including increased instruction and practice in phonemic awareness and word study, and several repeated readings — low-performing readers who were placed in difficult text experienced substantial improvement in accuracy, fluency, self-correction behaviors, and understanding of grade-appropriate text.

The four children we followed learned a great deal about words in the stories they read. Their improvement in accuracy, fluency, and self-correction behaviors is particularly convincing. While the increase in word accuracy may be interpreted by some as evidence of memorization due to repeated reading, the children's attention to errors and increase in self-correction behaviors suggest otherwise. As Clay (1979) suggested, self-corrections demonstrate that the children are aware that a message is being communicated in a text; when they make an error that distorts meaning, they return to the error and correct it. These students' self-correction behaviors indicate that they attended to both the word (or local) level and the meaning (or global) level of the text.

As in other studies (e.g., Dowhower, 1987; Samuels, 1979), repeated reading helped these first-graders develop familiarity with vocabulary, content, and style of text. It is likely that these factors influenced reading rate. These four students were able to read three times as many words per minute after rereading the selection as they did on the first reading. An average increase from 73% to 97% accuracy suggests that rereading made difficult text easier, changing frustration-level text into instructional-level text. This outcome was consistent with work published by Gonzales and Elijah (1975), who found that with older students, *one rereading* led to a change in reading performance from frustration to instructional level.

In addition to an increase in accuracy, self-correction behaviors, and fluency, these first-graders displayed an increase in their ability to retell stories. These results are consistent with those from earlier repeated reading studies (O'Shea, Sindelar, & O'Shea, 1985; Reutzel & Hollingsworth, 1993).

Conclusion

As a result of the increasing use of heterogeneous grouping in first-grade classrooms, many emergent and beginning readers are routinely instructed in common, grade-appropriate text for at least part of their instructional reading program. This practice is too often characterized by a "one-size-fits-all" philosophy that fails to provide children with the types of instructional adjustments that make difficult text easier to read. The risks of such an instructional approach are obvious. Just as with ability grouping, the children who are most dependent on effective instruction are likely to be hurt by instructional experiences that frustrate them and fail to meet their individual needs.

Our evidence suggests, on the other hand, that when teachers modify a grade-level curriculum by providing increased scaffolding and rehearsal, children can not only listen to and comprehend the selections, but also learn to read them. When teachers combine opportunities to read easy text with opportunities to listen to, reread, and respond to difficult text, first-graders can be expected to acquire both the word study strategies necessary for achieving eventual independence in reading *and* the vocabulary and concept knowledge that is achieved through exposure to age- and grade-appropriate curriculum.

References

Allington, R.L. (1980). Teacher interruption behaviors during primary-grade oral reading. *Journal of Educational Psychology, 72,* 371-377.

Allington, R.L. (1984). Content coverage and contextual reading in reading groups. *Journal of Reading Behavior, 16,* 85-96.

Ball, E.W., & Blachman, B.A. (1991). Does phoneme segmentation training in kindergarten make a difference in early word recognition and developmental spelling? *Reading Research Quarterly, 26,* 49-66.

Clay, M.M. (1979). *The early detection of reading difficulties.* New Zealand: Octopus Publishing.

Chall, J.S., Roswell, F.G., & Blumenthal, S.H. (1963). Auditory blending ability: A factor in success in beginning reading. *The Reading Teacher, 16,* 113-118.

Dowhower, S.L. (1987). Effect of repeated reading on second-grade transitional readers' fluency and comprehension. *Reading Research Quarterly, 22,* 389-406.

Gonzales, P.C., & Elijah, D.V. (1975). Rereading: Effect on error patterns and performance levels on the IRI. *The Reading Teacher, 28,* 647-652.

Hall, D., & Cunningham, P.M. (1992). Reading without ability grouping: Issues in first-grade reading instruction. In C.K. Kinzer & D.J. Leu (Eds.), *Literacy research, theory, and practice: Views from many perspectives. Forty-first Yearbook of the National Reading Conference* (pp. 235-241). Chicago: National Reading Conference.

Juel, C. (1990). Effects of reading group assignment on reading development in first and second grade. *Journal of Reading Behavior, 22,* 233-254.

Juel, C., & Roper/Schneider, D. (1985). The influence of basal readers on first grade reading. *Reading Research Quarterly, 20,* 134-151.

Morrow, L.M. (1988). Retelling as a diagnostic tool. In S. Glazer, L. Searfoss, & L. Gentile (Eds.), *Re-examining reading diagnosis: New trends and procedures* (pp. 128-149). Newark, DE: International Reading Association.

O'Shea, L.J., Sindelar, P.T., & O'Shea, D.J. (1985). The effects of repeated readings and attentional cues on reading fluency and comprehension. *Journal of Reading Behavior, 17,* 129-141.

Paratore, J.R. (1991). *Flexible grouping: Why and how.* Needham Heights, MA: Silver Burdett & Ginn.

Reutzel, D.R., & Hollingsworth, P.N. (1993). Effects of fluency training on second graders' reading comprehension. *Journal of Educational Research, 86,* 325-331.

Samuels, S.J. (1979). The method of repeated readings. *The Reading Teacher, 32,* 403-408.

6

Teaching Reading to Children, Adolescents, and Adults

Similarities and Differences

MARY E. CURTIS, Ph.D.

Boys Town Reading Center, Father Flanagan's Boys' Home, Omaha, Nebraska

Differences among the ways that children, adolescents, and adults learn have often been discussed in theory and research (for example, see Cross, 1981; Davidson & Koppenhaver, 1993; Kidd, 1973; Knowles, 1980). And, as anyone who has ever worked with beginning readers at varying ages knows, some very striking differences do exist. Older learners have had more exposure to print, and they have more knowledge about the functions that written language serves. Consequently, they are more cognizant of the barriers that a lack of literacy can present (Sticht & McDonald, 1992), and they have developed strategies for coping with their deficits when difficulties arise. Increased age also means increased experience with the learning process itself. For adolescents and adults

* An earlier version of this paper was presented at the annual meeting of the International Reading Association in Atlanta in May 1990.

who have yet to master reading, this often means memories of past failures, along with attitudes and beliefs about the unlikelihood of future success (Roswell & Chall, 1994).

Apart from the many differences among them, however, beginning readers of all ages share a significant feature: their level of reading development (Chall, 1987; Sticht, 1988). Moreover, for any of these beginners to become proficient in reading, they need to acquire similar kinds of knowledge and skills, and to learn to apply similar kinds of strategies (Chall, 1983).

My goal in this chapter is twofold: to discuss in more detail some of the similarities and differences that exist among children, adolescents, and adults who are learning to read, and to show how understanding these similarities and differences can help us to better understand how to develop reading abilities in adolescents and adults. To accomplish this, I will focus on three components of reading that theory and research have identified as important sources of developmental differences (Carroll, 1977; Chall, 1983; Perfetti, 1985; Stanovich, 1986): word identification, knowledge of word meanings, and comprehension. By looking more closely at each of these components, I believe that we will be in better position to identify which instructional approaches will work best with readers at varying ages.

Word Identification

A great deal of theory and research has examined the ways in which children learn to identify the words on a page (Adams, 1990; Chall, 1967). And, though there has been much disagreement about the best ways to teach children to identify words accurately (Chall, 1989), most now acknowledge that this skill is essential for children who are learning to read. Zemelman, Daniels, and Hyde (1993) have summarized current thinking on this issue as follows:

Effective teachers have a broad-based approach to teaching word analysis that includes wide contextual reading experiences, focused word study, and student writing. They spend their instructional time judiciously; they carefully balance direct phonics instruction with more holistic, integrated reading and writing activities, and are alert to the potential boredom of decontextualized drills. In any case, such brief, well-designed lessons in phonics should normally be concluded by the end of second grade. (p. 28)

The use of second grade as a milestone at which time most children master word identification is consistent with developmental theory (Chall, 1983). In practice, however, many adolescents and adults have not yet reached this stage. Results from a recent report on the National Adult Literacy Survey (NALS) suggest that nearly 25% of American adults read at or below a fourth-grade level, despite having spent an average of 10 years in school (Kirsch, Jenkins, Jungeblut, & Kolstad, 1993). For many of these individuals, the process of word identification and the knowledge of symbol–sound relationships it entails remain to be mastered.

Are the methods appropriate for teaching word identification to adolescents and adults different from those appropriate for children? Regardless of age, the critical concepts to be learned (e.g., the alphabetic principle, the process of blending) and the advantage of direct instructional approaches for teaching are the same. The elements that need to differ as a function of age are the contexts provided for instruction and the kinds of materials used.

Suppose we want to teach the rule of silent *e*. If our student is a child, we would show him or her familiar words (like *mad* and *hop*) that change vowel sound when *e* is added to the end (e.g., *made* and *hope*). With older beginning readers, however, such an approach must be enhanced. The words used need to include ones that are more appropriate to their level of cognitive development, and that provide them with challenge (e.g., words like *explode* and *envelope*), allowing learners the opportunity to put into use the knowledge that has just been acquired (Curtis & Chmelka, 1994). The words also need to be ones that learners can see immediate value in knowing; the link between the generative power of knowing how to analyze words and the demands of reading in the "real world" should be stressed.

In addition to accuracy in word identification, fluency is a critical aspect of reading development (Samuels, Schermer, & Reinking, 1992). Fluent word identification means that when a person recognizes a word, she does so in a more or less effortless way (i.e., without attention). Fluent word recognition allows the reader to focus her attention on comprehension — the process of constructing meaning from what is read. In terms of reading development, fluent reading (or "ungluing from print," as Chall, 1983, refers to it) is usually achieved by the fourth grade.

Since rate of reading is one manifestation of fluency, studies of reading rate can help us to understand the developmental course of fluency in readers of varying ages. Children who learn to read without difficulty typically make a dramatic jump in reading rate. By the end of the second grade, for example, most children are reading aloud at a rate of at least 70 words per minute (Durrell, 1955; Gilmore, 1952; Hasbrouck & Tindal, 1992), and silently at about 90 words per minute (Harris & Sipay, 1985; Spache, 1981). By the fifth grade, the oral reading rate of skilled readers has jumped to about 150 words per minute (Hasbrouck & Tindal, 1992), and rate of silent reading is 175–200 words per minute (Harris & Sipay, 1985).

For many adolescents and adults learning to read, the relationship between the development of accuracy and the development of fluency is different from that in children. In particular, many older readers who can read accurately at the fourth- and fifth-grade levels read aloud much more slowly than fourth- and fifth-graders do (Bristow & Leslie, 1988; Curtis, 1996b). With adolescents and adults, it is not at all unusual to find that the level at which they can read fluently lags several grades behind their accuracy level (Bristow & Leslie, 1988; Curtis, 1996b). In other words, for adolescents and adults, the process of "ungluing from print" does not seem to occur at the same grade levels, or in the same ways, as it does for children.

The reason for this lag seems to be different for different people.

For some, it seems to be a consequence of the process they use to identify the words on the page; they rely on cues that slow them down. For others, it signals the need for more practice with texts on which they are already accurate. For still others, it indicates that a learning disability underlies their difficulty in reading (Cicci, 1995).

Whatever the cause, adolescents and adults need help in dealing with a lack of fluency, particularly because it can overload their ability to remember and comprehend what they have read (Perfetti, 1985) and cause them to adopt inappropriate strategies to speed things up (Stanovich, 1980). Most importantly, lack of fluency can turn reading into a task to avoid, one that brings little satisfaction or enjoyment.

Chall (1983) has described the development of fluency in children as a process that "requires daring and reflecting on one's daring":

> The child learns implicitly that the correct word or answer is based not only on sounding, or only on memory, or only on context — it is based on all of these. The integration is more difficult than knowing each separately. So the reader in Stage 2 makes many mistakes, and he or she should be given this freedom, along with "tips" on how to make corrections. (p. 47)

Given their histories of failure, it should not surprise us that the development of fluency seems to be a more difficult hurdle for adolescents and adults than it is for children. This difficulty has a number of implications for instruction.

In older learners much more than in children, risk-taking has to be nurtured and continually reinforced. Errors need to be celebrated and used to measure growth (Shaughnessy, 1977). Great care must be taken to select reading materials that are worth the effort they require on the part of the learner. With adolescents and adults, if texts are not entertaining or providing interesting or useful information, motivation will be difficult to maintain (Venezky, 1991). Rationales for why methods and materials are being used need to be provided frequently and concisely. And feedback must be continually sought from the learners about their needs and the extent to which they view the reading instruction as addressing them.

Over the years, the process of recognizing words on a page seems to have generated more research (and more controversy) than any other aspect of reading. And in most people's minds, the capacity to carry out this process is what is meant by "being able to read." Fortunately, many adolescents and adults seem able to master this aspect of reading fairly quickly (Chall, 1987; Curtis, 1996a). However, as word identification is only one part of what it means to be literate, our prognosis for older learners needs to consider other components of reading as well.

Knowledge of Word Meanings

When children first learn to read, they already know the meanings of all the words they are learning to identify in print. In fact, by the beginning of grade 2, most children can read only about 10 percent of the 6000 or so words that they can understand when heard (Chall, 1983). Over the next couple of years of instruction, the reading knowledge and skills that children acquire help them to close the gap between the words whose meanings they know and those that they are able to read. By grade 3, children can read about one third of the 9000 or more words in their listening vocabularies. By middle school, for those children who have not experienced difficulties in learning to read, the gap is closed; at this point children are finally able to read all of the words whose meanings they know.

Now a new gap begins. Students begin encountering words that they are able to read, but for which they do not have meanings. This process has been referred to as "reading to 'learn the new' — new knowledge, information, thoughts, and experiences" (Chall, 1983, p. 20). Before this time, children have been learning to read materials that largely confirm what they already know. Now children are faced with the task of learning how to learn from the materials that they can read.

For adolescents and adults with reading difficulties, the developmental link between reading achievement and knowledge of word meanings is somewhat different from that found in children. As with younger beginning readers, older beginning readers know the meanings of many more words than they are able to identify in print. Consequently, in the process of learning to analyze words, older learners are also encountering a gap between words they can read and words they recognize when heard. In fact, because this gap is much greater in older beginning readers than it is in younger ones, older learners initially make more rapid progress in learning to read than younger students do (Sticht, 1988).

However, as they progress in the development of their word identification skills, adolescent and adult readers are much less likely than children to encounter words in text that are totally new to them. Moreover, problems unique to older learners begin to arise because, even though the words are not totally new, they are also not totally known. Confusion and frustration can quickly settle in, and interest and motivation quickly fade away.

As skilled adult readers, much of our knowledge about word meanings has been acquired incidentally, the result of our encounters with words in multiple contexts (Graves, 1986; Sternberg, 1987). Less-skilled adolescent and adult readers have also acquired knowledge about word meanings in this way, although the contexts in which they have encountered words are usually less varied and are frequently aural rather than written in nature. Older learners may recall hearing or seeing a particular word before, and may even be able to recall the context in which the word occurred. But often less-skilled adolescent and adult readers will find it difficult to separate the meaning of the word from the context in which they remember it occurring (Curtis, 1987). Consider the case of the man who assumed that *beneficial* must have something to do with money because he remembered that there used to be a company called "Beneficial Finance." Or the teen who defined *ancestor* as "one of your relatives who you don't see too much." Or the student who said a *controversy* was "something to do with government." Or the one who said about *desist*, "My high school teacher used to say that — cease and desist — I think it means sit down, shut up, and pay attention" (Curtis & Glaser, 1983).

Since adolescents and adults with reading difficulties can end up trying to apply incomplete or imprecise knowledge about word meanings, teachers need to continually seek out and reinforce their willingness to take risks concerning vocabulary questions during reading. In addition, older readers will often benefit from direct instruction in strategies for confirming (and refining, if necessary) their vocabulary knowledge (Sternberg, 1987).

Older readers can also benefit from direct instruction in words, meanings, and concepts, especially in areas on which they have missed out because they have not been reading. For instance, with at-risk older adolescents like those we work with at Boys Town, limited vocabulary knowledge is their most prevalent difficulty in reading (Curtis, 1996b). For the majority of these youth, not having done much reading is more of the problem than not being able to read. And by the time they reach late adolescence, they are caught in a vicious cycle: because their vocabularies are weak, their comprehension suffers; because their comprehension suffers, their vocabularies remain weak.

The findings from Boys Town youth are consistent with the pattern of results from a study of children from low-income backgrounds (Chall, Jacobs, & Baldwin, 1990). In spite of starting school with adequate intelligence, these children were found to be more than two years behind grade level in their knowledge of word meanings by the time they reached the 7th grade.

For adolescents and adults with histories of reading difficulties, a well-planned, systematic, and continuous program of vocabulary instruction may be critical for promoting further growth in reading abilities. Such a direct vocabulary intervention can provide students with multiple opportunities to encounter a wide range of word meanings in a variety of contexts. Participants can also be given activities that require them to process the words in an active, generative way (incorporating speaking and writing along with reading and listening). Distinctions among words' meanings should be stressed as much as their similarities (Curtis, 1996a).

Just as the development of vocabulary knowledge plays a central role in children's reading development from about grade 3 until grade 9 (Chall, 1983), lack of knowledge of word meanings is a major cause of reading problems in adolescents and adults. Hence, many of the same approaches used to promote vocabulary development in children can be adapted for meeting the vocabulary needs of older readers. In addition, however, as mentioned above, older readers tend to have a great deal of partial knowledge, derived from the contexts in which words have occurred, and background knowledge drawn almost entirely from their own experiences. These characteristics are critical for vocabulary lessons to address if they are to work effectively with older learners.

Reading Comprehension

When children first begin to learn to read, their ability to understand the meaning of what they are reading far surpasses their ability to read it (Chall, 1983; Sticht, Beck, Hauke, Kleiman, & James, 1974; Sticht & James, 1984). In other words, their lack of skill in identifying words places a limit, or "cap," on their comprehension (Carroll, 1977). Remove this cap or limit, as happens when we give them a listening task rather than a reading one, and they are able to understand written materials at levels higher than they can read (Curtis, 1980).

Deficits in word identification skills also limit what adolescents and adults are able to understand through reading. In spite of this, however, it is not at all unusual for older readers to be able to read texts aloud that are more difficult than the words they are able to read in isolation (Curtis, 1996b), or even to understand texts that they are unable to read aloud. Seeming contradictions like these underscore the need to recognize that older readers are often much more likely than younger ones to use prior knowledge and context to figure out what is on a page. In fact, helping adolescents and adults to realize how this strategy ultimately can (and cannot) help them to improve their reading should be an important instructional goal.

Another way in which older learners tend to be different from younger ones is in the relationship between their reading and listening levels. Numerous studies (summarized in Sticht & James, 1984) have found a developmental pattern in the correlations between listening and reading comprehension abilities, beginning with little or no relationship in the primary grades (see also Curtis, 1980) and rising to correlations as high as +.60 to +.70 by the 5th to 6th grades. In most adolescents and adults, regardless of reading level, reading and listening comprehension skills are highly correlated. This correlation is partly due to older beginning readers' heavy dependence on context to bypass their problems in word identification. In addition, low listening comprehension levels are related to the limited fund of general knowledge that characterizes many older learners with reading problems (Chall, Heron, & Hilferty, 1987).

Regardless of the reasons why, reading and listening skills tend to be more similar in older learners with reading problems than they are in children. Because of this, instruction for older learners needs to focus, from the start, on ways to help them to learn to comprehend better. Teaching students to ask questions about what is being read and teaching ways to answer those questions have been found to be effective techniques for adolescent poor readers (Anderson & Roit, 1993). Using writing to emphasize the importance of meaning in reading is a critical step for older learners as well (Sticht & McDonald, 1992). Teachers of adolescents and adults with reading problems also need to stimulate and encourage wide and independent reading and listening (Roswell & Chall, 1994), so that these older learners will acquire the background knowledge they need to enhance their abilities to understand and learn from what they read.

Summary

Methods of understanding and promoting reading development in children have long been influenced by the study of mature reading (Carroll, 1977). Using knowledge derived from research on skilled readers to inform instructional practices with children has not required that we treat children as miniature adults. And, although some have argued otherwise (Kazemek, 1988), using knowledge derived from the study of reading development in children to inform reading instruction in adolescents and adults does not require us to assume that younger and older learners have identical needs. Rather, it represents an acknowledgement that over a century's worth of theory and research, we have managed to learn something about literacy and literacy development. It also represents a recognition that understanding the best ways to develop literacy in adolescents and adults might possibly be accomplished by building on what we already know.

I have looked only briefly at three components of reading (word identification, knowledge of word meanings, and reading comprehension). For each, I have described some of the similarities and differences in the ways that each component develops in children, adolescents, and adults. I have also noted some implications that these similarities and differences have for instructional methods and materials.

With regard to word identification, I have argued that similar methods are appropriate for use with younger and older readers. However, the instructional context and content of instruction should be different for adolescents and adults. In particular, phonics-based approaches will be most effective with older learners when they are provided with tasks and materials that afford them opportunities to generalize and extend the concepts they are learning. Older students also require more encouragement and support for developing fluency than children do. Special attention needs to be paid to the kinds of materials used, as well, so that older learners remain convinced that the benefits of their struggle far outweigh the costs.

With regard to knowledge of word meanings, I have suggested that direct vocabulary instruction, along with strategies for acquiring new vocabulary from context, are effective ways to promote growth in reading ability, regardless of the student's age. When working with older students, however, two features of their vocabulary knowledge will be of particular importance for teachers to address. The first is the way in which much of their knowledge is tied to the particular contexts in which it has been acquired. The second has to do with limitations in their general word knowledge *per se,* the consequence of not having engaged in the same kinds of opportunities for learning new words, meanings, and concepts as older learners who did not experience difficulties in reading.

In terms of comprehension, I have suggested that older learners who have experienced difficulties in learning to read are more likely to benefit from direct instruction than children who are just learning to read. The methods I recommended included: teaching strategies for solving problems that can arise during reading; using writing as a tool for focusing on the meaning of what has been read; and expanding background knowledge via wide and varied independent reading and listening activities.

In 1967, when Jeanne Chall reviewed the evidence on the best way to teach children how to read, she cautioned that research must always be initiated and understood within the context of the work that has preceded it. Perhaps nowhere is this more critical for us to remember today than in the field of adolescent and adult literacy. As we search for solutions to the reading difficulties faced by older learners, let us be guided by what she warned us nearly 30 years ago:

> The existence of a controversy is in itself a phenomenon deserving serious study. We can no longer afford the luxury of anger and indiscriminate blaming. When a body of "truths" has been accepted in theory and practice for nearly fifty years, we must closely examine the foundation upon which it was built before replacing it with a new set of truths. The foundation for the new truths must be studied carefully as well. Otherwise we build on sand.
>
> (Chall, 1967, p. 305)

References

Adams, M.J. (1990). *Beginning to read.* Cambridge, MA: MIT Press.

Anderson, V., & Roit, M. (1993). Planning and implementing collaborative strategy instruction for delayed readers in grades 6-10. *The Elementary School Journal, 94,* 121-137.

Bristow, P.S., & Leslie, L. (1988). Indicators of reading difficulty. *Reading Research Quarterly, 23,* 200-218.

Carroll, J.B. (1977). Developmental parameters in reading comprehension. In J.T. Guthrie (Ed.), *Cognition, curriculum, and comprehension* (pp. 1-15). Newark, DE: IRA

Chall, J.S. (1967). *Learning to read: The great debate.* New York: McGraw Hill.

Chall, J.S. (1983). *Stages of reading development.* New York: McGraw-Hill.

Chall, J.S. (1987). Developing literacy ... in children and adults. In D. Wagner (Ed.), *Future of literacy in a changing world* (pp. 65-80). New York: Pergamon.

Chall, J.S. (1989). Learning to read: The great debate 20 years later. *Phi Delta Kappan, 70,* 521-528.

Chall, J.S., Heron, E., & Hilferty, A. (1987). Adult literacy: New and enduring problems. *Phi Delta Kappan, 69,* 190-196.

Chall, J.S., Jacobs, V.A., & Baldwin, L.E. (1990). *The reading crisis: Why poor children fall behind.* Cambridge and London: Harvard University Press.

Cicci, R. (1995). *"What's wrong with me?" Learning disabilities at home and school.* Baltimore: York Press.

Cross, P. (1981). *Adults as learners.* San Francisco: Jossey-Bass.

Curtis, M.E. (1980). Development of components of reading skill. *Journal of Educational Psychology, 72,* 656-669.

Curtis, M.E. (1987). Vocabulary testing and vocabulary instruction. In M.G. McKeown & M.E. Curtis (Eds.), *The nature of vocabulary acquisition* (pp. 37-51). Hillsdale, NJ: Erlbaum.

Curtis, M.E. (1996a). Intervention for adolescents "at-risk." In L.R. Putnam (Ed.), *How to be a better reading teacher* (pp. 231-239). Columbus, Ohio: Macmillan.

Curtis, M.E. (1996b). Reading strengths and needs of at-risk youth. *Contemporary group care practice: Research & evaluation, 6*(1).

Curtis, M.E., & Chmelka, M.B. (1994). Modifying the *laubach way to reading* program for use with adolescents with LDs. *Learning Disabilities Research & Practice, 9,* 38-43.

Curtis, M.E., & Glaser, R. (1983). Reading theory and the assessment of reading achievement. *Journal of Educational Measurement, 20,* 133-147.

Davidson, J., & Koppenhaver, D. (1993). *Adolescent literacy: What works and why.* New York: Garland.

Durrell, D.D. (1955). *Durrell analysis of reading difficulty.* Yonkers, NY: World Book.

Gilmore, J.V. (1952). *Gilmore oral reading test.* Yonkers, NY: World Book.

Graves, M.F. (1986). Vocabulary learning and instruction. *Review of Research in Education, 13,* 49-89.

Harris, A., & Sipay, E. (1985). *How to increase reading ability.* New York: Longman.

Hasbrouck, J.E., & Tindal, G. (1992). Curriculum-based oral reading fluency norms for students in grades 2 through 5. *Teaching Exceptional Children, 24,* 41-44.

Kazemek, F.E. (1988). Necessary changes: Professional involvement in adult literacy programs. *Harvard Educational Review, 58,* 464-487.

Kidd, J.R. (1973). *How adults learn.* Chicago: Follett.

Kirsch, I.S., Jenkins, L, Jungeblut, A., & Kolstad, A. (1993). *Adult literacy in America: A first look at the results of the national adult literacy survey.* Washington: US Department of Education.

Knowles, M. (1980). *The modern practices of adult education.* Chicago: Association Press.

Perfetti, C.A. (1985). *Reading ability.* New York: Oxford.

Roswell, F.G., & Chall, J.S. (1994). *Creating successful readers: A practical guide to testing and teaching at all levels.* Chicago: The Riverside Publishing Company.

Samuels, S.J., Schermer, N., & Reinking, D. (1992). In S.J. Samuels & A.E. Farstrup (Eds.), *What research has to say about reading instruction* (pp. 124-144). Newark, DE: International Reading Association.

Shaughnessy, M.P. (1977). *Errors & expectations: A guide for the teacher of basic writing.* New York: Oxford University Press.

Spache, G.D. (1981). *Diagnostic reading scales.* Monterey, CA: CTB/McGraw-Hill.

Stanovich, K.E. (1980). Toward an interactive-compensatory model of individual differences in the development of reading fluency. *Reading Research Quarterly, 16,* 32-71.

Stanovich, K.E. (1986). Matthew effects in reading: Some consequences of individual differences in the acquisition of reading. *Reading Research Quarterly, 21,* 360-407.

Sternberg, R.J. (1987). Most vocabulary is learned from context. In M.G. McKeown & M.E. Curtis (Eds.), *The nature of vocabulary acquisition* (pp. 89-105). Hillsdale, NJ: Erlbaum.

Sticht, T.G. (1988). Adult literacy education. *Review of Research in Education, 15,* 59-96.

Sticht, T.G., Beck, L.J., Hauke, R.N., Kleiman, G.M., & James, J.H. (1974). *Auding and reading: A developmental model.* Alexandria, VA: HumRR.

Sticht, T.G., & James, J.H. (1984). Listening and reading. In P.D. Pearson (Ed.), *Handbook of reading research* (pp. 293-317). New York: Longman.

Sticht, T.G., & McDonald, B.A. (1992). Teaching adults to read. In S.J. Samuels & A.E. Farstrup (Eds.), *What research has to say about reading instruction* (pp. 314-334). Newark, DE: International Reading Association.

Venezky, R.L. (1991). Catching up and filling in: Literacy learning after high school. In J. Flood, J.M. Jensen, D. Lapp, & J.R. Squire (Eds.), *Handbook of research on teaching the English language arts* (pp. 343-348). New York: Macmillan.

Zemelman, S., Daniels, H., & Hyde, A. (1993). *Best practice: New standards for teaching and learning in America's schools.* Portsmouth, NH: Heinemann.

7

A Study of Prediction Ability

LILLIAN R. PUTNAM, Ed.D.
Professor Emeritus, Kean College of New Jersey

"What do you think will happen next?"

"How do you think the story will end?"

These are the most common questions asked by reading teachers in comprehension lessons. Teachers instinctively know that asking children to predict events in a story or story endings has several advantages. Predictive questions:

- attract, focus, and retain attention.
- set a purpose for reading.
- bring confirmation or negation of the student's thoughts and ideas.
- provide an added incentive of interest.
- depend on knowledge to produce inferential thinking.
- indicate the level of the student's comprehension.

"Prediction" comes from two Latin words — *pre-,* meaning "before," and *dicto,* meaning "to say" — hence, to say what the remainder or ending of the story will be before the story is finished. It is interesting to note that as early as 1908, E.B. Huey was recommending prediction as an instructional strategy, with his statements about "push forward" and "forward tendency." Arthur Gates (1947) recognized the value of prediction; he suggested it as a remedial strategy for pupils who have specific difficulty thinking with and beyond the facts given, since these pupils read without relating the material to known facts.

Authors of contemporary reading instruction texts also recommend prediction as an effective instructional strategy. Lipson and Wixson (1991) suggest using word lists to predict story content, and also suggest using Prediction Monitor Guides. Harris and Sipay (1985) advocate prediction of story endings, and evaluation of those predictions after completion of reading. They urge discussion and "justification" of students' predictions from the story text.

Earlier Research

The professional literature is replete with suggestions that prediction is a good instructional strategy. Foley (1993) provides an overview of the importance of prediction and practice from 1960 to 1990. Hunt and Joseph (1990) compared the effectiveness of teacher questions to that of prediction-generating questions with low-achieving readers, and found the prediction-generating questions to be significantly superior.

Various factors have been shown to influence children's ability to make predictions. Nistler (1987) found that children who have been read stories aloud make better predictions about story endings when they read the same stories later themselves. This results because they are better aware of story components, character, plot, and theme. Chi (1989) reported that extensive listening activities could greatly improve prediction abilities when teaching Chinese language to young children. Vosniadou (1984) had preschool children through grade 3 listen to stories and act out the meaning of the ending. The enactments were classified as (1) unrelated, (2) literal, (3) correct, or (4) composite. She concluded that this is a developmental skill influenced by predictability and literal use of figures of speech.

Grant (1987) found that Native American children were often bewildered by white man's stories, particularly by the violence in fairy tales. These children lacked the cultural background to predict the endings of Western stories, although they may have been competent at prediction of stories in their own culture.

The Study

Despite the wealth of research on prediction-related instruction, there is little in the literature that indicates at what grade level children are first able to predict story endings, and what kinds of predictions they can make when listening to a story. Elementary school teachers know that children in grades 3, 4, and higher can make story ending predictions when reading. What is not known is whether or not young prereaders can make predictions of story endings when listening to stories, and if so, what kinds of predictions they can make.

This study sought answers to the following questions:

1. Can first-graders predict story endings?
2. If so, what kinds of predictions can they make?
3. Do these abilities change from fall to spring?

Pilot Study

A pilot study was conducted with first-graders to determine if the idea for the planned study seemed feasible. A condensed version of the folk story of Peter Rabbit was told to each of the 29 first-graders individually. They were told that only part of the story would be given, and that they would be asked to suggest an ending. At the point at which Peter is being chased by Farmer McGregor, children were asked to predict the story ending and draw a picture. Thirteen of the 29 first-graders were able to make a sensible prediction. This result provided encouragement to continue with the study.

Study with First-Grade Children

A full study was conducted with a total of 100 children in five different classrooms, in different urban and suburban districts (Putnam & Farber, 1984). The same format was used as in the pilot study. Each child was told individually, in a private setting, that part of a story would be told and that he or she would then be asked to suggest a story ending. This was done once in the fall and again in the spring.

The story selected by first-grade teachers for the study was *The Horse who Lived Upstairs,* by Phyllis McGinley (1957). It was chosen because of its interesting story line, and also because it was unknown to the children. The abbreviated story read to the children was as follows:

> Once there was a horse named Joey. He lived in an apartment in the city. He pulled a wagon with vegetables for his master to sell. But he was not happy. He wanted to live in the country where he would have a red barn to live in, and green fields to run in, so he was not happy. One day his old master said, "Joey, I don't need you anymore. I have bought a new truck, and the truck can carry my vegetables for me." So he took Joey out to the country to live. At first, Joey was very happy beause he had a red barn to live in, and green fields to run in. But they didn't feed him much at all. Poor Joey was very unhappy. One day his old master came back and said, "Joey, you know that new truck I bought? Well, I didn't like that truck at all, so I sold the truck." Now what do you think would happen next?

The responses were recorded and analyzed into one of three categories, as shown in Table 7-1. Divergent predictions are considered to be more sophisticated responses than convergent predictions, which in turn are considered more sophisticated than no prediction at all.

Table 7-2 presents the classification and comparison of fall and spring data for first-graders. Chi-square analysis showed chi-square = 5.11 and p > .05, with df=2 and N=100. There was no significant difference between the two distributions, which means that there was no significant improvement in ability to make predictions from fall to spring, although there was a trend toward more convergent predictions in the spring. It is particularly interesting that a few children were able to make divergent predictions even in the fall. Teachers were instructed to give no instruction or practice in predictive strategies during the year. This study shows that when listening to stories, some first-graders are able to make both convergent and divergent predictions of story endings.

Table 7-1
Types of Prediction Responses

Category	Criteria	Example
1. No prediction	No prediction	Joey was hungry.
	Simple repetition	Joey wanted a barn.
2. Convergent	Sensible, logical prediction	Master took Joey back. Joey pulled the wagon again.
3. Divergent	Sensible prediction but creative or unusual	Joey went home, and they got a new truck. Master put Joey on a better farm.

Table 7-2
Comparison of Fall and Spring Prediction Responses of First-Grade Children

	No Prediction	Convergent	Divergent	Total
Fall	53	34	13	100
Spring	33	50	17	100
	86	84	30	200

Study with Kindergarten Children

The question then arose, if first-graders were able to make predictions, could kindergarten children do it? To answer this question, a second study was done with 201 kindergarten children in 13 urban and suburban school districts (Putnam, 1991). The same story and format were repeated, as children were individually told the story and asked for a prediction of the story ending, in the fall and again in the spring. Table 7-3 shows the analysis and comparison of this data. With chi-square = 31.28, p < .001, df=2, and N=201, there was a highly significant difference between the fall and spring data. Many more children were able to make predictions in the spring.

An intriguing question arose as to whether children who performed well in prediction also performed well on Reading Readiness Tests. To answer this, the predictions of the children who scored in the top 10% on the California Reading Readiness Test were compared with the predictions of children in the bottom 10% of that test. Table 7-4 shows a comparison of the predictions of these two kindergarten groups. Numbers in the respective cells had "expected" frequencies too small to use the chi-square statistic, but inspection indicates there was only a minimal difference between the two groups. The highest and lowest scorers on the Reading Readiness Test performed almost equally well on the prediction test. This finding suggests that the skills tapped in the Reading Readiness Test are different from those tapped in the prediction of story endings.

Comparison of First-Graders and Kindergarteners

It was also interesting to compare the findings on prediction for first grade with those of the kindergarten group. Table 7-5 shows the comparison of these two groups. With chi-square = 12.81, p < .005, df=2, and N=301, there was a highly significant difference between the predictions of the two groups; first-graders made significantly more divergent predictions.

Table 7-3
Comparison of Fall and Spring Prediction Responses of Kindergarten Children

	No Prediction	Convergent	Divergent	Total
Fall	104	93	4	201
Spring	51	137	13	201
	155	230	17	402

Table 7-4
Comparison of Prediction Responses of Kindergarten Children in the Top 10% and Bottom 10% of Reading Readiness Test

	No Prediction	Convergent	Divergent	Total
Top 10%	5	12	0	17
Bottom 10%	4	12	1	17
	9	24	1	34

Table 7-5
Comparison of Prediction Responses of First-Grade Children and Kindergarten Children

	No Prediction	Convergent	Divergent	Total
First Graders	33	50	17	100
Kindergarten	51	137	13	201
	84	187	30	301

Study with Four-Year-Old Children

Eager to see what would happen with younger children, we repeated the project with a population of four-year-old children in six public and private day care centers in urban and suburban areas. As before, the same story was told orally to each child, one at a time, in a private setting. Each child was told that part of a story would be read, and that he or she would be asked to tell how it might end.

Table 7-6 presents the data for this four-year-old group. With chi-square = 0.20, p > .05, and df = 2, there was no significant difference between the fall and spring responses.

It was interesting to compare the responses of the four-year-old

Table 7-6
Comparisons of Fall and Spring Prediction Responses of Four-Year-Old Children

	No Prediction	Convergent	Divergent	Total
Fall	78	26	2	106
Spring	62	19	1	82
	140	**45**	**3**	**188**

Table 7-7
Comparisons of Prediction Responses of Four-Year-Old Children and Kindergarten Children

	No Prediction	Convergent	Divergent	Total
Kindergarten	51	137	13	201
4-Year-Olds	62	19	1	82
	113	**156**	**14**	**283**

children to those of the kindergarten children. Table 7-7 shows the comparison of these two groups. With chi-square = 53.7, p < .001, and df = 2, there was a significant difference between the responses of the four-year-old children in day care centers and those of the kindergarten children. The four-year-olds were significantly less able to predict story endings, and only one was able to make a divergent response. As with the other groups, the teachers stated that they had not deliberately taught prediction or given extensive practice in doing it.

During the sessions of story telling and questioning, it became very evident that the investigator's asking for a story's ending or "finish" caused the four-year-olds more consternation than was apparent in the older groups. The question resulted in some confusion: some children fingered parts of their clothing, twisted their hair, changed the subject, asked irrelevant questions about the investigator, talked about lunch, or just smiled sweetly, but gave no response at all. Frequently, diverting questions replaced an expected response: "Did you see my new sneakers?" "We're going to have birthday cake today for lunch." "Did you know I have a new baby brother?"

Summary

This paper answered the four questions raised initially, concerning prediction abilities of first-graders when listening to stories, and extended the study to kindergarten and four-year-old children in nursery schools and day care centers. It showed that both convergent and divergent predictions of story endings are possible for some first-graders, some kindergarteners, and some four-year-old children.

Both first-graders and four-year-olds showed no significant difference between their fall and spring predictions. Kindergarten children did display significant differences between fall and spring results, with many more children able to make convergent predictions in the spring.

A comparison between the groups showed that there was a highly significant difference between the predictions of first-graders and those of kindergarten children, with the first-graders giving more divergent responses. Some interesting examples of these were:

> Joey would go back with his master and pull the wagon again and he would work harder and make more money and then he'd be warm again and he'd be happy again.

> Joey'd go back to the city and he'd help his master find a better truck to pull the fruits and then he don't have to work no more but he'd be warm and happy and have a lot of food.

There was also a significant difference between predictions of kindergarteners and four-year-olds, with the younger children far less able to make any predictions at all. In general, the convergent and divergent responses increased respectively with age.

A practical question arose at the conclusion of this study: Should teachers encourage and promote prediction of story endings when children listen to stories at kindergarten and first-grade levels?

Our answer was this: Since kindergarten and first-grade children demonstrate this skill easily, it would be wise for teachers to have them practice the strategy routinely. Since four-year-old children seem to have considerable difficulty with this task, this writer believes there is little or no need to force the skill earlier. It could be taught casually and occasionally, but not as a systematic drill to augment an already full curriculum.

References

Chi, Y. (1989). The role of listening comprehension in classroom instruction. *Journal of the Chinese Language Teachers Association, 24,* 63-69.

Foley, C. (1993). Prediction: A valuable reading strategy. *Reading Improvement, 30,* 166-70.

Gates, A. (1947). *The improvement of reading.* New York, NY: Macmillan.

Grant, A. (1987). *Cultural specific materials: Stories by My Kobun and Mushoom.* Urbana, IL: ED 299085.

Harris, A., & Sipay, E. (1985). *How to increase reading ability.* New York: Longman.

Huey, E. (1908). *The psychology and pedagogy of reading.* Cambridge, MA: MIT Press.

Hunt, J., & Joseph, D. (1990). Using prediction to improve reading comprehension of low-achieving readers. *Journal of Clinical Reading, 3,* 14-17.

Lipson, M., & Wixson, K. (1991). *Assessment and instruction of reading disabilities.* New York, NY: HarperCollins.

McGinley, P. (1957). *The horse who lived upstairs.* Philadelphia: Lippincott.

Nistler, R. (November, 1987). *Reading aloud as contributor to child's concept of story.* Paper presented at the Annual Meeting of the National Council of Teachers of English. Los Angeles, CA.

Putnam, L. (1991). The growth of prediction of kindergarten children from fall to spring. *The Reading Instruction Journal, 34,* 5-11.

Putnam, L., & Farber, F. (1984). Convergent/divergent predictions from fall to spring of urban first graders. *The Reading Instruction Journal, 28,* 15-22.

Vosniadou, S. (1984). Sources of deficiency in the young child's understanding of metaphorical language. *Child Development, 55,* 1588-1606.

8

The Use of Connectives in Low-Income Children's Writing

Linking Reading, Writing, and Language Skill Development

VICKI A. JACOBS, Ed.D.

Harvard University

Over the past 25 years, theorists and practitioners have shown increased interest in the relation between reading (comprehension) and writing (composition) processes (e.g., Gold, 1981; Jensen, 1984; Meyer, 1982; Stotsky, 1975, 1982). One focus common to both reading and writing research has been on how ideas are semantically integrated, either for comprehension or for effective presentation of meaning in writing. The literature suggests that one way that both readers and writers might integrate information semantically is by using their knowledge of connectives.

Historically, there has been consistent interest in the nature of connectives (e.g., Huey, 1908; Ingham, 1896; Thorndike, 1917). That meaning, in part, inheres in relationships between ideas (Dewey, 1933) is illustrated in texts on logic (e.g., Beardsley, 1975; Kneller, 1966; Quine, 1950) wherein connectives both signal and prescribe the relations between logical propositions and clauses — influencing the truth-meaning statements that they help to form. *Not* signals denial; *and, both–and,* and *but* signal conjunction; *or* and *either–or* signal disjunction; *if–then* signals conditionality; and *if and only if* signals biconditionality (Schagrin, 1968).

Researchers in the psychology of logic have examined developmental trends in the use and understanding of logical connectives and the relation of that development to children's development of thinking as defined by Piaget (e.g., Greer, 1978, 1983; Neimark, 1970; Neimark & Slotnick, 1970; Shine & Walsh, 1971; cf. Jacobs, 1983, 1986). Such research has found that most children understand the concept of conjunction by the second grade, and that conjunction is easier to understand than disjunction. Disjunction is poorly understood until at least grade 6; the development of this concept proceeds through high school and, in some cases, into the college years. Some have argued that children cannot explain their use of disjunctive *or* until at least the onset of formal operations. The conditional *(if–then)* and biconditional *(if and only if)* have been found to be difficult for children at least through grade 11, with understanding improving over time.

In natural (oral) language, connectives serve both syntactic and semantic functions. Linguists have examined the development of children's use and understanding of natural language connectives in children's spontaneous speech during play and during interaction with peers or adults (e.g., Bloom, Lahey, Hood, Lifter, & Fiess, 1980; Katz & Brent, 1968; Scholnick & Wing, 1982; Silva, 1984; Sullivan, 1972; Wing & Scholnick, 1981; cf. Jacobs, 1986). Such study has found that, beginning at about age 1½, children show connection by juxtaposing sentences without the use of connectives. At about age 2, children begin to use *and,* employing it to signify different relations in the developmental order of addition, time, cause, adversity, and condition. Once children use *and* to signify multiple relations, they begin to use other connectives to express those relations, in roughly the same order as they begin to grasp the intended meanings (e.g., use of temporal *when* precedes use of causal *because,* which precedes use of concessional *unless,* which precedes use of conditional *if*). From the age of 5, children use an increasingly wider range of connectives to express an increasingly wider variety of connective meanings. However, through the age of 12, children frequently draw upon a very small pool of connectives in their oral language; *and* is used most frequently, followed by use of *so, but, when, then,* and *because.*

Research has also examined the nature of children's use and understanding of particular natural language connectives or relational meanings, including coordination, temporality, causality, and adversity. Acknowledging that the development of children's use or understanding of natural language connectives can be influenced by several factors (e.g., pragmatic, syntactic, grammatical, and cognitive factors), such study has found that children can generally use and explain their use of natural language connectives before they can use and explain their use of logical connectives (e.g., Clark, 1971, 1973; Clark & Clark, 1968; Greenfield & Dent, 1979, 1982; Hakuta, deVilliers, & Tager-Flusberg, 1982; Hood & Bloom, 1979; Katz & Brent, 1968; Lawton, 1977; Lust, 1977, 1981; Lust, Flynn, Chien, & Clifford, 1980; McCabe, Evely, Abramovitch, Corter, & Pepler, 1983; McCabe & Peterson, 1983, 1985; Werner & Kaplan, 1963).

The role of connectives has also been investigated in the context of discourse processing models, which seek to explain how readers integrate semantic and logical information to gain a coherent reading of text (e.g., Frederiksen, 1975; Haviland & Clark, 1974; Irwin, 1980; Just & Carpenter, 1980; Kintsch & van Dijk, 1978; Marshall & Glock, 1978-1979; Meyer, Brandt, & Bluth, 1980). In models of reading comprehension processes, connectives play a role both on a local or "micro" level (signaling links or specific semantic relations between propositions or clauses, or acting as syntactic indicators of clausal boundaries) and on a more global level (facilitating a coherent reading of text by signaling the relation between given and inferred information). Thus, in reading, connectives function both syntactically and semantically. Variables that can influence the comprehension of a connective or connective relation in printed text include the explicitness or implicitness of the presentation of the relation, syntactic factors, pragmatic factors, semantic factors, and cognitive factors (cf. Jacobs, 1983, 1986; Walmsley, 1977a, 1977b).

Models of written composition have acknowledged the role of connectives in discourse production (e.g., Britton, Burgess, Martin, McLeod, & Rosen, 1975; Emig, 1971); however, little empirical study has examined children's use of connectives in their writing. Some research has examined the syntactic role of connectives in the production of various linguistic structures, especially subordinate clauses (Evanechko, Ollila, & Armstrong, 1974; Hunt, 1965; Loban, 1976; O'Donnell, Griffin, & Norris, 1967). More recently, research has examined children's production of connectives as cohesive ties (e.g., Halliday & Hasan, 1976; King & Rentel, 1981, 1982, 1983). Trends do emerge in children's frequency of use of connectives in their writing (cf. Jacobs, 1983, 1986). The coordinate connectives that children most frequently use in their writing in grades 1 through 12 are *and, but,* and *so* (*or* and *yet* are less common and begin to be used later). The most frequently used subordinate connectives are *when* and *because.* The youngest students (in grades 1-2) use additive, temporal, and causal connectives more frequently than adversative or continuative connectives in narration.

As was once the case with reading research, study into writers' uses of connectives rarely draws upon findings from studies of oral acquisition and use of connectives. There is some evidence, however, that developmental use of connectives in children's writing recapitulates such use in oral language (cf. Jacobs, 1986). For example, as early as grade 1, writers primarily use *and* (and, to a lesser degree, *but, so,* and *then*); they use *and* robustly to signify addition, time, and cause. Soon after such robust use of *and,* children use other connectives that express more precisely the relations initially signified by *and.* Generally, older, secondary writers use a wider variety of connectives than do elementary writers; they also make more frequent use of the less common relations (e.g., condition, concession, manner, place, and purpose).

Little empirical study has examined the interrelation of reading and writing processes as reflected through readers' and writers' use of connectives. Researchers agree that, as semantic elements, connectives are part of the underlying logical structure of writing that, when used well, guides readers through shifts and changes in relational concepts (Holloway, 1981). Readers use the explicit connectives supplied to them in text to construct the structural relations between propositions and the semantic linkages between ideas (e.g., Campbell, 1980; Meyer, 1979, 1982; Meyer et al., 1980; Moe, 1978). If reading comprehension is defined as a cycle of communication between reader and writer, then use of connective signals could be a means for producing clearer writing and, subsequently, more effectual reading (Fahnestock, 1982; Marshall & Glock, 1978-1979; Meyer, 1982).

Little attempt has been made to synthesize findings concerning children's developmental use or understanding of connectives in their oral language, their reading, or their writing; there has been even less of an attempt to use such syntheses in research on the use of connectives in written language. Moreover, no research has examined the relation between children's use of connectives in their writing and their reading, writing, or language skill development. A positive relation has been found between socioeconomic status and children's use and/or understanding of logical connectives (Beilin, 1975; Suppes & Feldman, 1971), of natural language connectives in speech (e.g., Bernstein, 1971; Lawton, 1968; Loban, 1976), and of natural language connectives in the production of written discourse (King & Rentel, 1982; Lawton, 1968; Loban, 1976). However, little study has examined a low-income population for possible within-group variation in their written use of connectives or has compared that use with their more general reading, writing, and/or language skill development.

The Study

Background and Scope

The research that this section describes used as its data source a study, funded by the National Institute of Education (NIE), that examined the reading, writing, and language skill development of children from low-income families (Chall et al., 1982; see also Chall, Jacobs, & Baldwin, 1990; Snow, Barnes, Chandler, Goodman, & Hemphill, 1991).[1] The NIE study was a 2-year investigation of why some children from low-income families manage to continue successfully through critical stages of literacy acquisition while others are unable to meet increased challenge.

The NIE study provided a rich base of data for the examination of children's use of connectives in their writing and for the generation of hypotheses about the relations among the children's reading, writing, and language skill abilities in light of their use of connectives. First, the data allowed within-group examination of low-income children's writing for variation in connective use. Second, because the data were collected over two years, developmental trends could be observed by grade, cross-sectionally. Third, trends found in each grade over time could be compared to trends found in other developmental studies of use of connectives in oral language, reading, and writing. Finally, since the study included measures of reading, writing, and language ability; it allowed us to compare the children's scores on these measures to their use of connectives in their writing. What follows is a summary of the present study's methods, the most striking findings, and the implications of findings for both practice and future research. (See Jacobs, 1986, for more detailed analyses and discussion.)

Methods

Subjects. The subjects in the present study were the 30 children in the NIE study for whom both pre- and post-test reading, writing, and lan-

---

[1] The NIE study was proposed and conducted by Jeanne S. Chall and Catherine E. Snow as principal investigators, with Chall's major focus on literacy and language development and Snow's on home influences on literacy and language development. As a research assistant for the NIE study, I was responsible for collecting the reading and writing data and analyzing the writing data. The present study was not a part of the original NIE study's design; and I wish to thank both Jeanne Chall and Catherine Snow for granting me permission to use data from the NIE study for the present research.

guage data were available. (Ten subjects were in grade 2 at the end of the first year of the study and in grade 3 at the end of the second year; twelve were in grade 4 at the end of the first year and in grade 5 at the end of the second; the remaining eight were in grade 6 at the end of the first year and in grade 7 at the end of the second). All of the subjects qualified as "low income" (according to their eligibility for a free lunch program). Students were given preference for selection if they came from primarily English-speaking families and if they came from a classroom that had a cooperative teacher and a number of other potential subjects. Subjects were selected as above-average or below-average readers, based on a combination of factors (including initial recommendations of classroom teachers and standardized reading test results in the pupils' files). In addition, the present study classified the subjects as either above-average or below-average writers on the basis of their holistic ranks on the writing samples completed for the NIE study.

Measures. The subjects' reading, language, and writing skills were measured twice — at the end of each year of the study (when the children were finishing grade 2, 4, or 6, and again when they were finishing grade 3, 5, or 7). Reading skills were assessed using an experimental version of the Diagnostic Assessments of Reading and Trial Teaching Strategies (DARTTS; Roswell & Chall, 1992) — an individually administered, diagnostic, criterion-referenced test consisting of six subtests: word recognition, phonics, oral reading, word meaning, spelling, and silent reading comprehension. The language tests included measures of children's vocabulary (the WISC-R vocabulary test and a measure of precision and sophistication of word knowledge based upon performance on the WISC-R) and measures of meta-linguistic awareness, grammar, and "total language" (a score based on a combination of the four language measures). (All but the WISC-R vocabulary subtest were developed by Carol Chomsky.)

Writing was assessed by taking both narrative and expository samples; stimuli were based on those used by the National Assessment of Educational Progress (NAEP, 1972). The children were given ten minutes to complete each writing task. The narrative stimulus was a picture of an elderly woman standing in the vegetable section of a market, holding a package of tomatoes. The instructions to the students were the same as those used by the NAEP:

> Here is a picture of a woman with some tomatoes. Look at the picture for a while and think about what is going on. When you have decided, write a story that tells what is happening in the picture and what is likely to happen next.

The expository stimulus was an adaptation of the instructions used by NAEP:

> Many of us have a special person whom we look up to or admire for reasons that are very special to us. For example, some people admire and look up to famous sports players, to TV or movie stars, to a person in a story, or to a relative or friend. Write about whom you admire or look up to; tell who the person is and explain why you look up to this person.

Data Analysis. The present study used two kinds of measures to analyze its data. The first group of measures included those from the larger study that were related to connective use or that had been identified as powerful enough to be included in factor analyses. The reading measures used were the subjects' scores on the six subtests of the DARTS. The writing measures used included holistic and analytic ratings and rankings of various aspects of students' writing: overall holistic rating, overall holistic ranking, organization rating, content rating, and form rating. Writing measures also included counts of internal factors of writing, such as number and average length of T-units produced (a T-unit being a kernel sentence with embeddings such as dependent clauses; Hunt, 1965), average number of words not found on the Spache list of 1,000 common words (Spache, 1974), and average number of words not found on the Dale list of 3,000 familiar words (Chall & Dale, 1995).

The language measures used were the five measures of vocabulary, grammar, language awareness, and total language.

The second group of measures used in the study consisted primarily of counts of connectives and connective structures. Several of these measures had been used in earlier studies (e.g., Hunt, 1965; Loban, 1976); therefore, it was possible to compare the findings of the present study with those of earlier ones. These measures included counts of T-unit production, counts of production of coordinate connectives and coordinated structures, counts of writers' intended use of inter-T-unit *and*, counts of intra-T-unit connective use, and counts of production of subordinate connectives and subordinate clausal structures.

Results

1. What were the trends in the children's use of connectives in their writing according to grade?

Table 8-1 summarizes the children's first use of specific connectives and connective relations by grade in both narration and exposition. In both genres, the youngest children (grade 2) could express a variety of connective relations, using a variety of connectives. However, they primarily relied on three: additive relations (expressed overwhelmingly by *and*); temporal relations (expressed mostly by *and, then,* and *when*); and, to a lesser degree, causal relations (primarily expressed by *and, so,* and *because*). They only occasionally used conditional *(if)* relations, comparative relations, or other noun- and adjective-clause subordinators (e.g., *that,* deleted *that, what, who,* deleted *whom, why*). At grade 3, the children also expressed adversity *(but)* and manner (e.g., *like, how*).

Any other connective relations that even the oldest students (grades 6-7) used were first used at grade 4 — i.e., alternation *(or)*, general-to-specific *(for example)*, and concession *(even though)*. After grade 4, children rarely used any "new" connectives (and any new ones were mostly additive and temporal connectives). The oldest students (grades 6-7) did, however, use the less-common connective relations and connectives slightly more frequently than the youngest students (grades 2-3).

Table 8-1a
Earliest Use of Various Connectives and
Connective Relations — Narration

	Grade 2	Grade 3	Grade 4	Grade 5	Grade 6	Grade 7
Coordinate connectives	and so	but	or			
Conjunctive adverbs		then	soon	again also now		at that time finally
Relations expressed by coordinate connectives and conjunctive adverbs	addition time* cause*	adversity	alternative adversity*	addition		
Subordinate connectives	deleted that if that what when	because like who	even if how so [adj.] that [S] until where wherever	after		as (time) while
Relations expressed by subordinate connectives	time condition	cause direct discourse manner	comparison place			

* = used as an intended meaning for "and"
___ = expressed explicitly with coordinate connectives other than "and" or with conjunctive adverbs

Table 8-1b
Earliest Use of Various Connectives and Connective Relations — Exposition

	Grade 2	Grade 3	Grade 4	Grade 5	Gr. 6	Grade 7
Coordinate connectives	and; so	but		or; for		
Conjunctive adverbs	then	also	for example; still			
Relations expressed by coordinate connectives and conjunctive adverbs	addition	adversity addition	general-to-specific*	alternative		
	time* cause*			adversity*		
Subordinate connectives	because deleted that deleted whom if so [adj.] that [S] so [adv.] that [S] when who; why	how same as/like [S] that	-er than [S] even though more than [S] what wherever	as [adj.] as [S] even when like till whatever whenever		as (time)
Relations expressed by subordinate connectives	time cause condition comparison purpose	manner direct discourse	concession place			

* = used as an intended meaning for "and"

— = expressed explicitly with coordinate connectives other than "and" or with conjunctive adverbs

Throughout grades 2–7, children continued to use additive and temporal connective relations and connectives most frequently. The simplicity of the relations that the children used was ultimately reflected in the quality of their writing — both syntactically and semantically. Figure 8-1 (pp. 112-114) presents samples of average-rated writing at each grade (2–7) for both narration and exposition that illustrate that simplicity.

As Figure 8-1 illustrates, the youngest students (grade 2–3) generally produced the least sophisticated and least varied connective structures; their production could be considered a baseline for the production of connective structures by children in later grades. They produced the shortest, and thus the least "mature," T-units. They used little inter-T-unit coordination (using *and* almost exclusively) and even less intra-T-unit coordination. When they did use intra-T-unit coordination, they produced run-on lists, repeating *and* each time they added an element to the list. Their use of subordination was generally unvaried; they relied on only a few, very simple subordinators (especially *like*, temporal *when*, or causal *because*).

Students in grades 4–7 exhibited the same tendencies as the younger children. Although they used connectives and connective structures with greater frequency than younger students, they used them with only slightly more variation.

Considerable similarity emerged between how the children in the present study used connectives and connective relations in their writing and how children generally use connectives in oral language (see discussion above). The connectives (*and, so, but, then, when, because,* and *like*) and connective relations (addition, time, and cause) that the children used most frequently — and almost exclusively across grades — are the same ones that children use earliest in their oral language development (by the ages of 2–4). They are the simplest, list-like connectives and connective relations, and they are among the connectives that children use most frequently, through the age of 12, in both oral and written narration.

Figure 8-1
"Average"-ranked writing, grades 2-7

NARRATION

Grade 2: ALN1

T-unit #	Text
1	She's going to open it.
2	She's holding it up.
3	She's at a store.
4	And she's going to buy it.
5	She's going home and eating it.

Grade 3: PJN2

1   The woman has some tomatoes.

2   And she is looking for someone to throw them at

3   There are three tomatoes covered with a plastic sheet.

4   The old woman has glasses and a string of pearls and a new dress with stars on them.

Grade 4: JRN1

1   She [is] going to pay for it and go home and cook it and have supper with her family if she has one.

2   But even if she doesn't have a family, she will eat it anyway because she bought it.

3   And when you buy something you have to eat it.

4   She bought it from the store.

Grade 5: AJN2

1   This is an old lady looking for some big, red, juicy tomatoes.

2   She is going to buy some tomatoes.

3   When she gets home, she might make salad to eat for lunch.

4   She might also be picking up some tomatoes for her son's wife or a friend.

5   After maybe a week she will go back and get some more juicy tomatoes to eat or maybe lettuce this time.

6   She might not even get vegetables anymore.

7   She might get some nice, lean meat and have a cookout and have meat, Coke, hamburgers, hot dogs, and fruit punch.

Grade 6: RMN1

1   This is a woman that is going to buy some tomatoes.

2   She is looking back to see if anyone is coming.

3   So she can grab a lot because they are on sale.

4   And they are ripe and big.

Figure 8-1
"Average"-ranked writing, grades 2-7 (continued)

T-unit #	Text
5	If she doesn't get any now, she will never get them again.

Grade 7: CTN2

1	This is a picture of an old lady who is about to buy some tomatoes.
2	But she [is] yelling and screaming about how expensive they are.
3	So she [is] standing there wondering if she should buy or not.
4	So she decided to buy the tomatoes only for half price.
5	But if she did that, she would not be allowed in that particular store anymore.
6	So she went along with the idea of not being able to go in the store anymore.

EXPOSITION

Grade 2: LME1

1	My mother is special.
2	And I love her.
3	She gives us candy sometimes.
4	The candy has gum in it.

Grade 3: PJE2

1	[I admire] my mother and father because they buy me clothes and toys.
2	And [I admire] my friend too because my friend plays with me.
3	And he tells me jokes.

Grade 4: BKE1

1	I look up to my mother and father because [they] are the ones that beat all those T.V. stars, the story book people, and the sports people.
2	And you can trust them without a doubt.
3	And, if they gave me something, they won't be expecting anything back from me.
4	I really don't know what that word means.
5	But what they do for me I really admire them for.

Grade 5: CAE2

1	I admire the Celtics because basketball is my favorite sport and because of the great players they have like Robert Parish, Larry Bird, Kevin McHale, and the rest of the team.

Figure 8-1
"Average"-ranked writing, grades 2-7 (continued)

T-unit #	Text
2	The Celtics have been World Champions fourteen times.
3	And now they're working on their fifteenth time.
4	I also like the way they come back like last year.
5	The 76'ers only needed to win one more game.
6	And the Celtics had to win three.
7	But the Celtics won.

Grade 6: KFE1

1	Her name is X— X—.
2	She's my best friend in the class.
3	When I get mad at her, sometimes she says sorry right away.
4	She's very nice.
5	And she's not selfish or rude to me.
6	We've stayed friends a long time.
7	We've never had a big fight or quarrel because we're nice to each other.
8	I've got other friends.
9	But she's probably one of the nicest persons I've ever met.

Grade 7: TCE2

1	The person that I admire is a good friend of mine.
2	She has long black hair and is very pretty.
3	She's very nice.
4	We do a lot of things together.
5	We always have fun wherever we go like when we go to the movies on Saturday night with a couple of other people.
6	But the really only other reason why I like X— is because we never fight like me and my other friends.

2. What were the trends in the children's connective use according to genre?

The students' use of inter-T-unit *and* illustrates differences in the children's connective production by genre and underscores the exclusivity with which they used the simplest connective relations (addition and temporality) and connectives to represent those relations. Table 8-2 presents a summary of the children's use of inter-T-unit coordination over grades and genres.

Students at all grades used *and* (one of the least sophisticated connectives) more frequently than any other inter-T-unit coordinative connective. At grades 2–3, if children used any connectives at all, they usually used *and*. This was true for both narration and exposition. Trends in use of *and* in later grades differed by genre. In narration, use of *and* gradually decreased over the grades, as use of other coordinating connectives (such as *so, but,* and *or*) increased slightly. However, in exposition, use of *and* did not decrease appreciably over the grades. Only rarely, in later grades, did students use other coordinating connectives (e.g., *so, but, or,* and *for*) in their expositions. Thus, more varied use of coordinating connectives was characteristic of older students — especially in narration.

As already noted, in developmental studies of both oral and written language, children have been observed using *and* to signify a variety of relations before they use other connectives to express those relations more explicitly. In this study, this appeared to be true of the children's use of *and* in their writing. An additional study was made to determine the meanings that students may have intended for inter-T-unit *and*.[2] Table 8-3 presents measures of the children's intended meanings for inter-T-unit *and* on both genres.

In narration, children's writing across the grades was character-

---

[2] First, students' papers were corrected for spelling; and then each paper was typed as a list of T-units. Every time a coordinate connective introduced a T-unit, it was replaced with a blank. Then, five proficient adult writers were asked, separately, to fill the blanks with the relational meanings they felt the student might have intended for the blank (e.g., addition, time, adversity, cause, continuation, general-to-specific). Rater-agreement was reached when at least 3/5 raters supplied the same intended meaning of an inter-T-unit *and*.

Table 8-2a

Measures of Inter-T-Unit Connective Use — Narration

	Grade 2	Grade 3	Grade 4	Grade 5	Grade 6	Grade 7
Percent of students who used inter-T-unit coordinate connectives	70.00%	60.00%	91.70%	91.70%	87.50%	62.50%
Percentage of possible T-units introduced by inter-T-unit coordinate connectives	50.00%	39.60%	52.38%	58.35%	56.04%	46.16%
Of inter-T-unit coordinate connectives used, percent that was:						
and	90.91%	84.62%	54.29%	63.64%	71.43%	41.67%
so	9.09%	0	14.29%	15.91%	28.57%	20.83%
but	0	0	20.00%	15.91%	0	33.33%
or	0	15.38%	11.43%	4.55%	0	4.17%
for	0	0	0	0	0	0
nor	0	0	0	0	0	0
yet	0	0	0	0	0	0

Table 8-2b: Measures of Inter-T-Unit Connective Use — Exposition

		Grade 2	Grade 3	Grade 4	Grade 5	Grade 6	Grade 7
Percent of students who used inter-T-unit coordinate connectives		60.00%	90.00%	83.30%	100.00%	37.50%	100.00%
*Percentage of possible T-units introduced by inter-T-unit coordinate connectives		29.17%	53.74%	41.56%	56.96%	6.47%	35.02%
Of inter-T-unit coordinate connectives used, percent that was:	and	92.86%	88.00%	86.96%	86.96%	75.00%	60.00%
	so	7.14%	4.00%	0	0	0	15.00%
	but	0	8.00%	14.81%	8.70%	25.00%	25.00%
	or	0	0	0	2.17%	0	0
	for	0	0	0	2.17%	0	0
	nor	0	0	0	0	0	0
	yet	0	0	0	0	0	0

*grade 2, 4, 6 F=.0504 (no specific group differences)

Table 8-3
Measures of intended meanings for inter-T-unit *and* as percentage of total incidence

Narration	Grade 2	Grade 3	Grade 4	Grade 5	Grade 6	Grade 7
additive	10.00%	18.18%	36.84%	21.43%	30.00%	10.00%
temporal	80.00%	72.73%	10.53%	28.57%	30.00%	30.00%
causal	10.00%	0	26.32%	28.57%	20.00%	40.00%
adversative	0	0	5.26%	7.14%	0	10.00%
general-to-specific	0	0	0	0	0	0
rater disagreement	0	9.09%	21.05%	14.29%	20.00%	10.00%
Exposition	**Grade 2**	**Grade 3**	**Grade 4**	**Grade 5**	**Grade 6**	**Grade 7**
additive	53.85%	68.18%	78.26%	67.50%	100.00%	66.67%
temporal	15.38%	9.09%	4.35%	2.50%	0	8.33%
causal	7.69%	18.18%	8.70%	12.50%	0	25.00%
adversative	0	0	0	2.50%	0	0
general-to-specific	0	0	4.35%	5.00%	0	0
rater disagreement	23.08%	4.55%	10.00%	10.00%	0	0

ized by the temporal use of *and*. The youngest (grades 2–3) children's use of *and* was almost always intended to indicate temporal relations. Even though older writers used *and* to intend other relations (such as causation and condition), the entire sample's narrations could generally be characterized by a temporal, "and then" approach. (Refer to Figure 8-1.)

In exposition, the children used the connective *and* most frequently; moreover, their use of *and* did not decrease with age. One might expect the children to use *and* to intend cause/effect relations, since they were to have argued why they admired someone. Yet, quite strikingly, they used *and* almost exclusively in exposition to mean nothing more than "additional fact." Thus, while students' narrations seemed to progress from simple lists of temporal action to slightly more complex stories that incorporated cause/effect and condition, their expositions remained very simple, list-like accounts of facts. In fact, the children's expository use of *and* could be seen as an extension of the "and then" strategy that they used in their narrations.

The children's use and overuse of *and* could indicate their lack of awareness as writers of readers' needs to have relations expressed explicitly. Such lack of consideration could be a result of egocentricity (in a Piagetian sense), or simply of the misapplication of oral language discourse rules (wherein the speaker knows that the listener can ask for clarification when it is needed) to written language. In fact, the children used *and* in their writing with the same frequency that middle-class children use *and* in their oral language (a rate often thought to be excessive; cf. Loban, 1976; O'Donnell et al., 1967).

3. What was the relation between the children's written production of connectives and their performance on measures of writing, reading, and language?

Writing. A series of correlations was performed to determine the relation between measures of students' written production of connectives and other measures of their writing performance. Generally, the children who were above-average writers used more connective structures and more varied connective relations (i.e., subordination and/or coordination using connectives other than *and*). This was true at each grade level, and for both narration and exposition.

Reading. A series of correlation analyses was performed to determine the relation between measures of students' written production of connectives and measures of their reading performance. Across the grades, above-average writers also tended to be above-average readers, and be-low-average writers tended to be below-average readers.

Poorer readers/writers tended to rely on the least sophisticated con-nective structures (e.g., use of inter-T-unit *and* and of intra-T-unit coor-dination), if they used connective structures at all. Their production did not vary much across the grades. When below-average readers/writers did use connective structures, their production resembled the use in the earliest reading passages of the DARTTS (grade 1 on oral reading and grade 2 on silent reading comprehension). Generally, be-low-average readers/writers produced shorter or fewer connective struc-tures than they were able to read on the oral and silent reading subtest passages.

Better readers/writers used the more sophisticated connective struc-tures (e.g., inter-T-unit coordination using connectives other than *and*, and subordination). Above-average readers/writers generally produced connective structures with equal or slightly lower frequency or length than they were able to read. However, they, too, most frequently de-pended upon the simplest connectives and structures (e.g., intra- and inter-T-unit coordination).

Language. The most remarkable and significant relation between stu-dents' use of connectives and their language performance was that found between frequent use of more sophisticated connective structures (i.e., subordination and coordinate connectives other than *and*) and higher vocabulary performance. This was true across grades and genres. This relation might be explained by the fact that, in order to use connective relations more sophisticated than additive *and*, students must not only have knowledge of the connective's meaning, but also understand how to use the particular relational meaning it embodies with precision and sophistication. The vocabulary measures tested such ability.

It is worth noting that while the grade 4–5 cohort generally pro-duced connectives and connective structures differently (and in some cases, significantly differently) from the grade 2–3 cohort, the grade 6–7 cohort generally behaved in the same way as the grade 4–5 cohort.

This trend, in which the children seemed to show improvement relative to each other only through about grades 4–5, was also found in the larger NIE study for reading and language development and for writing development most generally. Much of the children's deceleration, beginning in the middle grades, could be related to their deceleration in acquiring new vocabulary knowledge.

4. What is the relation between trends in the children's written production of connectives and trends identified in the literature for different socio-economic groups?

As has been noted, the low-income children in the present sample most frequently used the same connectives (e.g., *and, but,* and *when*), connective relations (e.g., addition and time), and connective structures (e.g., inter- and intra-T-unit coordination) that children, on average, use most frequently in oral and/or written language (and especially in narration). What distinguished the present sample was the exclusivity with which they used them. Even the older subjects (grades 4–7) and the above-average writers, who used a slightly greater variety of connectives, connective relations, and connective structures than did the younger (grade 2–3) or below-average writers, seemed to rely primarily on only a handful of connectives, relations, and structures — those with which they probably had familiarity in oral language before entering school.

Implications for Practice

There may be several reasons for the children's restricted use of connectives in their writing. Such use may be influenced by their limited vocabulary knowledge and limited ability to use that knowledge with precision. As a group, the children lacked vocabulary knowledge of the more abstract, polysyllabic, literary words that are less common to oral language than to academic discourse. Generally, on vocabulary measures, neither the above-average readers nor the older children scored significantly above the fourth-grade level — a level characteristic of oral language. The children experienced little direct instruction in more academic vocabulary in their classrooms; what instruction they did receive consisted of copying definitions from the dictionary or completing workbook exercises. Rarely were students given the chance to use new vocabulary in varied contexts — either in their reading or in their oral or written expression.

Another possible reason for the children's restricted use of connectives in their writing may be related to their limited reading experience. Their reading instruction most frequently consisted of oral reading of basals and, much less frequently, of trade books or other reading for which vocabulary was ungraded. In fact, the children's connective use was similar to that found in most late-elementary basals (Robertson, 1968; Stoodt, 1970, 1972). The books that the children chose to read on their own were usually popular novels — narrations rather than literary or explanatory texts. Even in their expositions, the children's use of connectives resembled the connective use generally found in both oral and written narration.

The sample's restricted use of connectives in writing may also be related to a lack of instruction or practice in producing extended pieces of writing. The children were rarely asked to produce extended writing (i.e., longer than a sentence); when they were, they were usually asked to write about personal experiences. This was especially true in the earliest grades (2–4). Such accounts can easily be portrayed using the connectives and connective relations found most frequently in oral language and/or narration — the language that children already know and use well upon entering school.

Thus, the low-income children in this study appear to need earlier and increased guided exposure to vocabulary and language that are less common in oral language and more common in academic discourse. One way to provide such exposure is to read the children texts that use vocabulary and syntax more complex than what the children can read or use in oral language. Appropriate challenge is a critical consideration in choosing such texts, and there should be structured follow-up activity that engages the children in using new vocabulary and syntactic structures (Chall & Jacobs, in press).

The children also appear to need increased and guided opportunity to read and produce prose — in addition to narration. Inquiry-based content instruction could provide the children with guided opportunities to examine their own ideas, evaluate those ideas in light of new information, classify and rearrange ideas in some hierarchy of importance, decide how ideas are interrelated, and mark the interrelations with appropriate connections (cf. Hillocks, 1986; Richards, 1942). Writing can provide students with the means to analyze and synthesize content-based material, making connections among ideas (Fulwiler, 1983; Knoblauch & Brannon, 1983; Stock, 1986). Such writing can take the form of observation notebooks, dialectic journals (Berthoff, 1987), or other means that give students the chance to integrate their background knowledge with new information (cf. Elbow & Belanoff, 1989; Stotsky, 1984).

Finally, if instruction is to treat connectives not only as syntactic entities but also as semantic entities, then students must have opportunities to experience the symbiotic relation that appears to exist between connectives and context. Such practice should provide students with guided means by which they can experiment using connective relations more sophisticated than addition or time, while constructing their own meaning (cf. sentence-combining curricula such as those by Obenchain, 1977, and O'Hare, 1973, 1975).

Implications for Further Research

The present study faced several constraints that further research might address. A replicate study might draw upon a larger low-income sample, allow more time for the children to engage in the full writing process (including planning and revision), and use writing stimuli related to the contexts of the children's classrooms and curricula. Further study might also have the children produce explanations of why they are using certain connective relations in their writing and what relations they intend when they use *and*.

Despite these constraints, certain findings from the present study merit further investigation. For example, the study found that low-income children's use of connectives in their writing reflected some of the trends of use identified in the literature for oral language. Further examination is needed of the relation between developmental use of connectives in oral and in written language — longitudinally, between and within socio-economic status groups, and by genre. Such study could clarify the overlapping nature of oral and written language development and identify the areas of acquisition that are different. (For example, once children begin to use more explicit connectives than *and* in oral language, does robust use of *and* diminish?)

Although empirical studies have examined children's connective use in their reading and writing, little of that research has drawn from the extensive literature on the use of natural or logical connectives in oral language, and rarely are distinctions made between the nature of natural language and logical connectives. Further research should draw upon syntheses of findings on children's developmental knowledge of connectives in their speech, reading, and writing to determine the kind of knowledge of connectives that children at a particular age can be expected to possess.

The present study has tentatively established relations between children's abilities to use connectives in their writing and their general reading and writing performance. The question of how reading and writing skill development might be interrelated through children's use of connectives merits further investigation. Studies might investigate whether the connectives and connective relations that children use in their writing are the same as those they can comprehend, either implicitly or explicitly, in their reading. Such study would serve to clarify the effects of varying degrees of pragmatic support on the use and understanding of connectives or connective relations in reading, writing, and oral language.

Finally, the present study found a relation between students' written production of connectives and measures of vocabulary. The children were also found lacking in classroom exposure to and practice with the abstract, polysyllabic vocabulary used in discourse more academic or literary than oral language or narration. Such is the language of the more complex connective relations (e.g., condition and concession). Study in oral language acquisition and in the logical nature of connectives has found that some connective relations are harder than others for younger children to use and understand. However, study has also found that children's understanding of some of the more difficult relations can be accelerated (as early as age 6) through the use of instructional aids such as advanced organizers (Lawton, 1977). Further research could examine the effect of guided instruction in connectives on children's ability to use and understand them. Such instruction should provide students with the means to use their reading and writing skills for understanding — to make more sophisticated connections among ideas as they strive to become independent learners.

References

Beardsley, M.C. (1975). *Thinking straight: Principles of reasoning for readers and writers.* Englewood Cliffs, NJ: Prentice-Hall.

Beilin, H. (1975). *Studies in the cognitive basis of language development.* New York: Academic Press.

Bernstein, B. (1971). *Class, codes and control. Theoretical studies towards a sociology of language, Volume 1: Class, codes and control.* Boston, MA: Routledge & Kegan Paul.

Berthoff, A.E. (1987). Dialectical notebooks and the audit of meaning. In T. Fulwiler (Ed.), *The journal book.* Montclair, NJ: Boynton/Cook.

Bloom, L., Lahey, M., Hood, L., Lifter, K., & Fiess, K. (1980). Complex sentences: Acquisition of syntactic connectives and the semantic relations they encode. *Journal of Child Language, 7,* 235-261.

Britton, J., Burgess, T., Martin, N., McLeod, A., & Rosen, H. (1975). *The development of writing abilities* (pp. 11-18). London: Macmillan Education, Ltd.

Campbell, B.O. (1980, March). *Global and local textuality.* Paper presented at the Annual Meeting of the Conference on College Composition and Communication, Washington, DC. (ED 188 204)

Chall, J.S., & Dale, E. (1995). *Readability revisited: The new Dale-Chall readability formula.* Cambridge, MA: Brookline Books.

Chall, J.S., & Jacobs, V.A. (in press). The reading, writing, and language connection. In J. Shimron (Ed.), *Literacy and education.* Creskill, NJ: Hampton Press.

Chall, J.S., Jacobs, V.A., & Baldwin, L.E. (1990). *The reading crisis: Why poor children fall behind.* Cambridge, MA: Harvard University Press.

Chall, J., Snow, C., Barnes, W., Chandler, J., Goodman, I., Hemphill, L., & Jacobs, V. (1982, December 22). *Families and literacy: The contribution of out-of-school experiences to children's acquisition of literacy — A final report to the National Institute of Education.* Cambridge, MA: Harvard Graduate School of Education.

Clark, E.V. (1971). On the acquisition of the meaning of "before" and "after." *Journal of Verbal Learning and Verbal Behavior, 10,* 266-275.

Clark, E.V. (1973). How children describe time and order. In C.A. Ferguson & D.I. Slobin (Eds.), *Studies of child language development.* New York: Holt, Rinehart & Winston.

Clark, H.H., & Clark, E.V. (1968). Semantic distinctions and memory for complex sentences. *Quarterly Journal of Experimental Psychology, 20,* 129-138.

Dewey, J. (1933). *How we think.* Boston: D.C. Heath.

Elbow, P., & Belanoff, P. (1989). *A community of writers: A workshop course in writing.* New York: McGraw-Hill.

Emig, J. (1971). *The composing process of twelfth graders* (National Council of Teachers of English Research Report #13). Urbana, IL: National Council of Teachers of English.

Evanechko, P., Ollila, L., & Armstrong, R. (1974). An investigation of the relationship between children's performance in written language and their reading ability. *Research in the Teaching of English, 8,* 315-326.

Fahnestock, J. (1982). *Semantic and lexical coherence.* Unpublished manuscript (available from J. Fahnestock, Department of English, Pennsylvania State University, University Park, PA 16802).

Frederikson, C.H. (1975). Representing logical and semantic structure of knowledge acquired from discourse. *Cognitive Psychology, 7,* 371-485.

Fulwiler, T. (1983). Why we teach writing in the first place. In P.L. Stock (Ed.), *fforum: Essays on theory and practice in the teaching of writing.* Montclair, NJ: Boynton/Cook.

Gold, J.T. (1981, October). *Writing composition enhances reading comprehension.* Paper presented at the Annual Meeting of the College Reading Association, Louisville, KY. (ED 210 651)

Greenfield, P.M., & Dent, C.H. (1979). Syntax vs. pragmatics: A psychological account of coordinate structures in child language. *Papers and Reports on Child Language Development, No. 17.* Stanford University, CA: Department of Linguistics. (ED 191 266)

Greenfield, P.M., & Dent, C.H. (1982). Pragmatic factors in children's phrasal coordination. *Journal of Child Language, 9,* 425-443.

Greer, G.B. (1983). Comprehension of linguistic expressions of logical connectives. *Journal of Structural Learning, 7,* 189-191.

Greer, G.B. (1978). Comprehension of logical connectives in 9 to 16 year olds. *Journal of Structural Learning, 6,* 57-71.

Hakuta, K., de Villiers, J., & Tager-Flusberg, H. (1982). Sentence coordination in Japanese and English. *Journal of Child Language, 9,* 193-207.

Halliday, M.A.K., & Hasan, R. (1976). *Cohesion in English.* London: Longman Group Ltd.

Haviland, S.E., & Clark H.H. (1974). What's new? Acquiring new information as a process in comprehension. *Journal of Verbal Learning and Verbal Behavior, 13,* 512-521.

Hillocks, Jr., G. (1986). *Research on written composition: New directions for teaching.* Urbana, IL: National Council of Teachers of English.

Holloway, D.W. (1981). Semantic grammars: How they can help us teach writing. *College Composition and Communication, 32,* 205-218.

Hood, L., & Bloom, L. (1979). What, when, and how about why: A longitudinal study of early expression of causality. *Monographs of the Society for Research in Child Development: Serial No. 181, 44,* 1-40.

Huey, E.B. (1908). *The psychology and pedagogy of reading.* Cambridge, MA: The MIT Press.

Hunt, K. (1965). *Grammatical structures written at three grade levels* (National Council of Teachers of English Research Report #3). Urbana, IL: National Council of Teachers of English.

Ingham, C.S. (1896). *The conjunction "quod" in Saint Augustine's "De Civitate Dei."* Doctoral dissertation, Yale University, New Haven, CT. (ADD S0265014)

Irwin, J.W. (1980). Implicit connectives and comprehension. *Reading Teacher, 33,* 527-529.

Jacobs, V.A. (1983). *A missing link? The role of connectives in reading and writing processes.* Unpublished qualifying paper, Harvard Graduate School of Education.

Jacobs, V.A. (1986). *The use of connectives in low-income, elementary children's writing and its relation to their reading, writing, and language skill development.* Unpublished doctoral dissertation, Harvard Graduate School of Education, Cambridge, MA.

Jensen, J. (Ed.). (1984). *Composing and comprehending.* Urbana, IL: ERIC Clearinghouse on Reading and Communication Skills and the National Conference in Research in English.

Just, M.A., & Carpenter, P.A. (1980). A theory of reading: From eye fixations to comprehension. *Psychological Review, 87,* 329-354.

Katz, E.W., & Brent, S.B. (1968). Understanding connectives. *Journal of Verbal Learning and Verbal Behavior, 7,* 501-509.

King, M.L., & Rentel, V.M. (1981). *How children learn to write: A longitudinal study.* Washington, D.C.: National Institute of Education (Grant No. NIE-G-79-0137 and NIE-G-79-0039).

King, M.L., & Rentel, V.M. (1982). *Transition to writing.* Washington, D.C.: National Institute of Education (Grant No. NIE-G-79-0137 and NIE-G-79-0039).

King, M.L., & Rentel, V.M. (1983). *A longitudinal study of coherence in children's written narratives.* Washington, D.C.: National Institute of Education (Grant No. NIE-G-79-0137 and NIE-G-79-0039).

Kintsch, W., & van Dijk, T.A. (1978). Toward a model of text comprehension and production. *Psychological Review, 85,* 363-394.

Kneller, G.F. (1966). *Logic and language of education.* New York: Wiley.

Knoblauch, C.H., & Brannon, L. (1983). Writing as learning through the curriculum. *College English, 45,* 465-474.

Lawton, D. (1968). *Social class, language, and education.* New York: Schocken Books.

Lawton, J.T. (1977). The development of causal and logical connectives in children. *The British Journal of Educational Psychology, 47,* 81-84.

Loban, W. (1976). *Language development: Kindergarten through grade 12* (National Council of Teachers of English Research Report #18). Urbana, II.: National Council of Teachers of English.

Lust, B.C. (1977). Conjunction reduction in child language. *Journal of Child Language, 4,* 257-287.

Lust, B.C. (1981). Coordinating studies of coordination: A reply to Ardery. *Journal of Child Language, 8,* 457-470.

Lust, B.C., Flynn, S., Chien, Y.-C., & Clifford, T. (1980). Coordination: The role of syntactic, pragmatic, and processing factors in its first language acquisition in several languages. *Papers and Reports on Child Language Development, No. 19.* Stanford University, CA: Department of Linguistics, August 1980. (ED 197 616)

Marshall, N., & Glock, M.D. (1978-1979). Comprehension of connected discourse: A study into the relationships between the structure of text and information recalled. *Reading Research Quarterly, 14,* 10-56.

McCabe, A., Evely, S., Abramovitch, R., Corter, C., & Pepler, D. (1983). Conditional statements in young children's spontaneous speech. *Journal of Child Language, 10,* 253-258.

McCabe, A., & Peterson, C. (1983, April). *Developing comprehension vs. production of "because" and "so."* Paper presented at the Biennial Meeting of the Society for Research in Child Development, Detroit, MI. (ED 231 543)

McCabe, A., & Peterson, C. (1985). A naturalistic study of the production of causal connectives by children. *Journal of Child Language, 12,* 145-159.

Meyer, B.J.F. (1982). Reading research and the composition teacher: The importance of plans. *College Composition and Communication, 33,* 37-49.

Meyer, B.J.F. (1979, April). *Research on prose comprehension: Applications for composition teachers.* Paper presented at the Annual Meeting of the Conference on College Composition and Communication, Minneapolis, MN. (ED 174 999)

Meyer, B.J.F., Brandt, D.M., & Bluth, G.J. (1980). Use of top-level structure in text: Key for reading comprehension of ninth-grade students. *Reading Research Quarterly, 16*, 72-103.

Moe, A.J. (1978, November-December). *Cohesion as a factor in the comprehensibility of written discourse.* Paper presented at the Annual Meeting of the National Reading Conference, St. Petersburg Beach, FL.

National Assessment of Educational Progress (1972). Washington, D.C.: U.S. Government Printing Office.

Neimark, E.D. (1970). Development of comprehension of logical connectives: Understanding of "or." *Psychometric Science, 21*, 217-219.

Neimark, E.D., & Slotnick, N.S. (1970). Development of the understanding of logical connectives. *Journal of Educational Psychology, 61*, 451-460.

Obenchain, A.D. (1977). *Links to forceful writing, part I: Sentence power.* Reston, VA: Validated Writing Systems.

O'Donnell, C., Griffin, W.J., & Norris, R.C. (1967). *Syntax of kindergarten and elementary school children: A transformational analysis* (National Council of Teachers of English Research Report #8). Urbana, IL: National Council of Teacher of English.

O'Hare, F. (1973). *Sentence combining: Improving student writing without formal grammar instruction* (National Council of Teachers of English Research Report #15). Urbana, IL: National Council of Teachers of English.

O'Hare, F. (1975). *Sentencecraft: An elective course in writing.* Lexington, MA: Ginn.

Quine, W.V.O. (1950). *Methods of logic.* New York: Henry Holt.

Richards, I.A. (1942). *How to read a page.* New York: W.W. Norton.

Robertson, J.E. (1968). Pupil understanding of connectives in reading. *Reading Research Quarterly, 3*, 387-417.

Roswell, F.G., & Chall, J.S. (1992). *Diagnostic assessments of reading and teaching strategies.* Chicago, IL: Riverside Publishing Company.

Schagrin, M.L. (1968). *The language of logic: A programmed text.* New York: Random House.

Scholnick, E.K., & Wing, C.S. (1982). The pragmatics of subordinating conjunctions: A second look. *Journal of Child Language, 9*, 461-479.

Shine, D., & Walsh, J.F. (1971). Developmental trends in the use of logical connectives. *Psychonomic Science, 23*, 171-172.

Silva, M. (1984). Developmental issues in the acquisition of conjunction. *Papers and Reports on Child Language Development, No. 23.* Stanford University, CA: Department of Linguistics, 106-114.

Snow, C.E., Barnes, W.S., Chandler, J., Goodman, I.F., & Hemphill, L. (1991). *Unfulfilled expectations: Home and school influences on literacy.* Cambridge, MA: Harvard University Press.

Spache, G.D. (1974). *Good reading for poor readers.* Champagne, IL: Garrard Publishing Company.

Stock, P.L. (1986). Writing across the curriculum. *Theory into Practice, 25*, 97-101.

Stoodt, B. (1970, September). *The relationship between understanding grammatical conjunctions and reading comprehension: Final report.* U.S. Department of Health, Education and Welfare, Office of Education, Bureau of Research. (ED 045 331)

Stoodt, B. (1972). The relationship between understanding grammatical conjunctions and reading comprehension. *Elementary English, 49,* 502-504.

Stotsky, S.L. (1975). Sentence-combining as a curricular activity: Its effect on written language development and comprehension. *Research in the Teaching of English, 9,* 30-71.

Stotsky, S.L. (1982). The role of writing in developmental reading. *Journal of Reading, 25,* 330-339.

Stotsky, S.L. (1984). Imagination, writing, and the integration of knowledge in the middle grades. *Journal of Teaching Writing, 3,* 157-190.

Sullivan, L. (1972). Development of causal connectives by children. *Perceptual and Motor Skills, 35,* 1003-1010.

Suppes, P., & Feldman, S. (1971). Young children's comprehension of logical connectives. *Journal of Experimental Child Psychology, 12,* 304-317.

Thorndike, E.L. (1917). The understanding of sentences. *Elementary School Journal, 18,* 98-114.

Walmsley, S.A. (1977a, December). *Adolescents' understanding of logical connectives in a sentence memory task.* Paper presented at the Annual Meeting of the National Reading Conference, New Orleans, LA. (ED 161 001)

Walmsley, S.A. (1977b). Children's understanding of linguistic connectives: A review of selected literature and implications for future research. In P.D. Pearson (Ed.), *Reading: Theory, research and practice.* Clemson, SC: 26th Yearbook of the National Reading Conference.

Werner, H., & Kaplan, B. (1963). *Symbol formation.* New York: Wiley.

Wing, C.S., & Scholnick, E.K. (1981). Children's comprehension of pragmatic concepts expressed in "because," "although," "if," and "unless." *Journal of Child Language, 8,* 347-365.

9

Teaching Children with Reading Problems to Recognize Words

STEVEN A. STAHL, Ph.D.
The University of Georgia

This chapter reflects many of the themes of Jeanne Chall's work — teaching beginning reading (especially but certainly not only phonics instruction), reviewing research, teaching children with special needs in classrooms and clinics, and using research for policy decisions. I learned about all of these subjects from Jeanne. But more importantly, I learned from her a healthy skepticism. When I hear an assertion, the next thing I hear is Jeanne's voice crying "Where is the evidence?" The fields of reading and learning disabilities both have their share of assertions, some with evidence to back them up, but many without. Each of these assertions has its own associated instructional lore. These assertions and lore have been around so long without being questioned that they have acquired the status of fact. But being around for a long time does not prove that something is true; there has to be evidence supporting it.

The purpose of this paper is to examine some of these assertions about children with reading problems and their difficulties in learning to decode. Many of these assertions have been around for a long time, but have not been examined. The first part of this paper will discuss the importance for policy of the question of whether children with reading problems need special curricular adaptations. The second part of the paper will review research on whether special phonics programs are needed to teach children with identified reading problems.[1] In this section, I will suggest that children with reading problems may not need qualitatively different approaches so much as approaches that are more focused or avoid previous confusion, and that take their past failure into consideration. The third section of the paper will review the effects of a "Not-Phonics" approach to teaching children with reading problems, which we found to be effective at the University of Georgia Reading Clinic.

Different Programs for Different Children?

There are several assertions about children with reading problems — some that can be supported, others that cannot. First is the long-standing assumption that children with specific reading problems, especially those with learning disabilities, are qualitatively different from children with more general difficulties in learning (Gough & Tumner, 1986). This assumption suggests that children with learning disabilities are inherently different in some way from other children experiencing reading failure, and that these differences require separate programs. Initially, attempts were made to "fix" the child — to prepare the child to be a better learner and, through such preparation, to make the child "ready" to accept conventional reading instruction. These approaches have gradually been supplanted by more directed approaches to teaching reading, approaches that do not assume a particular etiology of the reading disability, but instead involve direct teaching of reading (e.g., Carnine, Silbert, & Kameenui, 1990). Although these approaches, such

---

[1] I use the term "children with reading problems" to indicate children who are in programs for learning disabled children or Title I (formerly Chapter I) for reading problems. Although LD students and Chapter I students are assumed to be distinct populations, researchers have found little difference between the two groups (Ysseldyke, Algozzine, Shinn, & McGue, 1982).

as Direct Instruction (Carnine et al., 1990), are increasingly used with all children in a school, usually schools in economically depressed areas, they are generally reserved for children having special problems with reading.

The shift from preparing children with learning disabilities to accept reading instruction to finding better instructional approaches for them represents progress, but it may have unintended consequences. With the shift to direct teaching of reading, programs for children with learning disabilities appear to have moved in two opposite directions. Some have come to resemble those used in regular class instruction (Allington, 1994; Haynes & Jenkins, 1986; Leinhardt, Zigmond, & Cooley, 1981). Other programs have used very different forms of instruction. Each of these two approaches has its own drawbacks.

The impulse to make reading instruction in resource rooms resemble that in regular classes comes from our application of knowledge in reading. As our conceptions of effective reading instruction change, it is likely that these conceptions will lead to similar implementations in regular and special education. Currently, whole-language approaches are widely used in regular education (Mullis, Campbell, & Farstrup, 1993); these approaches are also being recommended as applicable for learning-disabled children (Keefe & Keefe, 1993). These approaches have been thought to reflect our current knowledge of how children read (e.g., Goodman, 1986). However, if children have experienced failure in regular class programs, it is unlikely that they will make significant progress in essentially similar programs. This may be especially true for whole-language programs, which tend to be more effective with children from richer literacy environments (e.g., Stahl & Miller, 1989).

On the other hand, children with learning disabilities are often assumed to be different from those in regular classes. This assumption has led to the contrary impulse to provide approaches in the resource room that are distinctly different from, and often contradictory to, those used in regular classrooms. When there are significant differences, however, they are poorly integrated with the rest of the child's program, often leading to less than optimal learning. Allington and Johnston (1986) argue that if a child learns to read in a resource room setting using one approach — such as learning to decode phonetically controlled materials using a synthetic blending approach — but in the regular class learns a different approach, using less controlled materials with many words that must be learned by sight, the result is confusion. This confusion inhibits, rather than promotes, learning.

Underlying the segregation of children with reading problems is an assumption that these children are different from normally achieving children, at least in terms of the treatment they require. Such treatments may be as radical as the use of a totally different curriculum, or they may merely involve using smaller groups for instruction. This assertion of difference underlies programs such as Title I and special education programs for the learning-disabled, which have grown dramatically in the schools over the past two decades (Allington, 1994). For this assumption to be valid, we must be able to define "children with reading problems" in a way that identifies a population whose response to various treatments would differ from that of children with normal reading achievement. For example, several instructional methods, such as the Fernald and Gillingham approaches, have been proposed specifically for reading-disabled children (see Myers, 1978; Tierney, Readence, & Dishner, 1995). Others, such as Direct Instruction approaches (Carnine et al., 1990), are used considerably more for children who are identified as having reading problems than they are for normally achieving children.[2] If a child with reading problems responds best to treatments that are fundamentally different from the standard methods, she might need to be segregated in terms of academic programs so that she can be given these special treatments. However, if she does not need special treatments, she might best be integrated into regular class instruction, or taught along with garden-variety poor learn-

---

[2] Direct Instruction approaches are used with regular classes as well. "Direct Instruction" is capitalized to distinguish the specific approach (e.g., Carnine et al., 1990) from other approaches that call themselves direct instruction, but do not include the specific steps specified in this model.

ers with similar needs. Integrating children with reading problems into the regular class may require other accommodations, such as providing smaller group instruction or tutoring support (see Allington & Cunningham, 1995).

So, one question is whether special programs are required for children with reading problems, or whether these children can be accommodated using the same curriculum as regular-class children, possibly including some small group work. (This assumes, of course, that the regular class curriculum is of high quality; see Allington & Cunningham, 1995.) Before I review the research on special approaches for children with reading problems, I will review the reasons why children with reading problems may have problems with decoding.

Children With Reading Problems and Decoding

Children with reading problems tend to have greater difficulties with decoding than with comprehension; there is a fair amount of evidence supporting this assertion (e.g., van Ijzendoorn & Bus, 1994; Watson & Willows, 1995). As a result, these children receive much more instruction in decoding — both direct instruction in phonics and indirect instruction through phonics cues during teacher-directed oral reading — than competent readers (Allington, 1983). Yet despite this extra instruction, children with reading problems tend to fall further and further behind their competent peers as they progress through school (Stanovich, 1986). The question remains: if they get more instruction in phonics, why doesn't their decoding improve? If poor readers' specific difficulties are in decoding, why don't they catch up to their peers once they receive more instruction in that area?

Reading Problems as Cognitive Confusion

There have been many theories about the sources of children's reading problems. From the work of Samuel Orton, who stressed the role of letter reversals and posited a neurological base for such reversals (see

Orton, 1937), to more recent work positing that difficulty with phonological awareness (the ability to reflect upon sounds in spoken words) is the root of reading problems (e.g., Stanovich, 1986), many of these theoretical causes suggest that the child with reading problems suffers a confusion about one or more of the concepts underlying word perception. The work on visual difficulties — begun by Orton but continuing with work by Willows and her colleagues (e.g., Willows & Terepocki, 1993) — suggests that at least a subgroup of children with reading problems suffers confusions with orientation and visual recognition of letters. The work with phonological awareness suggests that children with reading problems focus not on the phonological aspects of words, but instead on semantic aspects. Thus, the "first sound of *cat*" may not be /k/ for the child with reading problems, but rather "the whiskers." Since an alphabetic language requires that children focus — at least partially — on the phonological aspects of words in order to map speech to print, a failure to reflect on sounds will impair learning to read (e.g., Adams, 1990). The difference between reading-impaired children and normally achieving readers may lie in their basic print concepts, such as directionality, but most likely involves their conceptions of basic literacy terms such as *word, letter, sentence,* and so on (Hare, 1984). Some researchers have stressed metacognitive differences in the ways that children with reading problems and competent readers view the function of reading (e.g., Garner & Kraus, 1981). They find that children with reading problems tend to view reading as largely a decoding task, while competent readers view the process as one of getting meaning or enjoyment from text (see Baker & Brown, 1984).

These characteristics of children with reading problems — visual confusions, difficulties with phonological awareness, poorly established print concepts, and metacognitive differences — may not apply to all such children. Also, these characteristics may not be the *causes* of the problems. Some have suggested, for example, that differences in phonological awareness are themselves rooted in genetic differences (e.g., Olson, Wise, & Rack, 1989). The same has been suggested of visual perception differences (Willows & Terepocki, 1993).[3] Differences in print concepts are likely the results of different experiences with print (see Adams, 1990). Metacognitive differences may arise from the different instruction that children with reading problems get, rather than being a cause of those problems (see Allington, 1983). Ignoring such possible underlying causes of the reading problems, we might consider these differences — visual confusions, lack of phonological awareness, poor print concepts, or metacognitive differences — to be *proximal causes* of reading problems, since we can easily see how differences in these areas might impact children's reading directly. Furthermore, these factors can be addressed directly, through instructional interventions, whereas direct intervention may not be possible for genetic or neurological substrates.

Each of these proximal causes represents a basic confusion about one of the basic understandings necessary for children to learn to read. In order to read, one must be able to reliably distinguish between *b* and *d*, one must be able to recognize that the first sound of *cat* is /k/, and that the purpose of reading is to understand the text, not just to mouth the words correctly. Confusions of these basic concepts would certainly interfere with learning to read.

Effects of Fragmented Instruction

Viewing children with reading problems as essentially *confused*, rather than perceptually, neurologically, or emotionally impaired (although they certainly may be all or some of these), may explain their response to instruction. Children with reading problems are usually not only served in the regular classroom, but also given additional instruction by a Title I teacher, or a special education teacher, and possibly by an additional specialist (Allington, 1994). In some areas, this instruction

[3] Willows and her colleagues hold a minority view. Many people have argued, in contrast, that visual confusions, such as those between *b* and *d*, are not rooted in neurology or basic perception, since they are easily remediated. For example, Bracey and Ward (1980) were able to remediate reversals quickly, using behavior management. If reversals can be remediated quickly, it is assumed, then their roots are not deep-seated.

cannot supplant the instruction in the regular class, but must supplement it. Given the multiplicity of programs for children with reading problems, it is inevitable that these children are going to receive different and often conflicting instruction. One teacher might stress the use of context and beginning letters; another might teach synthetic phonics or stress another strategy. The result may be that children with reading problems have to learn *more* than children without such problems, since they need to master separate reading programs for each specialist they deal with (Allington, 1994).

Dealing with instruction from multiple viewpoints, especially when one starts off with a basic confusion about the nature of alphabetic reading, may compound the confusion. This might explain why, even though children with reading problems get more instruction in phonics, they continue to have difficulties in decoding words.

The continued failure of children with reading problems to learn to read has emotional effects on them, and these effects must be taken into account when designing instruction. Because of their continued failure, in spite of the "help" from a variety of professionals, children increasingly believe themselves to be incapable of learning. The resulting "learned helplessness" (Butkowsky & Willows, 1980) or "passive failure" (Johnston & Winograd, 1985) makes children with reading problems increasingly unwilling to make the effort to master reading, since they believe that such effort will be fruitless. In our clinic, I have repeatedly seen children who, when confronted with a type of materials with which they have failed before, turn themselves off and resist instruction. It may be that earlier they were not ready for such instruction. For example, children without adequate phonological awareness may not be capable of understanding some types of phonics instruction, because they lack the root concept. If confronted with the same type of instruction later on, even when they understand phonological awareness and have the background to receive that instruction, they may resist it because of their memory of earlier failure. Furthermore, because of their exposure to multiple types of instruction in different settings, children with reading problems have failed with many types of instruction, and thus are resistant to more types of instruction.

These two characteristics of children with reading problems — their confusion about basic processes and their learned helplessness — suggest three principles for effective word identification instruction for this group of children. First, effective phonics instruction needs to avoid offering confusing information. To avoid confusing information, phonics instruction for children with reading problems should be highly focused, avoid extraneous concepts, and begin systematically from a beginning. This beginning could include letters and sounds in a synthetic phonics program, or a set of learned words in an analytic program. Children with specific reading difficulties seem to require direct instruction to acquire word analytic strategies (see Carnine et al., 1990). In contrast, a program of analytic phonics, which assumes a high degree of phoneme awareness, was indistinguishable from a whole-word method in promoting recognition of a set of words and did not result in transfer to untaught words (Lovett, Warren-Chaplin, Ransby, & Borden, 1990).

Second, effective word identification instruction for a child with reading problems must use methods different from those with which the child has previously failed. This may involve knowing the child and his or her instructional history. But even without knowing a child's specific instructional history, one can choose a method that has not been commonly used. It is my opinion that many of the successes we have had at the University of Georgia Reading Clinic have been due to our use of approaches different from those already tried, rather than to the inherent superiority of the approaches that we chose.

Third, good phonics instruction for children with reading problems needs to take phonological awareness into account. As noted earlier, there is a large body of research documenting the difficulties that children with reading problems have in reflecting upon phonemes in spoken words (see Adams, 1990). There is some evidence (Stahl & Murray, 1994) that a relatively low level of phoneme awareness — the ability to segment an initial consonant or onset — is adequate for a child to begin to learn to read. There is further evidence (Stahl & Murray, in press) that initial consonant segmentation is related to the notion of phoneme identity (Byrne & Fielding-Barnsley, 1993). Phoneme identity is the recognition that the /s/ in *sand* is the same sound as the /s/ in *sock* or in *sit*. Phoneme identity concepts can be taught along with letter–sound correspondences (Murray, 1995). This is done by providing a concrete symbol, the letter, for an abstract sound, the phoneme. Students learn that the sounds are the same across different words through the concrete mediator of the letters. Only those phonological awareness training programs that introduce letters or other concrete markers for phonemes have been successful in improving reading achievement (Wagner & Rashotte, 1993). Phoneme identities are taught in phonics programs such as the ones reviewed above, which directly teach the relations between letters and sounds. In contrast, analytic phonics approaches, such as those used in the basal reading programs of the 1970s and 1980s, rely upon the student's having phonological awareness and do not provide that phoneme identity knowledge. Quality phonics instruction for children with reading problems, through the simultaneous introduction of letters and sounds, would provide phonological awareness training, and thus eliminate one source of confusion.

Two of these three themes — the need for systematicity and the need for novelty — will recur over and over in the following section. The third, the need for phonological awareness instruction, is met in one way or another by all of the programs reviewed, but not necessarily by regular classroom reading instruction. This section will review research dealing with methods either specifically designed for children with reading problems or commonly recommended for use with this population.

Teaching Decoding to Children with Reading Problems

Synthetic phonics programs, such as the Orton-Gillingham approach and its variants and the Distar approach (Englemann & Bruner, 1969), have a long history in classroom and clinic. More recently, work at the

Benchmark School has led to the increased popularity of analogy and compare/contrast approaches for children with reading problems. These approaches both fit the criteria for effective phonics instruction for this population: they both tend to be clearly focused, and they tend to be new to the students who have experienced repeated failure with other approaches. There is, however, little research available on either approach.

I reviewed the research dealing with three classes of approaches — Orton-Gillingham–based approaches, Direct Instruction approaches (Distar and its followers), and Compare/Contrast–based approaches. To summarize the basic findings of that review, all of the programs reviewed were successful in improving the reading of children with reading problems. None of the programs was markedly superior to the others, or markedly superior to quality conventional programs with the same goals. None of these programs was well-researched, in spite of their longevity and widespread implementation. There were very few controlled studies, either experimental, single-subject, or qualitative. Instead, many of these programs relied on testimonials or logical argument for support. All of these programs could be considered promising, and I would recommend that clinicians know how to use each of them.

Contrary to many assertions, it does not seem to be the case that children with severe reading problems need highly structured programs, such as the Orton-Gillingham and Distar programs. Lovitt and Hurlburt (1974) and Lovitt and DeMier (1984) found that the highly structured Orton-Gillingham approach did not work appreciably better than a less structured linguistic approach; O'Connor, Jenkins, Cole, and Mills (1993), Kuder (1990), and Serwer, Shapiro, and Shapiro (1973) failed to find that the Distar program produced higher achievement than less structured approaches. As long as the content was the same, children with reading problems learned equally well from highly structured and less structured programs. On the other hand, Kline and Kline (1975) found that the Orton-Gillingham approach *did* produce significantly greater achievement than school-based programs, which were presumably based on basal reading materials. Such materials use an analytic phonics strategy, which both requires a great deal of phonological sophistication to follow the teaching and adds a great deal of extraneous information (Adams, 1990). As mentioned earlier, Lovett et al. (1990) failed to find that an analytic program produced better achievement than a whole-word method.

In the research reviewed above, these programs were the sole phonics instruction provided. This fact seems to be important, given the perspective that children with reading problems are confused about basic reading concepts. Owing to the nature of controlled research, the alternative program used as a control in each case (usually a linguistic approach) was also the only instruction given. At Benchmark School, the word identification program is carried out not only in language arts classes, but also in content area classes for middle school children. Consistency of instruction seems to be important in helping children with reading problems learn to decode.

Phonics and "Not-Phonics"

As noted earlier, children with reading problems have generally received a great deal of phonics instruction, usually teaching conflicting procedures, often during the same school year. The result is that these different procedures compound the problems these children have in decoding. As part of a diagnostic procedure, I have children verbalize their strategies as they read through text. It is not uncommon to run into a child with a history of reading problems, such as a fourth-grader reading at a pre-primer level, who verbalizes three or four different strategies as he goes through a text — using context here, "sounding out" there, analogy on another word — without having a coherent reason for using a particular strategy. The programs discussed above train the child to use one strategy consistently to identify unrecognized words, and thus eliminate some of the confusion.

The emphasis on phonics also keeps a child at what Chall (1983) called the Decoding stage, in which children are focused on word reading. Progress in reading depends on moving a child *through* this stage, toward automaticity in decoding and the efficient orchestration of word recognition skills in context. This progress can be made through practice in reading, using both wide reading (a variety of different materials) and repeated readings of the same material. For wide reading, I recommend that at least half (and preferably more) of the child's reading time be spent reading connected text, usually whole stories or expository texts. Emphasizing text reading gives the child needed practice and avoids over-stressing decoding instruction. In addition to wide reading, repeated reading is often useful in helping children progress through this automaticity stage (Samuels, 1988).

Repeated Readings

A number of studies have found that repeated readings of the same text lead to general improvements in word recognition and comprehension. There have been two major types of strategies for using repeated reading with children with reading problems. The first is simply having children read text over and over, with adult or peer feedback. Samuels (1988) reviewed a series of studies all showing the effectiveness of repeated readings in developing both fluency and comprehension. The second is *assisted reading,* in which the child reads repeatedly with an adult or a tape, with the assistance gradually faded so that the child reads independently. Heckelman (1969) called this approach the "neurological impress" method (N.I.M.), for reasons best lost in time. In the original N.I.M., the tutor was to sit beside the child, reading into his or her "dominant ear" and jointly pointing to the text. Today, it can be done without such embellishments. Chomsky (1978) had third-grade students who were accurate but slow decoders practice reading books along with a tape recorder until they had reached an adequate level of fluency. Over the course of four months, her approach proved successful in dramatically improving their reading comprehension ability.

Richek and McTeague (1988) found that having Chapter I children read "series" books using an assisted-reading strategy led to gains in word recognition and comprehension. Milobar (1991) found that it was not necessary for one to use a series book; children made equivalent gains using non-series books. However, both Lorenz and Vockell (1979) and Strong and Traynelis-Yurek (1983) found that a modified neurological impress approach failed to produce greater gains in reading skill than traditional remedial reading approaches. Homan, Klesius, and Hite (1993) found that repeated and non-repeated approaches produced similar gains with children with reading problems. They concluded it was the sheer amount of practice, not whether the readings were repeated, that led to the gains.

It may be not the repeating itself that leads to gains, but rather the use of repetition to scaffold children's reading of more difficult material. Richek and McTeague (1988) used material (*Curious George*) that students could not read on their own, and created an instructional environment in which they could read it. Mikkelsen (1981) found that assisted reading had its greatest effects on frustration-level material. Repeated or assisted readings might affect children's reading of frustration-level material in two ways. First, the use of difficult material is highly motivating. Children who have suffered repeated failure in reading are willing to work very hard to learn material "at their grade level," rather than easy material; in our clinical work with repeated readings, we have heard this from children a number of times. Second, such material (at least for children in second grade and up) is too long to efficiently memorize, especially when the criteria for task success is both accurate word calling and increased rate. Therefore, a student is forced to use word-level cues, supported by memory, to identify words. The need to use word-level cues forces a child to integrate information about phonics, which may be half-learned from previous fragmented instruction, into text reading.

Supported Contextual Reading

In the University of Georgia Reading Clinic, we have been using a variant of repeated reading/assisted reading — *supported contextual read-*

ing — with children with severe reading problems. The assumption behind the use of this technique is that children with reading problems have a great deal of phonics knowledge, but do not integrate it. Instead of having children repeat what they know in a different form, we have found a great deal of success in forcing them to use what they know about words as they read (using repeated readings) text that is relatively difficult for them. This technique, like most of those discussed in this article, is not new (see Heckelman, 1969; Hoffman, 1987), but is presented as an alternative for children with histories of reading difficulties.

In supported contextual reading, children are given material that is considerably above their instructional reading level and supported as they learn to read that material orally. Typically, we use material that is one or two years above the child's instructional level, depending on my judgment of how much effort the child is willing to put forth and how much frustration the child can handle. The first lesson usually begins with the tutor reading the selection out loud to the child. The tutor and student discuss the selection, using questions, a story map, or any other technique deemed appropriate. The purpose of this discussion is to make sure that the student understands, before repeated readings, that the purpose of reading is to comprehend the text. Handling comprehension first allows the student to concentrate on word recognition.

The next step is typically *echo reading,* in which the teacher reads a paragraph and the child echoes it back, pointing to each word with his or her finger as it is read. Echo reading introduces the words.

After this lesson, we send the book home for the child to read with his or her parents. The reading is assisted; that is, as the child has a problem with a word, the parent gives the word immediately and writes it down to be worked with later. The parent(s) and the tutor are instructed not to provide any cueing (such as "What does this word begin with?"), for fear of having the child use confusing cues. We have both the tutor and the parent use this procedure.

The child reads the same materials over the course of several lessons until the material is mastered. Sometimes the tutor reads along with the child, using *impress reading* techniques (Heckelman, 1969). In impress reading, the tutor and the child read the same material chorally, with the tutor phasing his or her voice out as the child can take over. Sometimes, we use tapes to support a child's reading. There was one child who traveled an hour and a half to the clinic for each lesson. We had him listen to the tape in the car and read along, pointing to each word as he read it, using the cassette player.

We do not use predictable materials, since the context may provide so much support that the child does not use information from the words at all (see Johnson, 1995). We use material that is long and complex, suitable for the child's level of comprehension. The material used is so complex and long (usually our selections are at least 1000 words in length) that it cannot be memorized. Instead, we hypothesize, the children use cues from their memory of the stories, along with cues from the words in the text, to successfully master each story. Using the word-level information requires the students to utilize previously learned phonics information, supported by context.

This supported contextual reading procedure has produced dramatic results. With the first child — a fifth-grade boy reading at a first-grade level who had previously been given extra help from any source available — his reading improved to a third-grade level at the end of a six-week intensive summer program using these procedures. The second child with whom we tried this method — a third-grade girl reading initially at a pre-primer level — is now in the fourth grade and reading at the early fourth-grade level. We have begun this approach with a third child, a fourth-grade boy. This child, with a somewhat weaker tutor than the others, made gains from the first-grade to the second-grade reading level over the course of a single seven-week tutoring session. Given that these children had all received sympathetic instruction in their respective schools, to little avail, the success of this approach is promising.

A Classroom Approach. Based on procedures developed for second-grade instruction in our Fluency-Oriented Reading Instruction program (Stahl, Heubach, & Cramond, 1994), we developed a model for classroom instruction. This approach, similar to Hoffman's (1987), is an attempt to use repeated readings in a classroom program to develop fluent and automatic word recognition in second-graders. The program consists of three parts — (a) a home reading program in which students are encouraged to read 20 minutes per day at home, (b) a choice reading program in which students read materials of their own choosing (and usually near their instructional level) either alone or with a partner during the school day, and (c) a redesigned basal reading lesson. The redesigned basal reading lesson, illustrated in Figure 9-1, is similar to the repeated readings discussed above.

These lessons were given to all students in the class, using the second-grade basal reader. Since students in the class vary considerably in initial reading level, this material is well above the level of many children in the class, and below the level of others. However, over the two years that we collected data, children at all initial ability levels made roughly the same amount of progress: roughly two years of growth in instructional level on an informal reading inventory in the school year (average progress 1.78 years in the first year, 1.72 years in the second year). For the first year, all children who began the second grade reading at a primer level or higher could read at the second-grade level by the end. Many of those reading below the primer level were also able to read second-grade material. In fact, of the 85 students in the first year, only 3 were still unable to read the second-grade passage by the end of the year. For the second year, the results were similar. All children but 2 (out of 105) initially reading at a primer level or higher could read the second-grade passage by the end of the year.

A child reading at a primer level or higher would be in Chall's (1983) Stage 2 of reading, the confirmation and fluency stage. To progress through this stage, a child needs to practice reading, so that the word recognition skills begun in Stage 1 (Decoding) become automatic.

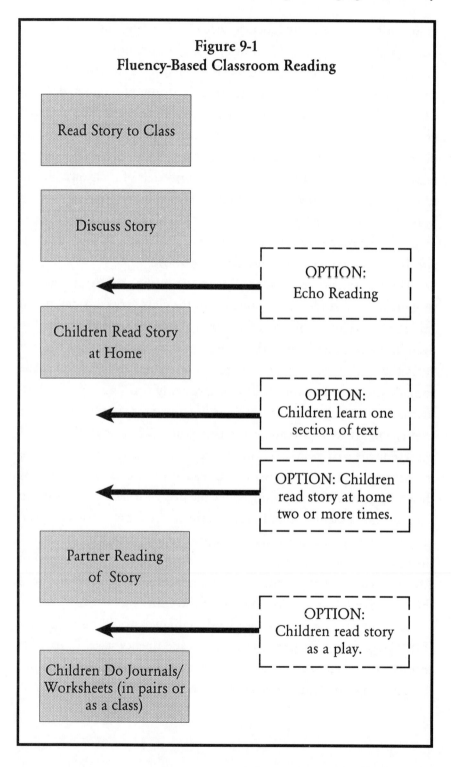

Figure 9-1
Fluency-Based Classroom Reading

Read Story to Class

Discuss Story

OPTION:
Echo Reading

Children Read Story
at Home

OPTION:
Children learn one
section of text

OPTION: Children
read story at home
two or more times.

Partner Reading
of Story

OPTION:
Children read story
as a play.

Children Do Journals/
Worksheets (in pairs or
as a class)

Bringing It All Together

The paradox of children with reading problems is that they get more phonics instruction than children reading at expected levels, yet they have continued difficulties decoding words. I have argued that the large amount of phonics instruction, especially when it includes multiple approaches to phonics, may serve to confuse the child rather than eliminate any difficulties with phonics. I recommend a two-pronged solution — first, providing a clear and consistent program of phonics instruction, and second, providing copious amounts of reading of connected text, possibly through supported contextual reading of material well above the children's instructional levels.

The phonics instruction should be systematic, so as to provide a clear strategy for the child to decode an unknown word. Synthetic phonics approaches, such as the Orton-Gillingham approach and the Distar approach, teach children to "sound words out" and give ample practice in this process. Compare/contrast approaches teach children to compare unknown words to words they already know and to evaluate their guesses in terms of the context. A review of the scant research available suggests that both of these approaches are effective, but that neither is appreciably more effective than other, systematic approaches to teaching phonics. What is important is that a consistent approach be used, and used well.

For children with reading problems, an approach to teaching phonics should be novel, to avoid the passive failure reaction that sets in when children encounter material with which they have already failed. Part of teaching children with reading problems is convincing them that they *can* learn to read, despite their experience to the contrary.

Phonics instruction should also take into account phonological awareness. Good instruction — especially for children with reading problems, but for others as well — should explicitly teach that spoken words can be broken into sounds and that letters can be mapped onto these sounds. The methods shown in this paper to be successful with children with reading problems teach phonological awareness as part of the process of teaching letter-sound correspondences. Conventional phonics instruction, at least as used in the basal reading programs of the 1970s and 1980s, seemed to require that the child have some awareness as a prerequisite to success.

Finally, phonics instruction should not predominate. Instead, the major emphasis should be on providing children opportunities to read connected text. Sometimes this text should be used to reinforce the letters and sounds taught, as in the Orton-Gillingham or Distar approaches, but one should also use children's literature such as the books suggested by Trachtenburg (1990). At other times, children should read material that is relatively easy for them. And at still other times, children should read material that is more difficult than what they could handle on their own, using supported contextual reading techniques such as assisted reading or repeated readings.

These principles are similar to those used in the Harvard Reading Laboratory in the late 1970s. We were taught to teach skills, but not to overwhelm students with them — to provide distributed rather than massed practice. We were also taught to provide students with a great deal of practice reading connected text — at least half of the time, if not more.

Different Programs for Different Children?

It should be pointed out that the principles discussed above apply to children making adequate progress as well as to those who are struggling. Indeed, one interpretation of the literature we reviewed is that techniques specially developed for children with reading problems, such as the Orton-Gillingham approach or the Distar approach, seem to be no more effective than other, conventional techniques that have similar characteristics. A review of research in teaching comprehension strategies to children with reading problems (Lively, Stahl, Pickle, & Kuhn, 1995) has concluded that techniques suitable for this population had similar effects on children making adequate progress in reading. Therefore, children with reading problems did not appear to need different approaches for comprehension instruction.

I learned from Jeanne Chall that educational policy needs to be supported by research, and that research should be used to review and reexamine policy decisions. The reason for the policy of classifying children is to better match children with appropriate instruction — instruction that is supposed to be provided by a specially trained teacher. If children with reading problems do not need specially designed instruction, then we may want to rethink our segregation of these children in programs for the "learning disabled" or "reading disabled," and instead try to redesign instruction to meet the needs of all children in the school. It may be that children with reading problems differ from others in their need for instructional support, rather than in their need for different programs. Providing different degrees of instructional support might require not special out-of-class programs, but rather the proper amount of support early on, and, if failure persists, more focused and targeted instruction, allowing for their previous experiences with failure from their initial instruction.

References

Adams, M.J. (1990). *Beginning to read: Thinking and learning about print.* Cambridge, MA: MIT Press.

Allington, R.L. (1983). The reading instruction provided readers of differing reading abilities. *The Elementary School Journal, 83,* 549-559.

Allington, R.L. (1994). Critical issues: What's special about special programs for children who find learning to read difficult. *Journal of Reading Behavior, 26,* 95-116.

Allington, R.L., & Cunningham, P.M. (1995). *Schools that work: Where all children read and write.* Reading, MA: Addison-Wesley.

Allington, R.L., & Johnston, P. (1986). The coordination among regular classroom reading programs and targeted support programs. (ERIC Document Reproduction Service ED 293 922)

Baker, L., & Brown, A.L. (1984). Metacognitive skills and reading. In P.D. Pearson (Ed.), *Handbook of reading research* (pp. 353-394). White Plains, NY: Longman.

Bracey, S.A., & Ward, J. (1980). "Dark, dark went the bog": Instructional interventions for remediating "b" and "d" reversals. *Reading Improvement, 17*(2), 104-111.

Butkowsky, I.S., & Willows, D.M. (1980). Cognitive-motivational characteristics of children varying in reading ability: Evidence for learned helplessness in poor readers. *Journal of Educational Psychology, 72,* 408-422.

Byrne, B., & Fielding-Barnsley, R. (1993). Evaluation of a program to teach phonemic awareness to young children: A 1-year follow-up. *Journal of Educational Psychology, 85*, 104-111.

Carnine, D., Silbert, J., & Kameenui, E. (1990). *Direct instruction reading* (2nd ed.). Columbus, OH: Charles E. Merrill.

Chall, J.S. (1983). *Stages of reading development*. New York: McGraw-Hill.

Chomsky, C. (1978). When you still can't read in third grade? After decoding, what? In S.J. Samuels (Ed.), *What research has to say about reading instruction* (pp. 13-30). Newark, DE: International Reading Association.

Englemann, S., & Bruner, E. (1969). *Distar Reading Program*. Chicago: SRA.

Garner, R., & Kraus, C. (1981). Good and poor comprehender differences in knowing and regulating reading behaviors. *Educational Research Quarterly, 6*, 5-12.

Goodman, K.S. (1986). *What's whole in whole language*. Portsmouth, NH: Heinemann.

Gough, P.B., & Tumner, W.E. (1986). Decoding, reading, and reading disability. *Remedial and Special Education, 7*, 6-10.

Hare, V.C. (1984). What's in a word? A review of young children's difficulties with the construct "word". *The Reading Teacher, 37*, 360-364.

Haynes, M.C., & Jenkins, J.R. (1986). Reading instruction in special education resource rooms. *American Educational Research Journal, 23*, 161-190.

Heckelman, R.G. (1969). A neurological-impress method of remedial reading instruction. *Academic Therapy Quarterly, 4*, 277-282.

Hoffman, J. (1987). Rethinking the role of oral reading. *Elementary School Journal, 87*, 367-373.

Homan, S.P., Klesius, J.P., & Hite, C. (1993). Effects of repeated readings and nonrepetitive strategies on students' fluency and comprehension. *Journal of Educational Research, 87*, 94-99/

Johnson, F.R. (1995, December). *Learning to read with predictable text: What kinds of words do beginning readers remember?* Paper presented at the annual meeting of the National Reading Conference.

Johnston, P.H., & Winograd, P.N. (1985). Passive failure in reading. *Journal of Reading Behavior, 17*, 279-301.

Keefe, C.H., & Keefe, D.R. (1993). Instruction for students with LD: A whole language model. *Intervention in school and clinic, 28*(3), 172-177.

Kline, C.L., & Kline, C.L. (1975). Follow-up study of 216 dyslexic children. *Bulletin of the Orton Society, 25*, 127-144.

Kuder, S.J. (1990). The effectiveness of the DISTAR reading program for children with learning disabilities. *Journal of Learning Disabilities, 23*, 69-71.

Leinhardt, G., Zigmond, N., & Cooley, W. (1981). Reading instruction and its effects. *American Educational Research Journal, 18*, 343-361.

Lively, M., Stahl, S.A., Pickle, J.M., & Kuhn, M. (1995, December). *Teaching reading comprehension to learning disabled children: A review.* Paper presented at the annual meeting of the National Reading Conference, New Orleans, LA.

Lorenz, L. & Vockell, E. (1979). Using the neurological impress method with learning disabled readers. *Journal of Learning Disabilities, 12,* 420-422.

Lovett, M.W., Warren-Chaplin, P.M., Ransby, M.J., & Borden, S.L. (1990). Training the word recognition skills of reading disabled children: Treatment and transfer effects. *Journal of Educational Psychology, 82,* 769-780.

Lovitt, T.C., & DeMier, D.M. (1984). An evaluation of the Slingerland method with LD youngsters. *Journal of Learning Disabilities, 17,* 267-272.

Lovitt, T.C., & Hurlburt, M. (1974). Using behavior-analysis techniques to assess the relationship between phonics instruction and oral reading. *Journal of Special Education, 8,* 57-72.

Mikkelsen, V.P. (1981). The effects of a modified neurological impress method on developing reading skills. (ERIC Document Reproduction Service ED 209 638)

Milobar, D. (1991). Does a connected series make a difference? "Curious George" revisited. (ERIC Document Reproduction Service ED 336 729)

Mullis, I.V.S., Campbell, J.R., & Farstrup, A.E. (1993). *NAEP 1992 Reading Report Card for the Nation and the States.* Washington, DC: Office of Educational Research and Development, U.S. Department of Education.

Murray, B.A. (1995). *Which better defines phoneme awareness: Segmentation skill or identity measures?* Unpublished doctoral thesis, University of Georgia.

Myers, C.A. (1978). Reviewing the literature on Fernald's technique of remedial reading. *The Reading Teacher, 31,* 614-619.

O'Connor, R.E., Jenkins, J.R., Cole, K.N., & Mills, P.E. (1993). Two approaches to reading instruction with children with disabilities: Does program design make a difference? *Exceptional Children, 59,* 312-323.

Olson, R.K., Wise, B.W., & Rack, J.P. (1989). Dyslexia: Deficits, genetic aetiology, and computer-based remediation. *Irish Journal of Psychology, 10,* 494-508.

Orton, S.T. (1937). *Reading, writing, and speech problems in children.* New York: W.W. Norton.

Richek, M.A., & McTeague, B.K. (1988). The "Curious George" strategy for students with reading problems. *The Reading Teacher, 42,* 220-226.

Samuels, S.J. (1988). Decoding and automaticity: Helping poor readers become automatic at word recognition. *The Reading Teacher, 41,* 756-760.

Serwer, B.L., Shapiro, B.J., & Shapiro, P.P. (1973). The comparative effectiveness of four methods of instruction on the achievement of children with specific learning disabilities. *Journal of Special Education, 7,* 241-249.

Stahl, S.A., Heubach, K., & Cramond, B. (1994, December). *Fluency oriented reading instruction: A second year evaluation.* Paper presented at the annual meeting of the National Reading Conference, San Diego, CA.

Stahl, S.A., & Miller, P.D. (1989). Whole language and language experience approaches for beginning reading: A quantitative research synthesis. *Review of Educational Research, 59*(1), 87-116.

Stahl, S.A., & Murray, B.A. (1994). Defining phonological awareness and its relationship to early reading. *Journal of Educational Psychology, 86*, 221-234.

Stahl, S.A., & Murray, B.A. (in press). Understanding the relations between phoneme awareness and reading. In J. Metsala & L. Ehri (Eds.), *Beginning reading,* .

Stanovich, K.E. (1986). Matthew effects in reading: Some consequences of individual differences in the acquisition of literacy. *Reading Research Quarterly, 21*, 360-407.

Strong, M.W., & Traynelis-Yurek, E. (1983). Behavioral reinforcement within a perceptual conditioning program of oral reading. (ERIC Document Reproduction Service ED 233 328)

Trachtenburg, P. (1990). Using children's literature to enhance phonics instruction. *The Reading Teacher, 43*, 648-653.

Tierney, R.J., Readence, J., & Dishner, E. (1995). *Reading strategies and practices*. Boston: Allyn & Bacon.

van Ijzendoorn, M.H., & Bus, A.G. (1994). Meta-analytic confirmation of the nonword reading deficit in developmental dyslexia. *Reading Research Quarterly, 29*, 267-275.

Wagner, R.K. & Rashotte, C.A. (1993, April). *Does phonological awareness training really work? A meta-analysis.* Paper presented at the annual meeting of the American Educational Research Association, Atlanta, GA.

Watson, C., & Willows, D.M. (1995). Information-processing patterns in specific reading disability. *Journal of Learning Disabilities, 28*, 216-231.

Willows, D.M., & Terepocki, M. (1993). The relation of reversal errors to reading disabilities. In D.M. Willows, R.S. Kruk, & E. Corcos (Eds.), *Visual processes in reading and reading disabilities*. Hillsdale, NJ: Lawrence Erlbaum Associates.

Ysseldyke, J.E., Algozzine, B., Shinn, M.R., & McGue, M. (1982). Similarities and differences between low achievers and students classified learning disabled. *Journal of Special Education, 16*, 73-85.

10

Common Reading Problems And Tools To Diagnose Them

EDWARD FRY, Ph.D.
Professor Emeritus, Rutgers University

Classroom teachers faced with the problem of what to do with disabled readers must have certain tools to work with. Plumbers and auto mechanics wouldn't be very useful if all they had was a theoretical knowledge of plumbing or a theoretical knowledge of automotive engineering; they need tools. They need wrenches and screwdrivers. Teachers too must have certain tools; academic tools are necessary for improving the reading and writing ability of disabled students. The tools[1] described below are designed to help teachers evaluate their students' reading abilities and develop appropriate instructional interventions.

Can the student read? Tool I — Oral Reading Test

The first question a teacher faces with a disabled reader — or, in fact, with any reader — is "What is his present reading ability?" Do not go

---

[1] These tools are copyrighted by the author for commercial purposes (sale), but teachers or professors may reproduce enough copies of any or all of them for their students.

Tool 1
ORAL READING TEST

Examiner's Copy and Record Sheet
For Determining Independent and Instructional Reading Levels

Student's Name _____ Date _____

Examiner _____ Class _____

	1st Testing	2nd Testing	3rd Testing
Date	_____	_____	_____
Total Score: Independent Reading Level	_____	_____	_____
	Grade	Grade	Grade
Instructional Reading Level	_____	_____	_____
	Grade	Grade	Grade

Directions: Student reads aloud from Student copy. Teacher marks this copy. If student can't read a word or mispronounces it, just say "Go on" and count it as an error (underline word). Do not tell the student the missed word. Stop the test when the Frustration Level is first reached. Paragraph numbers are grade levels.

			1st Testing	2nd Testing	3rd Testing
No. 1-A	**Errors**	**Level**			
Look at the dog.	0-2	Indep.	☐	☐	☐
It is big.	3-4	Instr.	☐	☐	☐
It can run.	5-6	Frust.	☐	☐	☐
Run, dog, run away.	**Speed:**	Fast	☐	☐	☐
		Avg.	☐	☐	☐
		Slow	☐	☐	☐
		V. Slow	☐	☐	☐
No. 1-B	**Errors**	**Level**			
We saw the sun.	0-2	Indep.	☐	☐	☐
It made us warm.	3-4	Instr.	☐	☐	☐
Now it was time to go home.	5-6	Frust.	☐	☐	☐
It was a long way to walk.	**Speed:**	Fast	☐	☐	☐
		Avg.	☐	☐	☐
		Slow	☐	☐	☐
		V. Slow	☐	☐	☐

Tool 1
ORAL READING TEST

		1st Testing	2nd Testing	3rd Testing

No. 2-A

The door of the house opened and a man came out. He had a broom in his hand. He said to the boy sitting there, "Go away." The boy got up and left.

Errors	Level	1st Testing	2nd Testing	3rd Testing
0-2	Indep.	☐	☐	☐
3-4	Instr.	☐	☐	☐
5-6	Frust.	☐	☐	☐
Speed:	Fast	☐	☐	☐
	Avg.	☐	☐	☐
	Slow	☐	☐	☐
	V. Slow	☐	☐	☐

No. 2-B

The family ate their breakfast. Then they gave the pig his breakfast. It was fun to watch him eat. He seemed to like it. He is eating all of it.

Errors	Level	1st Testing	2nd Testing	3rd Testing
0-2	Indep.	☐	☐	☐
3-4	Instr.	☐	☐	☐
5-6	Frust.	☐	☐	☐
Speed:	Fast	☐	☐	☐
	Avg.	☐	☐	☐
	Slow	☐	☐	☐
	V. Slow	☐	☐	☐

No. 3-A

When the man had gone, the boys were surprised to see how many boxes he had left in their little back yard. Right away they began to pile them on top of each other. They made caves and houses. It took so long that lunch time came before they knew they were hungry.

Errors	Level	1st Testing	2nd Testing	3rd Testing
0-2	Indep.	☐	☐	☐
3-4	Instr.	☐	☐	☐
5-6	Frust.	☐	☐	☐
Speed:	Fast	☐	☐	☐
	Avg.	☐	☐	☐
	Slow	☐	☐	☐
	V. Slow	☐	☐	☐

No. 3-B

The man became angry because his dog had never talked before, and, besides, he didn't like its voice. So he took his knife and cut a branch from a palm tree and hit his dog. Just then the palm tree said, "Put down that branch." The man was getting very upset about the way things were going and he started to throw it away.

Errors	Level	1st Testing	2nd Testing	3rd Testing
0-2	Indep.	☐	☐	☐
3-4	Instr.	☐	☐	☐
5-6	Frust.	☐	☐	☐
Speed:	Fast	☐	☐	☐
	Avg.	☐	☐	☐
	Slow	☐	☐	☐
	V. Slow	☐	☐	☐

Tool 1
ORAL READING TEST

No. 4

Tbree more cowboys tried their best to rope and tie a calf as quickly as Red, but none of them came within ten seconds of his time. Then came the long, thin cowboy. He was the last one to enter the contest.

		1st Testing	2nd Testing	3rd Testing
Errors	**Level**			
0-2	Indep.	☐	☐	☐
3-4	Instr.	☐	☐	☐
5-6	Frust.	☐	☐	☐
Speed:	Fast	☐	☐	☐
	Avg.	☐	☐	☐
	Slow	☐	☐	☐
	V. Slow	☐	☐	☐

No. 5

High in the hills they came to a wide ledge where trees grew among the rocks. Grass grew in patches and the ground was covered with bits of wood from trees blown over a long time ago and dried by the sun. Down in the valley it was already beginning to get dark.

Errors	**Level**			
0-2	Indep.	☐	☐	☐
3-4	Instr.	☐	☐	☐
5-6	Frust.	☐	☐	☐
Speed:	Fast	☐	☐	☐
	Avg.	☐	☐	☐
	Slow	☐	☐	☐
	V. Slow	☐	☐	☐

No. 6

Businessmen from suburban areas may travel to work in helicopters, land on the roof of an office building, and thus avoid city traffic jams. Families can spend more time at summer homes and mountain cabins through the use of this marvelous craft. People on farms can reach city centers quickly for medical service, shopping, entertainment, or sale of products.

Errors	**Level**			
0-2	Indep.	☐	☐	☐
3-4	Instr.	☐	☐	☐
5-6	Frust.	☐	☐	☐
Speed:	Fast	☐	☐	☐
	Avg.	☐	☐	☐
	Slow	☐	☐	☐
	V. Slow	☐	☐	☐

Errors	**Level**			
0-2	Indep.	☐	☐	☐
3-4	Instr.	☐	☐	☐
5-6	Frust.	☐	☐	☐
Speed:	Fast	☐	☐	☐
	Avg.	☐	☐	☐
	Slow	☐	☐	☐
	V. Slow	☐	☐	☐

Tool 1
ORAL READING TEST

		1st Testing	2nd Testing	3rd Testing

No. 7	Errors	Level			

The President of the United States was speaking. His audience comprised two thousand foreign born men who had just been admitted to citizenship. They listened intently, their faces aglow with the light of a newborn patriotism, upturned to the calm, intellectual face of the first citizen of the country they now claimed as their own.

Errors	Level	1st	2nd	3rd
0-2	Indep.	☐	☐	☐
3-4	Instr.	☐	☐	☐
5-6	Frust.	☐	☐	☐
Speed:	Fast	☐	☐	☐
	Avg.	☐	☐	☐
	Slow	☐	☐	☐
	V. Slow	☐	☐	☐

(If the last paragraph is read at the Independent Level, use a silent reading test to determine advanced reading levels.)

---

by age, grade placement, or previous teachers' comments. Find out for yourself quickly and easily by using Tool 1, a set of *Oral Reading Paragraphs*. It only takes a few minutes to administer, and it will give you an estimation of the student's reading grade level. This estimate won't be perfect, but it is certainly a lot better than a wild guess.

Is the material at an appropriate level?
Tool 2 — Readability Graph

Now that you know the student's approximate reading ability level, what do you do next? You give the student books, stories, and articles that he or she can read successfully. This is called *matching* the book to the student, and it is an important step in creating a successful reader. Disabled readers have already had plenty of unsuccessful exposure to reading materials. What you want to do is to create a pattern of success. This is fairly easy to do if you use the *Readability Graph* for judging the

Tool 2
READABILITY GRAPH

Directions: Randomly select three 100-word passages from a book or an article. Plot the average number of syllables and the average number of sentences per 100 words on this graph to determine the grade level of the material. Choose more passages per book if great variability is observed, and conclude that the book has uneven readability. Few books will fall in the gray area, but when they do, grade level scores are invalid.

Count proper nouns, numerals, and initializations as single words. Count one syllable for each symbol. For example, *1945* is 1 word and 4 syllables, and *IRA* is 1 word and 3 syllables.

Example:	SYLLABLES	SENTENCES
1st 100-Word Passage	124	6.6
2nd 100-Word Passage	141	5.5
3rd 100-Word Passage	158	6.8
AVERAGE	141	6.3

READABILITY: 7th GRADE (see dot plotted on graph).

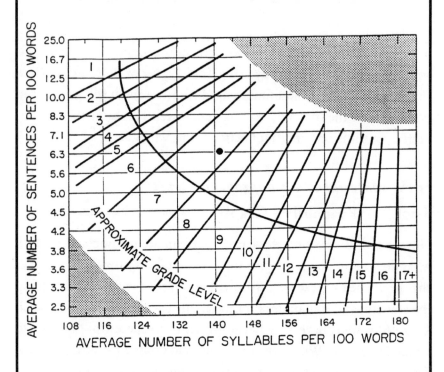

difficulty of books. (If you don't want to use the graph to determine the difficulty of a book, find a list of materials that are already graded.)

Note that the oral reading test indicates three different reading levels. The *frustration level* should be avoided because it generates more failure. The *instructional level* can be used in oral reading lessons and in reading assignments, since someone else is around to help with hard words or difficult passages. But the *independent level* is most useful for silent reading practice and pleasure reading. It is true that if a student is highly motivated to read something, as with a teenager who is studying for a driver's license, he will read materials at the frustration level — but most of the time, for most reading, you should use something easier.

What if I don't like tests and readability?
Tool 3 — The 1 Out Of 20 Rule

If you don't want to use the Oral Paragraphs and the Readability Graph, you can use the *1 Out Of 20 Rule.* Simply have the student read a section out of a proposed book, and count on your fingers the number of mistakes he makes. If he makes about one mistake in every 20 words, the text is approximately at his instructional level. If he makes less than one mistake in every 20 words, it is at his independent level, and he can successfully read it on his own most of the time. But if your student makes more than one error in 20 words, the text is at the frustration level; at this level, reading instruction is difficult, and independent silent reading for any length of time is rather unlikely.

Every shortcut has its price. The 1 Out Of 20 Rule is a shortcut eliminating the need for the Oral Paragraphs and the Readability Graph. Its benefits are speed and simplicity, since no paperwork is required. The drawbacks are that it is less accurate and takes up more teacher time in the long run. In other words, you have to use the 1 Out Of 20 Rule procedure for every student every time she selects a new book. You also can't measure a student's progress using various books, as you can with the re-administration of a test. There are some advantages to using readability measures; once you know the readability level of a book, it never needs to be calculated again, and you know you can suggest it to any student with the appropriate reading ability.

Of course you want to select the best literature, the most interesting subjects, and the widest variety of material for students to read. But don't overlook the text's inherent difficulty or readability level if you want to be successful with disabled readers, or with any developing reader for that matter. Librarians can be a great help with selecting appropriate books and materials.

Does the student know basic words? Tool 4 — Instant Words

People who are unfamiliar with reading research are usually amazed to find out that approximately half of all reading material is composed of just 100 of the most common words, and that the most common 300 words — the *instant words* — comprise 65% of all written material. It makes sense to teach the most common words because they come up all the time. You can hardly write a sentence without using some of them, and you certainly can't read a whole paragraph of anything without coming across many of them. So make sure your students know them. They should know how to read them without hesitation, as well as how to spell them, so their writing can proceed smoothly and they don't have to look up a word like *their* or, worse yet, avoid using it and thus distort their stories.

Because these words are so crucial, you really need Tool 4, the 300 Instant Words. If you or a tutor have the time, have the student read every word over several sessions. But for a quicker overview, just having the student read every 10th word will give you an idea of his basic sight-reading vocabulary. Do the same thing with spelling testing. Then teach any unknown words, using flash cards, sentence context, spelling lessons, correction during oral reading or story writing, repetition, encouragement, and games.

Tool 4
INSTANT WORDS

These are the most common words in English, ranked in frequency order. The first 25 make up about a third of all printed material. The first 100 make up about half of all written material, and the first 300 make up about 65 percent of all written material. These words are also called "sight words" because fluent reading depends on the ability to recognize them instantly, on sight. Make sure your student knows most of the first 100 words before teaching the second 100. Teach only a few at a time to keep the student's success rate high. Use these words for flash cards, games, spelling lessons, or just reading down the column.

Column 1 Words 1-25	Column 2 Words 26-50	Column 3 Words 51-75	Column 4 Words 76-100
the	or	will	number
of	one	up	no
and	had	other	way
a	by	about	could
to	words	out	people
in	but	many	my
is	not	then	than
you	what	them	first
that	all	these	water
it	were	so	been
he	we	some	called
was	when	her	who
for	your	would	oil
on	can	make	sit
are	said	like	now
as	there	him	find
with	use	into	long
his	an	time	down
they	each	has	day
I	which	look	did
at	she	two	get
be	do	more	come
this	how	write	made
have	their	go	may
from	if	see	part

Tool 4
INSTANT WORDS

The Second Hundred Instant Words

Column 5 Words 101-125	Column 6 Words 126-150	Column 7 Words 151-175	Column 8 Words 176-200
over	say	set	try
new	great	put	kind
sound	where	end	hand
take	help	does	picture
only	through	another	again
little	much	well	change
work	before	large	off
know	line	must	play
place	right	big	spell
years	too	even	air
live	means	such	away
me	old	because	animals
back	any	turned	house
give	same	here	point
most	tell	why	page
very	boy	asked	letters
after	following	went	mother
things	came	men	answer
our	want	read	found
just	show	need	study
name	also	land	still
good	around	different	learn
sentence	form	home	should
man	three	us	American
think	small	move	world

Common suffixes: -s, -ing, -ed, -er, -ly, -est

Tool 4
INSTANT WORDS

The Third Hundred Instant Words

Column 9 Words 201-225	Column 10 Words 226-250	Column 11 Words 251-275	Column 12 Words 276-300
high	saw	important	miss
every	left	until	idea
near	don't	children	enough
add	few	side	eat
food	while	feet	face
between	along	car	watch
own	might	miles	far
below	close	night	Indians
country	something	walked	really
plants	seemed	white	almost
last	next	sea	let
school	hard	began	above
father	open	grow	girl
keep	example	took	sometimes
trees	beginning	river	mountains
never	life	four	cut
started	always	carry	young
city	those	state	talk
earth	both	once	soon
eyes	paper	book	list
light	together	hear	song
thought	got	stop	being
head	group	without	leave
under	often	second	family
story	run	later	it's

Are the instant words enough? Tool 5 — Picture Nouns

Are the instant words enough for reading instruction? No, certainly not. They comprise one important element in an overall instructional pattern, but certainly not a total vocabulary building program. For example, the instant words have many "structure words" such as *the* and *of.* While these words are absolutely necessary for reading and writing, you can't write a very interesting story using just instant words, particularly those near the beginning of the list. For this reason, I have developed 100 *picture nouns,* which can be taught along with the instant words and other beginning reading teaching methods. The picture nouns are concrete words whose referents can be easily visualized; for many students, these words are much easier to learn than the instant words. You can teach the picture nouns in the same ways you teach the instant words, using games, spelling, writing sentences, etc.

The picture nouns have one additional characteristic that might be helpful: they are presented in meaningful clusters of five words each. Clusters like "Toys" and "Food" are conceptual categories. If you want to teach thinking skills, you can put words from several categories of picture nouns on cards, mix them up, and have the student sort them into categories. Alternatively, you can mix up the words from several categories, write them on the board, and have the children copy them into correct categories — but first ensure, through discussion, that the students know what each word means. The picture nouns are also helpful in teaching English as a second language (ESL) to students who are not native speakers.

Can he sound out new words? Tool 6 — Phonics Survey

The term *phonics* refers to an understanding of the phoneme–grapheme relationship. Many teachers like to teach some phonics because it helps students to sound out unknown words, saving them from having to ask for assistance or, worse yet, stopping reading. Phonics knowledge is a long way from making perfect spellers or even perfect readers,

Tool 5
100 PICTURE NOUNS

These words are intended to supplement the first 300 Instant Words for use in beginning or remedial reading instruction. These words can be made into flash cards with the word on one side only, or cards with the word on one side and a picture on the other.

1. People	6. Furniture	11. Numbers 6-10	16. Farm Animals
boy	table	six	horse
girl	chair	seven	cow
man	sofa	eight	pig
woman	chest	nine	chicken
baby	desk	ten	duck

2. Toys	7. Eating Objects	12. Fruits	17. Workers
ball	cup	fruit	farmer
doll	plate	orange	policeman
train	bowl	grape	cook
game	fork	pear	doctor
toy	spoon	banana	nurse

3. Numbers 1-5	8. Transportation	13. Plants	18. Entertainment
one	car	bush	television
two	truck	flower	radio
three	bus	grass	movie
four	plane	plant	ball game
five	boat	tree	band

4. Clothing	9. Food	14. Sky Things	19. Writing Tools
shirt	bread	sun	pen
pants	meat	moon	pencil
dress	soup	star	crayon
shoes	apple	cloud	chalk
hat	cereal	rain	computer

5. Pets	10. Drinks	15. Earth Things	20. Reading Things
cat	water	lake	book
dog	milk	rock	newspaper
bird	juice	dirt	magazine
fish	soda	field	sign
rabbit	malt	hill	letter

Tool 6
PHONICS SURVEY

This survey gives a general idea of the amount of phonics skills known by the student.

Name _____

Examiner _____ Date _____

Student reads nonsense words using phonics rules. Teacher checks box to right of line according to amount known.

	Perfect	Knew Some	Knew None

Section I — Easy Consonants and Short Vowels
Charts 1 & 2

			Perfect	Knew Some	Knew None
TIP	NEL	ROM	☐	☐	☐
DUP	CAV	SEB	☐	☐	☐

Section 2 — Harder Consonants and Long Vowels
Charts 3 & 5

					Perfect	Knew Some	Knew None
KO	HOAB	WAJE	KE	YATE	☐	☐	☐
ZEEX	QUIDE	YAIG	ZAY	SUDE	☐	☐	☐

Section 3 — Consonant Digraphs and Difficult Vowels
Charts 4, 6, & 7

				Perfect	Knew Some	Knew None
WHAW	THOIM	PHER	KOYCH	☐	☐	☐
OUSH	CHAU	EANG	HOON	☐	☐	☐

This survey may be repeated at a later date after more phonics instruction, or the teacher can make up nonsense words for testing or instruction.

but for many students it is definitely a help — and sometimes a little help is all that we mere teachers can provide.

If you would like to quickly get some idea of a student's phonics ability, try using Tool 6 — the Phonics Survey. Let the student read the nonsense words aloud and you will quickly get an idea of his or her "sounding-out" ability. You can also ask students to sound out unknown words during any reading lesson and take notes on weaknesses, such as long vowels.

Some teachers have incredibly strong feelings about phonics; they love it or they hate it. The funny thing is that those who dislike the idea of teaching phonics often like the idea of "invented spelling." If you don't like the idea of teaching phonics in reading lessons, consider working on students' abilities to "invent" spellings (for words they have not been taught).

How much phonics? Tool 7 — Phonics Charts

It is not the purpose of this article to lay out a whole phonics curriculum, but Tool 7 — the Phonics Charts of vowel sounds and consonant sounds — will give you a quick overview of most of the phonics skills needed by competent readers. These skills will help your students in learning to spell many words. Furthermore, they will have a difficult time using the pronunciation symbols in any dictionary if they do not have at least this much familiarity with phonics.

The Vowel Sounds Chart and the Consonant Sounds Chart lay out all the basic phonics curriculum content on just two pages. Start at the top with the basic sounds and work your way down to the exceptions. To teach phonics, you will need more example words for each sound. You can find these in *The Reading Teacher's Book of Lists* or other publications. Don't bore your student with a lot of phonics drills devoid of meaning, but bear in mind that we have an alphabetic language with a good deal of correspondence between the printed letter or letter cluster and the speech sound.

Tool 7

PHONICS CHARTS

VOWEL SOUNDS

Short Vowels

a — at	/a/
e — end	/e/
i — is	/i/
o — hot	/o/
u — up	/u/

Long Vowel
Digraphs

ai — aid	/ā/
ay — say	/ā/
ea — eat	/ē/
ee — see	/ē/
oa — oat	/ō/
ow — own	/ō/

Diphthongs

oi — oil	/oi/
oy — boy	/oi/
ou — out	/ou/
ow — how	/ou/

Long Vowels
Open Syllable Rule

a — baby	/ā/
e — we	/ē/
i — idea	/ī/
o — so	/ō/
u — duty	/ū/

Schwa

u — hurt	/ə/
e — happen	/ə/
o — other	/ə/

Vowel y

y — try	/ī/
y — funny	/ē/

Double O

oo — soon	/o͞o/
oo — good	/oo/
u — truth	/o͞o/
u — put	/oo/

Long Vowels
Final E Rule

a — make	/ā/
e — here	/ē/
i — five	/ī/
o — home	/ō/
u — use	/u/

Vowel Plus R

er — her	/r/
ir — sir	/r/
ur — fur	/r/
ar — far	/är/
ar — vary	/ār/
or — for	/ôr/

Broad O

o — long	/ô/
a (1) — also	/ô/
a (w) — saw	/ô/
a (u) — auto	/ô/

Vowel Exceptions

ea — bread	/e/	*ea* makes both a long and a short E sound.
e (silent) — come		*e* at the end of a word is usually silent and sometimes makes the preceding vowel long.
y — yes	/y/	*y* is a consonant at the beginning of a word. (yes) *y* is long I in a one syllable word or middle. (cycle) *y* is long E at the end of a polysyllable word. (funny)
le — candle	/əl/	final *-le* makes a schwa plus L sound.
al — pedal	/əl/	final *-al* makes a schwa plus L sound also.
ul — awful	/əl/	final *-ul* makes a schwa plus L sound also.

Tool 7 (Continued)
PHONICS CHARTS

CONSONANT SOUNDS

Single Consonants

b	h	n	v
c	j	p	w
d	k	r	y
f	l	s	z
g	m	t	

Consonant Digraphs

ch as in "church"
sh as in "shoe"
th (voiced) as in "this"
th (voiceless) as in "thin"
wh (h-w blend) as in "which"

Important Exceptions

qu = /kw/ blend as in "quick"
    (the letter "q" is never used
    without "u")
ph = /f/ sound as in "phone"
c = /s/ before i, e, or y as in "city"
c = /k/ before a, o, or u as in "cat"
g = /j/ before a, o, or u as in "good"
x = /ks/ blend as in "fox"
s = /z/ sound at the end of some
    words, as in "is"
ng = /ng/ unique phoneme, as in
    "sing"

Rare Exceptions

ch = /k/ as in "character"
ch = /sh/ as in "chef"
ti = /sh/ as in "attention"
s = /sh/ as in "sure"
x = /gz/ as in "exact"
s = /zh/ as in "measure"
si = /zh/ as in "vision"

Silent Consonants

gn = /n/ as in "gnat"
kn = /n/ as in "knife"
wr = /r/ as in "write"
gh = /-/ as in "right"
ck = /k/ as in "back"

Beginning Consonant Blends

(r family)	(l family)	(s family)	(3 letter)	(no family)
br	bl	sc	scr	dw
cr	cl	sk	squ	tw
dr	fl	sm	str	
fr	gl	sn	thr	
gr	pl	sp	spr	
pr	sl	st	spl	
tr		sw	shr	
wr			sch	

Final Consonant Blends

ct – act	mp – jump	nt – ant	rk – dark
ft – lift	nc (e) – since	pt – kept	rt – art
ld – old	nd – and	rd – hard	st – least
lt – salt	nk – ink		

Does the student understand what he reads?
Tool 8 — Comprehension Questions

Certainly most people would agree that there is no point in reading anything if you don't understand it. There are a lot of varied opinions on how comprehension should be taught, but most teachers are comfortable with individual or group discussion following the reading of a book or shorter passage.

Tool 8 is a set of *Comprehension Questions* that can be used in oral discussion or even written responses or reports. You shouldn't try to use them all at once, but the list can help you by suggesting a variety of question types to stimulate thinking about any reading passage. Use some questions with children's literature, some with newspaper articles, some with a set of directions, etc.; in other words, the applicable questions will vary according to the type of reading material.

What is he interested in? Tool 9 — Interest Inventory

Most people — children and newly literate adults included — tend to read material that interests them. You can often find out about students' interests just by talking to them or by observing what they do for a period of time. But sometimes you miss even major interests because you don't have any systematic approach to finding out about them. The *Interest Inventory,* Tool 9, provides one way of determining student interest. It is a set of questions ranging over several broad areas. You can add your own questions to make it even more meaningful in your teaching situation.

Use this Interest Inventory as a tool, as a guide for informal discussion, or as a story starter in a writing exercise. If you don't want to use it all at once, use just a question or two per day for a few days. Showing interest in your students' interests is a powerful motivation tool. And knowing a student's interests can be very helpful in suggesting books or articles to read.

Tool 8

COMPREHENSION QUESTIONS

These are just some suggested question types. Select some of the ones you like, or ones that best suit the type of book or story the students have read. Use them for discussion groups or individual writen responses. Two important guidelines are (1) to use a variety of different questions and (2) that not too many questions request directly stated facts.

Opinion: Did you like this book? Why?

Comparison: Is this better than a similar story or article?

Sequence: What happened first? Next? Before the ... ?

Setting: Where does the story or action take place? Would it be different in a different location?

Main Idea: What point is the writer making? What is this book all about? What would be a better title?

Characters: What is the hero really like? Who is the worst or weakest character?

Style: Is this a fable, a biography, or an essay? Is the writing style informal, believable, or difficult?

Newspaper Questions: Who? What? Why? When? Where? How?

Conclusion: How did the story end? What would be a better ending?

Summary: Retell the story (article) in your own words. Briefly tell us what the story was all about.

Tool 9
INTEREST INVENTORY

Outside of school, the thing I like to do best is _____.

In school, the thing I like best is _____.

If I had a million dollars, I would _____.

When I grow up, I will _____.

I hate _____.

My favorite animal is _____.

The best sport is _____.

When nobody is around, I like to _____.

The person I like best is _____.

Next summer I hope to _____.

My father's work is _____.

My mother's work is _____.

When I grow up, I will be _____.

I like to collect _____.

The things I like to make are _____.

My favorite place to be is _____.

The best book I ever read was _____.

The best TV show is _____.

My favorite school subjects are _____.

What are some good teaching methods for disabled readers?
Tool 10 — Some Tips

This article is not really a discussion of teaching methods; it is the presentation of some tools to use in teaching disabled readers. The tools work for normal readers as well, because disabled readers are usually not very different from normally achieving students. Their one definitive characteristic is that they read below normal levels for their age or grade placement. As with any other students, their educational progress will be better if you teach them at an appropriate level.

The tools presented here certainly imply some teaching methods or strategies, but these few additional tips might also help you.

> *Tip 1.* Give plenty of reading practice. Have the students read in class and at home every day. You learn to read, in part, *by reading.*

> *Tip 2.* Have the students reread short reading selections several times until they achieve good fluency. (*Fluency* here is defined as reading aloud without hesitation and without errors. Some teachers would call this *automaticity*.)

> *Tip 3.* Give plenty of writing practice. As with reading, you learn to write by practicing writing. Have students write stories, poems, notes, reports, advertisements, directions, and business letters. Correct the students' writing and have them study their errors, then rewrite the assignments correctly.

> *Tip 4.* Have students improve their vocabulary by studying new words. Make a list of the unknown words each student encounters while reading. Do this for sight vocabulary (words in speaking vocabulary but unknown in print) and for meaning vocabulary (words unknown even in speaking vocabulary). Have the students study their lists and use the words in oral and/or written exercises. It is also helpful to teach word roots and words that come up in other school subjects.

Tip 5. Make sure that your student experiences some success every day. If your student fails in a lesson, make subsequent lessons easier and shorter, or select easier books for reading practice. Build little successes on little successes. Both you and the student will enjoy the lessons more.

Conclusion

I hope that you will like and use at least one of these tools or tips. The teaching of reading is a very important and worthwhile enterprise, and I'd like to think that I'm one of your partners in this task.

References

Tool 1 — Oral Reading Paragraphs
Tool 6 — Phonics Survey
Tool 8 — Comprehension Questions
Tool 9 — Interest Inventory
  Fry, E. (1992). *How To Teach Reading*. Laguna Beach, CA: Laguna Beach Educational Books.

Tool 2 — Readability Graph
  Fry, E. (1977). Fry's readability graph: Clarification, validity, and extensions to Level 17. *Journal of Reading, 21*(3), 242-252.

Tool 3 — The 1 Out Of 20 Rule
  Betts, E. (1957). *Foundations of reading instruction*. New York: American Book.

Tool 4 — Instant Words
  Fry, E. (1993). *Reading teachers book of lists (3rd ed.)*. Englewood Cliffs, NJ: Prentice Hall.

Tool 5 — Picture Nouns
  Fry, E. (1987). Picture nouns for reading and vocabulary improvement. *The Reading Teacher, 41*(2), 185-191.

Tool 7 — Phonics Charts
  Fry, E. (1993). *The Beginning Writer's Manual*. Laguna Beach, CA: Laguna Beach Educational Books.

11

The "Double-Deficit" Hypothesis

Implications for Diagnosis and Practice in Reading Disabilities

MARYANNE WOLF, Ed.D., & MATEO OBREGÓN, M.A.
Tufts University

The overarching goal of this chapter is to present a new conceptualization of developmental reading disorders that integrates reading research on phonological-core deficits and cognitive neuropsychological research on naming-speed deficits. It is no coincidence that these two research areas represent longstanding interests of Jeanne Chall. This work and its ultimate goal — bringing insights from the neurosciences to life in our classrooms — began within the Harvard Reading Laboratory and the divergent intellectual perspectives that thrived there under Professor Chall's guidance. The second author was the student of the first author, and the first author was the student of Professor Chall. Thus, this chapter represents two generations of the influence of Jeanne Chall, and the potential blueprint for another generation of work to come.

The largest focus of research and intervention on reading disabilities in the last two decades has been on the critical role of phonological processes in the failure to learn to read. With roots both in Chall's (1967, 1983) comprehensive accounts of how children learn to read and in psycholinguistic research (Shankweiler & Liberman, 1972), this body of work has established that severely impaired English-speaking readers have early, continuing difficulties with phonological awareness, segmenting and blending individual sounds, and using phonological codes in short-term memory (Kamhi & Catts, 1989; Perfetti, 1985; Shankweiler & Liberman, 1972; Stanovich, 1986; Stanovich & Siegel, 1994; Vellutino, Scanlon, & Tanzman, in press; Wagner, Torgesen, & Rashotte, 1994). This research in the reading area represents what Stanovich has called one of the few scientific success stories (Stanovich, 1992). Its principal insights represent a major part of the conceptualization to be described here.

A parallel body of evidence based on work in the cognitive sciences and neurosciences has shown that impaired readers are also characterized by naming-speed deficits (Bowers, Steffy, & Tate, 1988; Denckla & Rudel, 1974, 1976a, b; Geschwind, 1972; Spring & Davis, 1988; Wolf, 1982, 1991a; Wolff, Michel, & Ovrut, 1990a, b; Some researchers have categorized naming-speed deficits as part of a more general phonological problem (Wagner & Torgesen, 1987). Evidence will be presented here that indicates the independent contribution of naming speed to reading and the compelling reasons to classify naming-speed problems as a second core deficit in reading disorders, largely separate from phonological processes.

If naming-speed and phonological-decoding deficits are independent, specific deficits, then there will, in principle, be two single deficit subgroups and a possible double-deficit subgroup (i.e., a phonological-deficit subgroup of readers with no naming-speed deficits, a naming-speed deficit subgroup of readers with no phonological decoding problems, and a subgroup with both deficits). The last group would be hypothesized to include the most impaired readers because of their lack of available compensatory capacities in either phonological or timing processes. Yet present practice, with its primary emphasis on phonology, either would ignore children with solely naming-speed deficits because their phonological decoding skills are intact, or would offer these children inappropriate intervention in phonologically based skills. Similarly, half of the difficulties exhibited by double-deficit readers would be unaddressed by conventional intervention.

The two purposes of this chapter are: (a) to present an overview of a research program on the development of children's naming and naming speed, with a discussion of the implications of this research for diagnosis, assessment, and intervention in developmental reading disorders; and (b) to argue that deficits in the processes underlying naming speed and phonological deficits represent two independent and interacting core deficits in developmental dyslexia. This position is the basis for the emerging "Double-Deficit" Hypothesis for developmental dyslexia (Bowers & Wolf, 1993b; Wolf & Bowers, 1995). The diagnostic measures, teaching methods, and interventions suggested by this hypothesis differ significantly from those currently practiced and will be treated briefly in the final section of the paper.

Theoretical Background

The cross-disciplinary perspective employed in this work was first developed in the Harvard Reading Laboratory during the directorship of Jeanne Chall and her colleagues, Helen Popp and Carol Chomsky, and lab affiliates, Martha Denckla, Norman Geschwind, Anthony Bashir, and Peter Wolff. The rich and diverse influences of each of these researchers and their separate disciplines helped shape the origins of the present research program. Critical to the overall goals has been the integration of several of their research traditions: cognitive, experimental, and educational psychology research on normal reading abilities; psycholinguistic research on language development; and neuropsychological research on language and reading pathology (e.g., aphasias and dyslexias). For example, in the earlier studies of this program, neurophysiological findings on language and reading pathology in brain-damaged patients were used to help construct measures to study the precursors and early development of reading abilities.

A second major aspect of this research program involves an approach to address developmental issues of cognition and learning in the cognitive neuroscience field. For example, to pursue a more comprehensive understanding of the developmental dyslexias, Ellis (1987) stressed the need to find cognitive systems that develop earlier than reading and yet utilize many of the same components. The notion was that if such a system could be found, we could probe this system before reading is acquired to study both what is necessary for normal reading acquisition and what is predictive of reading failure.

A major premise of the present research program is that the naming or word-retrieval system represents a unique, early developing system that (a) incorporates many of the major components utilized by reading (e.g., visual, phonological, conceptual, semantic, and memory processes); (b) possesses the critical characteristics of an automatic system through its rapid rates of processing; and (c) is relatively independent from IQ (Bowers et al., 1988). A key assumption of this research is that the time and subprocesses used for rapid access and retrieval[1] of a verbal label in the act of naming are related at some level to the time and subprocesses used to access and retrieve a word rapidly in reading. According to this view, examination of the early development of naming and naming speed provides an important window for understanding major components that will be used later in reading.

The theoretical rationale behind this view is based on a convergence of findings from the directions of research discussed earlier. Neuropsychologists Goodglass and Kaplan and their colleagues (Goodglass & Kaplan, 1972; Goodglass, 1980) demonstrated that naming is a complex process that is fairly easily probed and highly susceptible to disruption from any of its underlying components. They found that naming problems were the most frequently observed characteristic of every form of aphasia, regardless of the lesion site. In other words,

---

[1] The terms *rapid access* and *retrieval* do not refer to any specific information-processing model of the brain; rather, they are used metaphorically to refer to the subprocesses involved in finding words.

what we call naming is only the surface of interconnecting perceptual, cognitive, and linguistic subprocesses, each of which is necessary for the normal retrieval of words to occur. Goodglass's work highlighted how different kinds of naming tasks emphasize different kinds of subprocesses.

In both early and recent reading research, many investigators (Adams, 1990; Badian, 1995; Bond & Dykstra, 1967; Chall, 1967; Jansky & de Hirsch, 1972; Johnson & Myklebust, 1964; Wolf, 1991a) have found that one of the single best predictors of later reading achievement is the kindergarten and preschool child's letter naming abilities. What was less known until recently is why this might be so and which aspects of letter-naming (e.g., accuracy, speed, retrieval, and/or receptive linguistic knowledge) are predicting which components of later reading behavior (see Badian, 1995).

The unraveling of this simple question is something akin to a cognitive mystery story that links various research traditions, one of which goes back to the extraordinary insights of neurologist Norman Geschwind concerning the development of naming in children. On the basis of work in alexia and anomia, Geschwind (1972) hypothesized that the best predictor of reading readiness might be the young child's ability to name colors. The principle was that color naming, like reading, requires all the processes underlying the retrieval of a verbal label for an abstract visual symbol, yet does not require that the child know letters.

Denckla and Rudel (1976a, b) pursued this hypothesis in a series of studies with average and dyslexic readers. They found that color-naming speed, rather than color-naming accuracy, differentiated reading groups. Based on this finding, they designed Rapid Automatized Naming (RAN) tasks, in which the child names 50 stimuli as rapidly as possible (e.g., 5 common letters, 5 digits, 5 colors, or 5 pictured objects, repeated randomly 10 times on a board; see Figure 11-1). Denckla and Rudel found impressive relationships between reading performance and naming speed for all of these categories. They found a clear ability to differentiate dyslexic children from average readers, as well as from

---

Figure 11-1
A sample of the letters on the Rapid Automatized Naming (RAN) board used for measuring naming-speed abilities.

```
o  a  s  d  p  a  o  s  p  d

s  d  a  p  d  o  a  p  s  o

a  o  s  a  s  d  p  o  d  a

d  s  p  o  d  s  a  s  o  p

s  a  d  p  a  p  o  a  p  s
```

---

other learning-disabled children (Denckla & Rudel, 1976b).

Over the last two decades, the results of a large group of cross-sectional studies demonstrated that most dyslexic children exhibit a particular deficit or set of deficits in visual naming speed. That is, they show deficiencies or disruptions in the process underlying the precise rapid access and retrieval of visually presented linguistic information. More precisely, dyslexic children are significantly slower to name the most basic and most familiar visual symbols (i.e., letters, digits, colors, or simple pictured objects) than any of the following groups: *average peers* (Ackerman & Dykman, 1993; Ackerman, Dykman, & Gardner, 1990; Bowers et al., 1988; Bowers & Swanson, 1991; Denckla & Rudel,

1976b; Fawcett & Nicolson, 1994; Spring & Capps, 1974; Wolf, 1982); other *learning-disabled* children (Denckla & Rudel, 1976b; Felton & Brown, 1990); *garden-variety reading-impaired* children (a term used by Gough & Tumner, 1986, to describe children whose poor reading performance is commensurate with their achievement or IQ levels; Badian, 1994; Wolf & Obregón, 1992); and *reading-age matched* children (average readers selected because they match the reading age of the dyslexic subjects; Wolf, 1991a; Wolf & Segal, 1993, 1995). Furthermore, this deficit appears unrelated to IQ (Bowers et al., 1988; Spring & Davis, 1988), rate of articulation (Ackerman & Dykman, 1993; Ellis, 1981; Obregón, 1994; see, however, Nicolson & Fawcett, 1994), memory (Bowers et al., 1988), and reading exposure (Wolf, 1991a).

The naming-speed deficit appears to be more powerful with serial than with discrete (or isolated) presentation of visual symbols and pictured objects (Swanson, 1989; Wagner et al., 1994; Wolff, Michel, & Ovrut, 1990a). The deficit characterizes dyslexic readers throughout their development, from prereading in kindergarten (Wolf, Bally, & Morris, 1986) through adulthood (Felton & Wood, 1989; Flowers, 1993; Wolff, Michel, & Ovrut, 1990a, b). Finally, in severely impaired populations, the naming-speed deficit appears to be more predictive for alphanumeric symbols (letters and numbers) than for colors or objects (Wolf et al., 1986).

This literature helps provide the answer to one piece of our letter-naming question. It appears that the processes underlying the rapid retrieval of automatically coded symbols — i.e., letters and numbers — are involved in the formation of the reading process, as well as its malfunction. This, of course, does not preclude the separate predictive contribution of letter-name knowledge, documented by a large separate literature (see review in Adams, 1990). However, it does suggest the separate importance of the cognitive processes involved in rapid retrieval and timing.

In a recent dyslexic twin study, Olson, Forsberg, and Wise (1994) found evidence for the heritability of phonological deficits. Wolff and Melngailis (1994) have also found evidence of the heritability of a temporal aspect of reading dysfunction. Furthermore, in a multigenerational bimanual coordination study, Wolff, Melngailis, Obregón, and Bedrosian (in press) found that dyslexic children with impaired temporal resolution (measured as the inability to maintain a fast tapping rhythm) had at least one parent with similar motor coordination deficits. Dyslexic children without motor coordination deficits came from families where the dyslexic members had no tapping difficulties. To our knowledge, these findings represent the first behavioral evidence that is suggestive of a possible genetic role of timing factors in the developmental dyslexias.

Perfetti, Finger, and Hogaboam (1978) questioned whether the rapid naming findings were limited to naming speed for continuous or serial presentation of visual stimuli, or whether dyslexic children were also slower to name individually presented stimuli (e.g., in a computerized, discrete-trial format). Results of their work indicated that naming speed under discrete-trial conditions failed to differentiate good and poor reading groups. Results of newer, more extensive work (Bowers & Swanson, 1991; Fawcett & Nicolson, 1994; Levy & Hinchley, 1990; Wolff et al., 1990a, 1990b; Wolff, Michel, Ovrut, & Drake, 1990), however, indicate two findings. First, deficits in discrete-trial presentation have been found when the poor reader group is large enough and severely impaired (Bowers & Swanson, 1991; Wolff et al., 1990a). Second, generalizations between the two types of tasks are inappropriate because the requirements underlying the serial and discrete tasks differ significantly, with the requirements for serial naming being a closer approximation of the reading process (see discussion in Wolf, 1991a). This is evidenced in various factor analyses when both isolated and serial naming tasks are included (see Wagner et al., 1994). In a recent discrete-format study, Fawcett and Nicolson (1994) found that the naming speed of 17-year-old dyslexic subjects was closest to that of 8-year-old control subjects.

Other types of naming tasks have also differentiated severely impaired readers from average peers. For example, confrontation picture-naming tasks, in which subjects are asked to name pictured objects, have been shown to be both powerful differentiators of reading groups

(Goswami & Swan, 1994; Guilford & Nawojczyk, 1988; Haynes, 1994; Wolf & Goodglass, 1986; Wolf & Obregón, 1992) and strong, early predictors of later reading performance (Scarborough, 1989). This prediction is particularly robust with regard to reading comprehension (Wolf & Obregón, 1989).

The research to be presented in the following sections is situated in the research direction just described. It represents a systematic effort to understand both the development of various types of word-retrieval processes and the underlying relationship between deficits in specific aspects of naming (particularly naming speed) and specific aspects of reading.

The first question studied was whether developmentally evolving relationships existed between particular kinds of naming tasks and particular kinds of reading tasks at specific stages of reading development (see Chall, 1983; Frith, 1985; Snowling, 1987). The second question was whether different subgroups of impaired readers could be distinguished (in general or by specific subtype) from average readers on various carefully designed tests of naming and/or naming speed. The third question examined the capacity to predict later reading abilities.

To pursue this developmental-differential approach, we developed a research program with seven phases. Phase I involved the construction of a neurolinguistic model of word retrieval and reading. Phase II used a cross-sectional study to investigate the ability of a battery of reading tasks to differentiate average and impaired readers. Phase III comprised an 8-year longitudinal investigation of the development of naming and reading skills and their predictive relationships. Phase IV, an intervention program based on the results of this research effort, was recently completed with children at a residential school for dyslexic children. The research to be reported in this paper represents a first attempt to summarize the first four phases of the work and to connect them to the fifth and sixth phases — a cross-linguistic study of German-speaking children and a re-analysis of data to test the notion of the Double-Deficit Hypothesis. The seventh phase of this research explores the nature of the naming-speed deficits. A brief description of each phase follows.

Phase I: Theoretical Model of the Naming Process

Phase I involved the construction of a model of word retrieval that incorporates developmental dimensions. Briefly, according to this model, naming requires at a basic level: (1) attention to the stimulus; (2) visual perception and memory; (3) conceptual knowledge of the stimulus; (4) integration of conceptual information with stored lexical (i.e., phonological and semantic) information; (5) access and retrieval of the phonological label; (6) motoric activation leading to the articulation of the stimulus label; and (7) rapid rates of processing within and across all the individual subprocesses. External factors such as stimulus clarity, rate of presentation, word frequency, and familiarity level were also included in the model. These components of the naming model were used as the basis for selection of the psychometric measures that were employed in the next phases.

The battery of instruments was chosen for the tasks' ability to probe any disruption in the major components and processing variables in the developing naming and reading systems. (For detailed description, see Wolf, 1982, 1991b.)

Phase II: Early Cross-sectional Findings

Phase II involved the empirical validation of the naming-reading battery and explored the differentiation power of this battery with a cross-sectional study of 64 children (32 average readers, 32 severely impaired readers) from 6 to 11 years of age. Results indicated (a) a strong, general relationship between word-retrieval and reading measures ($r = .74$; $p < .001$) and (b) the robust ability of a word-retrieval battery to differentiate average from severely-impaired readers (Wolf, 1982). All measures, except a receptive vocabulary measure and a visually distorted perceptual measure (modeled after a task by Bisiach, 1966), differentiated reading groups at all ages at the p < .001 level. Naming measures that emphasized speed appeared to be particularly powerful in differentiating average from impaired readers. (These initial phases formed the basis of my dissertation work, supervised by Professors Popp, Chall, and Denckla.)

Phase III: Longitudinal Investigation of Naming Processes in Child Development

Phase III comprised an 8-year longitudinal effort to chart the development of carefully defined word-retrieval processes and to study the predictive relationships between these processes and specific reading operations. Subjects included 115 children from three schools (of varying socioeconomic status) who were tested from kindergarten to grade 4 and again in grade 7 (Wolf et al., 1986). After excluding subjects who were missing any year of data, 8 children were classified as dyslexic readers, 24 as garden-variety poor readers, and 43 as average-to-able readers (Wolf & Obregón, 1989). The second-grade performance of 17 average subjects was used as a reading-age-matched comparison. A group of bilingual children was also studied, but is not included in these analyses.

There are several central findings in these longitudinal analyses that help to clarify previous controversies in the literature. The first is the persistently severe, specific nature of the visual naming-speed deficit in dyslexic readers (see Figure 11-2 on the next page). Consistent, significant naming-speed differences on the continuous-naming tests were found between dyslexic and garden-variety poor readers, as well as between fourth-grade dyslexic readers and second-grade reading-age-matched average readers (Wolf & Obregón, 1989; Wolf & Segal, 1993). Furthermore, in contrast to the conclusions reached by Walsh, Price, and Cunningham (1988), this deficit appears to be obdurate over time (from kindergarten through grade 7) for the very impaired readers in this sample.

The second provocative finding is the sustained deficit in general word retrieval (i.e., confrontation naming and semantic fluency) that

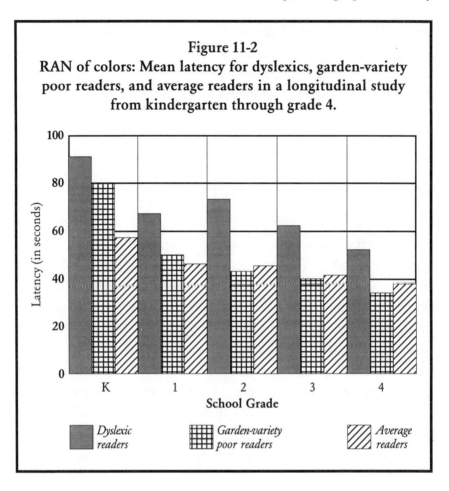

Figure 11-2
RAN of colors: Mean latency for dyslexics, garden-variety poor readers, and average readers in a longitudinal study from kindergarten through grade 4.

appears among all impaired readers, but for different reasons in the dyslexic and in the garden-variety poor reader groups. Dyslexic subjects appear to have depressed naming performance based on faulty retrieval of known words, while in the garden-variety poor readers, the same depressed naming performance is based on limited vocabulary knowledge (Wolf & Obregón, 1992). In recent work by Haynes (1994) at the Harvard Reading Lab, this pattern was found on the Boston Naming Test (Kaplan, Goodglass, & Weintraub, 1983) for dyslexic and average reader comparisons, but not for garden-variety poor readers. However, this exact pattern of results was replicated in a study by Goswami and Swan (1994), using a carefully controlled confrontation naming task.

Third, longitudinal analyses indicated clear developmental patterns of reading prediction according to age and the type of reading and naming (Wolf, 1991b). For example, early naming speed is most predictive of later word recognition, and early semantic-related confrontation naming is more predictive of later reading comprehension. The entire battery in kindergarten is highly predictive of each form of fourth-grade reading, but is most robust in its prediction of fourth-grade reading comprehension. After grade 2, two cognitive developmental changes are occurring that change the naming-to-reading predictive relationships: rapid processing (or automaticity) emerges, and the underlying requirements involved in naming and reading become more differentiated. This pattern of developmental differentiation helps reconcile earlier results by Perfetti et al. (1978), who found no relationship between third-grade naming speed and third-grade reading comprehension. That is, little or no relation between these particular tasks would be expected by grade 3, because naming speed predicts word recognition, and it predicts comprehension only through comprehension's shared variance with word recognition (Bowers & Swanson, 1991; Spring & Davis, 1988). The data strongly reinforce Stanovich's (1986) general conclusions about the changing relationships among individual cognitive tasks and identify some of the specific relationships between particular naming and reading processes in development.

Phase IV: Intervention

Phase IV is the most applied and speculative phase in our research (Segal & Wolf, 1993; Wolf & Segal, 1995), and holds particular promise for practitioners. The underlying question is: if naming-speed deficits must now be considered a separate type of deficit in our diagnosis and assessment, can they be successfully addressed in our intervention efforts? There exists only a very small group of studies that have directly attempted to intervene in retrieval problems of poor readers (Bowers, 1993; Levy & Hinchley, 1990), although there are very good studies in work with language-impaired children (German, 1992; McGregor & Leonard, 1989).

To address this question, we conducted two pilot training studies with dyslexic readers. Each training study emphasized the interconnectedness (Curtis, 1987) of reading skills, name-retrieval difficulties, processing speed, and depth of reading vocabulary knowledge (see Beck, Perfetti, & McKeown, 1982). We incorporated a notion of a developmental continuum of word knowledge, based on Beck, Perfetti, and McKeown's (1982) work in vocabulary intervention. They described levels of lexical access as moving from unknown, to acquainted, to highly familiar or established (see also Kameenui, Dixon, & Carnine, 1987). Further, they proposed that in order to understand the meaning of a word in depth, children must be aware of "commonly accessed meaning components" and a word's connection with other concepts, as demanded by the particular context (Beck et al., 1982, p. 507). We integrated these concepts in our approach to depth of vocabulary (see Segal & Wolf, 1993) and integrated it with general and specific strategies for rapid, accurate word retrieval. Our notion was that fast and accurate retrieval could occur best for words that are highly familiar and that possess rich associations for the reader. A variety of different strategies were then taught to aid both faster retrieval and a more flexible set of strategies for word-finding difficulties. For some words, visual mnemonic strategies (see Wing, 1990) were used. (For example, to retrieve the word *barometer* the students were taught to visualize a "tall Baron Meter," carrying numerous measurement devices.)

In the first study, 28 dyslexic readers (12-14 years old) were selected from a residential school for dyslexic children. They received an 8-week intensive program of language games and exercises aimed at both increasing the breadth and depth of their knowledge of a specific group of words and improving their ability to retrieve these and related words rapidly and accurately. Word-specific and general strategies were designed to aid flexibility during word-finding problems.

Findings from the pre- and post-test battery comparisons indicated substantial improvement in both quantitative measures of expressive vocabulary and qualitative gains for (a) depth of vocabulary knowledge for the trained words; (b) the ability to give associations; and (c) the ability to use diverse linguistic contexts. Perhaps of most importance, improved naming rate on an untrained specific, continuous naming-speed task was demonstrated. These results indicate that some aspects of word-retrieval problems in dyslexic readers may be amenable to treatment and that gains in retrieval rate may be generalizable to other tasks (see Wolf & Segal, 1995).

In the second study, an elaborated intervention program emphasized this same approach with a less intensive time allotment per day over a longer period of time (6 months). For this study, we selected 31 adolescent dyslexic readers, some with and some without pronounced word-retrieval problems. We specifically investigated (a) whether greater gains in retrieval speed and vocabulary would be found in dyslexics with prominent retrieval deficits; and (b) whether the effects of retrieval intervention generalized to produce reading gains in these subjects. In other words, if improvements in naming performance result in improved reading skills for this retrieval-deficit subgroup, but not for the non-deficit poor reader group, we would have additional evidence for the core-deficit role of retrieval processes. Post-test data indicated significant gains on all qualitative vocabulary measures for the targeted words, but no improvement in retrieval *rate* for untrained stimuli. The most important result was that significant gains in reading comprehension for the retrieval-deficit training group were found (Feinberg, 1995). A more elaborated set of interventions that include the principles from this study, an automatic, computerized orthographic-recognition component, and established phonological components (Lovett et al., 1994) is under development by Morris, Lovett, and our lab in a four-year NICHD study.

Summary From Phases I through IV:
An Emerging Reconceptualization

The first four phases of research summarized here lead to several conclusions and questions. First, the name-retrieval system emerges as a powerful predictor of reading ability, and it satisfies the search in the neurosciences (Ellis, 1985) for earlier developing, cognitive systems that employ subprocesses and processes similar to reading. Second, naming speed appears to be largely independent of phonological awareness measures in the prediction of reading. Third, these cumulative data indicate the presence of a specific core deficit in visual naming speed among many dyslexic readers, which distinguishes them from other impaired readers and reading-age matched children and is not a function of reading exposure, IQ, memory, or articulation (see Obregón, 1994).

Many American researchers, however, have been reluctant to consider naming-speed deficits as specific core deficits, in addition to the well documented phonological-core deficits, for two reasons. First, problems with phonological processes are generally regarded as the major source of reading disabilities (Wagner, Torgesen, Laughon, Simmons, & Rashotte, 1993). Second, many researchers explain naming-speed deficiency as another manifestation of phonological problems. Naming speed has been variously described as phonological encoding (Naslund & Schneider, 1991) and retrieval from phonological memory (Wagner & Torgesen, 1987). We have long concurred about the central role played by phonological processes in reading disabilities. We believe, however, that explanations of reading failure based solely on phonology (or on any other single factor) are insufficient when applied to a process as complex as reading and when used to explain the extraordinary heterogeneity of impaired readers. Furthermore, the cumulative data strongly support the independence of the two deficits and the need to understand the implications of a two-deficit model for assessment and intervention. Bowers and Wolf (1993b; Wolf & Bowers, 1995) argue strongly for such a reconceptualization, based on (a) the independent contribution (beyond phonology) of naming speed to word recognition in reading; (b) the relative lack of correlations between naming speed and performance on conventional phonological awareness measures; (c) data from other language systems; and (d) a re-analysis of longitudinal samples in the U.S. and Canada according to performance on phonological decoding tasks, naming-speed tasks, or both. A brief overview of some of these points, which includes perspectives from the two most recent phases of this research program, is presented in the following sections.

Data from Other Languages

Significant naming-speed deficits have been demonstrated in German-speaking children (Schneider & Naslund, 1992; Wimmer, 1993; Wimmer & Hummer, 1990; Wolf, Pfeil, Lotz, & Biddle, 1994), Dutch-speaking children (Yap & van der Leij, 1991), and Spanish-speaking children (Novoa & Wolf, 1984; Novoa, 1988). This is particularly important because these three languages span a continuum of orthographic regularity, and thus provide an opportunity to disentangle timing problems from demands placed upon phonological processes by a language's irregularity. In English, the irregularity of the orthography is represented in sometimes difficult, inconsistent grapheme-phoneme correspondence rules. For example, in English spoken in the Midwestern states of the United States there are 19 separate phonemes represented by the five vowels (Naslund, 1990) and multiple digraph pronunciations (e.g., *ea* is pronounced in five different ways in "The bear's heart beats early for bread." This lack of "transparency" in the English language places heavy demands on phonological processes in learning to read. In contrast, German vowel sounds come closer to a one-to-one correspondence with their grapheme representations (Valtin, 1989). The more regular German orthography makes the acquisition of sound-symbol correspondence rules a simpler task for the young German reader. These characteristics of the German writing system provide researchers with an excellent opportunity to test the relationship between naming speed and reading development in a language where the phonological coding factors are partially controlled.

Wimmer's (1993) data in the German language demonstrated that young German dyslexic readers (grades 2 through 4) have less pronounced difficulties in standard phonemic segmentation tasks and in word-recognition accuracy for words and pseudowords than English-speaking dyslexic children. However, German dyslexics have significant problems in naming speed and a "pervasive speed deficit for all types of reading tasks" (Wimmer, p. 2). Further, digit-naming speed was the best predictor of reading differences in German dyslexic children.

Phase V: Cross-linguistic Evidence

To further examine the development of naming speed and its potential relationship to reading failure in German readers, a fifth, cross-linguistic phase of our research program was begun as an extension of some aspects of work by Wimmer and by Naslund and Schneider. Wolf et al (1994) systematically investigated the "pervasive speed deficit" using an expanded series of naming- and reading-speed instruments and a variety of phonological measures modeled after tasks commonly used in German-speaking and English-speaking populations.

Although all the analyses are not yet complete, several early findings offer important insights for both research and teaching. First, the data with German-speaking impaired readers replicates findings by Wimmer (1993), Naslund (1990), and others: the majority of these children have pervasive speed deficits across all naming and reading measures (which include tests of real and nonsense words). Compared with English-speaking children, the phonological awareness deficits of German readers were far less pronounced. The phonological decoding of nonsense words was likewise less impeded in average and poor German readers (except in the most impaired readers, who exhibited deficits in both naming speed and phonological tasks).

Perhaps most unexpected was the finding of significant differences in the development of automaticity between second-graders taught by traditional German reading methods (whose emphases are on structured, phonic rules in German) and by relatively new, less traditional methods (whose emphases are equivalent to whole-language principles). The code-structure class performed significantly faster on every measure pertaining to the development of automaticity, as measured by six naming-speed and six reading-speed tasks. A second analysis was conducted for fourth-grade students, comparing groups who had been taught with these two different curricular types in grade 2. No significant differences were found on these measures by grade 4. Foorman (1994) has suggested that although no differences in automaticity were found in grade 4, differences in comprehension and other untested aspects of fluency might appear later for these children. This assertion is based on the possible effects of a slower attainment of automaticity on later reading. A longitudinal follow-up to explore these and other issues is in progress by Lotz.

Phase VI: The "Double-Deficit" Hypothesis

On the basis of these cumulative data, Bowers and Wolf (1993a, b; Wolf & Bowers, 1996) developed an alternative conceptualization of reading disabilities that integrates the phonological and the naming-speed literature. As mentioned in the introduction, four groups are hypothesized: a no-deficit, average reading group; a naming-speed deficit group with intact phonological skills; a phonological-deficit group with intact naming-speed skills; and a double-deficit group. To test this hypothesis, Wolf and Bowers (1996) conducted a re-analysis of their longitudinal samples of good and poor readers in Canada and the United States along two dimensions: the presence or absence of naming-speed deficits and of phonological-decoding deficits. Fourth-grade average readers and the phonological-deficit subgroup differed on the phonological decoding measure, but were similar in naming speed. Average readers and the naming-speed subgroup, in contrast, differed in naming speed but were similar in phonological decoding skills. Thus we see a clear differentiation of two subgroups with independent deficit patterns that were maintained across all the reading variables tested.

The most typical patterns of results for the reading variables from repeated measures MANOVA are represented by performance on the Gray Oral Reading Test (Gray, 1967), which reflects oral word-recognition skills in connected text, and the Gates-MacGinitie Reading Comprehension test (Gates & MacGinitie, 1978). Average readers had significantly higher scores than the three reading-deficit subgroups. The two single-deficit subgroups performed significantly higher than double-deficit readers and significantly lower than average readers, and appeared fairly similar to each other in oral reading and comprehension. However, because the single deficit groups differed significantly from each other on underlying phonological and automaticity tasks, we would argue that the groups' similar (poor) performance in oral reading and comprehension arose from two entirely different sources. The double-deficit group was the most impaired across all language and reading measures tested, except the Peabody Picture Vocabulary Test (Dunn & Dunn, 1979) — a vocabulary measure that is highly correlated with IQ. In other words, it appears that when children have deficits in both areas, neither phonological nor automaticity compensatory processes are available to them.

Phase VII: Experimental Investigations into the Nature of Naming-Speed Deficits

In our current work, we are pursuing two different experimental directions in order to discover what underlies the behavioral evidence of naming-speed deficits. Various investigators have suggested that this phenomenon may have its source in either articulatory processes or the visual scanning processes required in the serial formats of the Rapid Automatized Naming (RAN; Denckla & Rudel, 1976a, b) and Rapid Alternating Stimulus (RAS; Wolf, 1986) naming tasks.

Work by Obregón (1994) has clarified both questions with the aid of a recently designed computer program that digitizes the speech stream during continuous naming performance on the RAN task. This study demonstrated that dyslexic children spend the same amount of time as other children articulating the target item names and visually scanning from one line to the next line. However, dyslexic children spend two to three times longer than average counterparts in the intervals between words. Although the RAN task is not designed to challenge the children phonologically, the data indicate that dyslexic children's problems with naming of familiar items is directly related neither to an articulation problem nor to visual scanning issues.

Furthermore, in this fine-grained time analysis, Obregón (1994) found similar patterns of duration in dyslexic and average readers reading various sequences of target words. For example, dyslexic and average readers took nearly the same amount of time to articulate the individual targets *red* and *black*, and both groups took significantly longer to say the target sequence *black red* than to say *red black*. This similarity in the duration patterns of target sequences for dyslexic children and for their average-reading counterparts — together with the similar amounts of time taken to articulate the target words — offers some evidence that the same underlying cognitive mechanisms or subprocesses were being used successfully in both groups of children, albeit more slowly by dyslexic readers.

In current investigations into the nature of naming-speed deficits, members of our laboratory have begun collaborating with neuropsychologist Philip Holcomb. Together, we have begun to use the evoked response potential (ERP) paradigm to explore possible differences in brain electrical activity between dyslexic and average readers during various aspects of silent naming and reading tasks. The ERP paradigm will allow us to locate possible cortical sources of different naming-speed and behavioral deficits.

Implications for Diagnosis and Practice

In a recent article on early identification and remediation of reading difficulties, Hurford et al. (1994) were disappointed to find that their identification battery based on phonological and IQ tasks failed to classify one segment of at-risk children. The Double-Deficit Hypothesis speaks directly to this issue. Its first implication is that our current diagnostic batteries should also include naming-speed tasks, because phonological tasks do not identify one important subgroup of at-risk children. The best known naming-speed tasks, the RAN and the RAS, can easily be constructed and administered by a teacher. Because each of these tasks takes approximately one minute to administer, they are time-efficient additions to any kindergarten battery. Most importantly, the capacities of kindergarten naming-speed measures to predict later reading ability are equal to those of the more commonly used phonological measures. Regression analyses and fourth-grade reading outcome measures indicate that prediction capabilities are substantially increased by their joint inclusion (Wolf & Bowers, 1995). In other words, if a kindergarten teacher could only use two instruments, we would suggest a measure of phonological awareness and a measure of letter, digit, and color naming speeds.

The second implication of the Double-Deficit Hypothesis concerns our understanding of the heterogeneity of the dyslexic population. The phonological research over the last decade has contributed greatly to our understanding of one critical source of disruption in reading acquisition. The naming-speed literature has begun to direct our attention to another source: those processes underlying the rapid, precise retrieving of visually presented linguistic information. Unlike phonological problems, naming-speed deficiency is not itself a primary source of the reading problem; rather, it is an index of underlying temporal processing difficulties that may well extend beyond language. Questions of whether the naming-speed phenomenon is connected to the transient visual problems found in many dyslexic readers by Lovegrove and his colleagues (Lovegrove, Garzia, & Nicolson, 1990), to the cognitive speed aptitude in reading rate discussed by Carver (1995), or to the temporal and auditory processing difficulties in some poor readers discussed by Tallal, Miller, and Fitch (1993) are of keen importance, but are unresolved at present. There is substantive research that indicates timing problems in motoric areas and naming-speed difficulties in the same dyslexic children (Nicolson & Fawcett, 1990, 1994; Wolff et al., 1990).

Perhaps most important to our understanding will be future linkages between behavioral data and underlying neurophysiological evidence. Current cytoarchitectonic research in the cognitive neurosciences suggests that the architecture and organization of cells in some dyslexic brains may be different not only in regions involved in language, but also in regions outside of what are traditionally understood as language areas. For example, differences in cell migration, cell size, and myelination have been found in the magnocellular systems (i.e., systems of cells responsible, among other things, for the rapid processing of perceptual information) in visual and auditory regions of the thalamus (Galaburda, Menard, & Rosen, 1994; Livingstone, Rosen, Drislane, & Galaburda, 1991).

Naming speed may ultimately prove to be a simple index in the language domain of a broader, more domain-general problem of timing in dyslexic children (see Wolf, 1991a). Indeed, this hypothesis is a critical aspect of our future research studies. However, there are causal implications for reading acquisition directly associated with the behavior of slowed letter-naming speed. If an early reader is slow in identifying individual letters, then these letters in a word will not become "activated in sufficiently close temporal proximity to allow the child to become sensitive to letter patterns" (Bowers, Golden, Kennedy, & Young, 1994, p. 203). Bowers and Wolf (1993a, b) describe three potentially interrelated ways in which slow visual naming speed contribute to reading failure: (a) by preventing the appropriate amalgamation of phonological and orthographic identities at subword and word levels of representation (Berninger, 1990; Ehri, 1992); (b) by limiting the quality of orthographic codes in memory (Berninger, 1990, 1994); and (c) by increasing the amount of repeated practice needed to unitize codes before memory representations of adequate quality are achieved.

Regardless of whether naming speed reflects a language-specific or a more general underlying timing problem, this deficit is independent of phonological problems in some children, and interacts with phonological weakness in others. It is essential for diagnosis and intervention that we test for both types of processing difficulties in individual children. It is equally important that we recognize that other types of reading deficits are possible. The Double-Deficit Hypothesis is a metaphor for moving us beyond unitary hypotheses so that we will be more open to the heterogeneity of our readers, and more aware of the importance of understanding and testing for naming-speed deficits as well as phonological deficits. We do not assume that children's deficits are restricted to these two deficit patterns, but we are convinced that both are critical to understand.

The third implication of the Double-Deficit Hypothesis concerns teaching that matches our best understanding of reading acquisition and failure. There is little doubt that the German data reported here demonstrates the importance of learning decoding principles in a regular language, if automaticity is to develop on schedule. How much more important, then, are such emphases in an orthography that is less regular, like English? For children who are lagging behind in development for any environmental or physiological reason or who are at risk for reading failure, the need to develop automatic letter and word recognition skills is critical.

The Double-Deficit conceptualization has implications not only for assessing and understanding reading deficits, but also for addressing the skills all children need to become fluent users of written language. In our view, it calls for explicit emphasis on phonological skills that range from syllable and phoneme segmentation through decoding. And it calls for explicit attention to ensuring that these skills — from letter identification to letter cluster and word identification — become automatic. Children at risk for naming-speed deficits are known to require far more practice in these skills than other children (Bowers et al., 1994; Reitsma, 1983). The extensive use of practice may well be opposed by those whose teaching philosophy emphasizes the natural induction of decoding principles through connected text reading. The implication of our work is that for many children, this assumption of natural induction leads to failure.

Thus, perhaps the most important implication from these data concerns teaching methods that exclude explicit emphasis on letter-sound rules and their automatization (e.g., the conservative forms of whole-language teaching). Such approaches, despite their high motivational appeal for students and teachers, may well be depriving at-risk children of the fundamental tools they need to become fluent readers.

A more carefully orchestrated approach that systematically introduces specific phonological and decoding skills, and gradually introduces book and story material, appears to be the best integration of what we know about the reading process. Both emphases are essential; they should not be decoupled in our primary classrooms. If this implication reminds the reader of conclusions reached 30 years ago in *The Great Debate* (Chall, 1967), it is no coincidence.

A related implication concerns matching the content of intervention to reader abilities. Exceptional progress has been made in treating phonologically based reading problems. For example, programs by Foorman, Fletcher, and Francis (1994) and by Torgesen and Wagner (1994) have made great strides in addressing the difficult reading problems of large-scale populations of children. Most recently, Lovett et al. (1994) have demonstrated the powerful ability of several code- and strategy-based interventions to change the reading ability of impaired readers. The results of these programs are especially noteworthy in that generalization to untrained materials was shown. The importance of such gains in treatment efficacy cannot be overstated.

Our work suggests that such treatments need to be expanded beyond phonological emphases if we are not to overlook the subgroups of children without a phonological basis for their disability. Furthermore, if — as our data indicate — the most impaired readers prove to have double deficits, then current treatment practice is largely ignoring half of their deficits.

The problem is complicated by the paucity of efforts that address automaticity and fluency in young impaired readers. With the exception of several researchers (see Bowers, 1993, 1995; Frederiksen, Warren, & Rosebery, 1985; Levy & Hinchley, 1990; Segal & Wolf, 1993; Wolf & Segal, 1995), there is little appropriate intervention that includes automaticity and retrieval training for at-risk populations. Bowers (1995) has suggested that repeated reading practice may be particularly helpful for children with rate problems; her research has shown that these children need many exposures to a word before it is learned. Our own preliminary research in intervention is mixed-positive and needs replication. We have shown partial success in helping older impaired readers increase retrieval speed for basic symbols, clear gains in helping them increase word knowledge and acquiring retrieval strategies, and some generalization of improvements to their reading comprehension.

Conclusions

In summary, the Double-Deficit Hypothesis described in this paper offers an alternative conceptualization of reading disorders that places equal importance on the roles of phonological factors and naming-speed factors for diagnosis, prediction, and remediation. This conceptualization is supported by 15 years of cross-sectional, longitudinal, cross-linguistic, and digitized speech-stream studies into the nature of naming-speed deficits. According to this hypothesis, two single-deficit subgroups of relatively less impaired readers are classified, and the most profoundly impaired readers are shown to have both phonological and naming-speed deficits. The implications of the research program described are significant for practice in classroom and clinical settings: they emphasize the importance of early, careful diagnosis along the axes of phonological awareness and naming speed, explicit teaching of sound-symbol correspondence rules, and guided practice of automaticity skills for letter and word recognition. The two most important goals for future research that have emerged are: (1) the systematic investigation of processes across various modalities (language, vision, motor, audition) in the same reading-disabled children; and (2) the study of interventions based on both phonology and automaticity at younger ages. The latter research directions form the basis for a three-city, 4-year NICHD-sponsored reading intervention project among members of our lab, Dr. Maureen Lovett in Toronto, and Dr. Robin Morris in Atlanta.

Acknowledgments

The authors wish to acknowledge with gratitude the support of the Stratford Foundation, Educational Foundation of America, and Biomedical Support Grants for the first phases of this work; the Fulbright Research Fellowship and the Tufts Eliot-Pearson Department of Child Study Fund for Faculty Support for research conducted in Germany; and the National Institute for Child Health and Human Development's Shannon Award, for ongoing intervention research. Particular thanks is expressed to Professor Patricia Bowers at the University of Waterloo and to past and present members of the Tufts Developmental Neurolinguistics Laboratory: Heidi Bally, Kathleen Biddle, Charles Borden, Kathy Feinberg, Jennifer Keates, Cindy Krug, Cory Lewkowicz, Ruth Lotz, Haleh Rakni, and Denise Segal.

We are very grateful to Claudia Pfeil and Ruth Lotz for their assistance in the German research phase. The cooperation of Frau Bott and Herr Belusa and their teachers, Frau Schiller, Frau Heymann, Frau Luttge, and Frau Dohring from Rothenburg Schule and Kronach Schule in Berlin was extraordinary.

References

Ackerman, P.T., & Dykman, R.A. (1993). Phonological processes, confrontation naming, and immediate memory in dyslexia. *Journal of Learning Disabilities, 26*(9), 597-609.

Ackerman, P.T., Dykman, R.A., & Gardner, M. (1990). Counting rate, naming rate, phonological sensitivity, and memory span: Major factors in dyslexia. *Journal of Learning Disabilities, 23,* 325-327.

Adams, M.J. (1990). *Beginning to read: Thinking and learning about print.* Cambridge, MA: MIT Press.

Badian, N.A. (1994). Do dyslexic and other readers differ in reading-related cognitive skills? *Reading and Writing. 6*(1), 45-63.

Badian, N.A. (1995). Predicting reading ability over the long term: The changing roles of letter naming, phonological awareness, and orthographic processing. *Annals of Dyslexia, XLV,* 79-96.

Beck, I.L., Perfetti, C.A., & McKeown, M.G. (1982). Effects of long-term vocabulary instruction on lexical access and reading comprehension. *Journal of Educational Psychology, 74,* 506-521.

Berninger, V.W. (1990). Multiple orthographic codes: Key to alternative instructional methodologies for developing orthographic-phonological connections underlying word identification. *School Psychology Review, 19,* 518-533.

Berninger, V.W. (1994). *The varieties of orthographic knowledge, Vol. I: Theoretical and developmental issues.*. Dordrecht, The Netherlands: Kluwer.

Bisiach, E. (1966). Perceptual factors in pathogenesis of anomia. *Cortex, 2,* 90-95.

Bond, G., & Dykstra, R. (1967). The cooperative research program in first-grade reading instruction. *Reading Research Quarterly, 2,* 5-142.

Bowers, P.G. (1993). Text reading and rereading: Predictors of fluency beyond word recognition. *Journal of Reading Behavior, 25,* 133-153.

Bowers, P.G. (1995, March). *Re-examining selected reading research from the viewpoint of the double-deficit hypothesis.* Paper presented at the Society for Research in Child Development, Indianapolis, IN.

Bowers, P.G., Golden, J., Kennedy, J., & Young, A. (1994). Limits upon orthographic knowledge due to processes indexed by naming speed. In V.W. Berninger (Ed.), *The varieties of orthographic knowledge, Vol. I: Theoretical and developmental issues* (pp. 173-218). Dordrecht, The Netherlands: Kluwer.

Bowers, P.G., Steffy, R., & Tate, E. (1988). Comparison of the effects of IQ control methods on memory and naming speed predictors of reading disability. *Reading Research Quarterly, 23,* 304-309.

Bowers, P.G., & Swanson, L.B. (1991). Naming speed deficits in reading disability: Multiple measures of a singular process. *Journal of Experimental Child Psychology, 51,* 195-219.

Bowers, P.G., & Wolf, M. (1993a). Theoretical links among naming speed, precise timing mechanisms and orthographic skill in dyslexia. *Reading and Writing: An Interdisciplinary Journal, 5*(1), 69-85.

Bowers, P.G., & Wolf, M. (1993b). *A "Double-Deficit Hypothesis" for developmental reading disorders.* Paper presented at the Society for Research in Child Development, New Orleans, LA.

Carver, R.P. (in press). Reading for one second, one minute, or one year from the perspective of reading theory. *Journal for the Scientific Study of Reading.*

Chall, J.S. (1967). *Learning to read: The great debate.* New York: McGraw-Hill.

Chall, J.S. (1983). *Stages of reading development.* New York: McGraw-Hill.

Curtis, M.E. (1987). Vocabulary testing and vocabulary instruction. In M.G. McKeown & M.E. Curtis (Eds.), *The nature of vocabulary acquisition* (pp. 37-51). Hillsdale, NJ: Erlbaum.

Denckla, M.B., & Rudel, R. (1974). Rapid "automatized" naming of pictured objects, colors, letters and numbers by normal children. *Cortex, 10,* 186-202.

Denckla, M.B., & Rudel, R.G. (1976a). Naming of objects by dyslexic and other learning-disabled children. *Brain and Language, 3,* 1-15.

Denckla, M.B., & Rudel, R.G. (1976b). Rapid automatized naming (R.A.N.): Dyslexia differentiated from other learning disabilities. *Neuropsychologia, 14,* 471-479.

Dunn, L.M., & Dunn, L. (1979). *Peabody picture vocabulary test* (rev. ed.). Circle Pines, MN: American Guidance Service.

Ehri, L.C. (1992). Reconceptualizing the development of sight word reading and its relationship to recoding. In P.B. Gough, L.C. Ehri, & R. Treiman (Eds.), *Reading acquisition* (pp. 107-143). Hillsdale, NJ: Erlbaum.

Ellis, A.W. (1981). Visual and name coding in dyslexic children. *Psychological Research, 43,* 201-218.

Ellis, A.W. (1985). The cognitive neuropsychology of developmental (and acquired) dyslexia: A critical survey. *Cognitive Neuropsychology, 2,* 169-205.

Ellis, A.W. (1987). On problems in developing culturally-transmitted cognitive modules: Review of P.H.K. Seymour, "Cognitive analysis of dyslexia." *Mind and Language, 3,* 242-251.

Fawcett, A.J., & Nicolson, R.I. (1994). Naming speed in children with dyslexia. *Journal of Learning Disabilities, 27*(10), 641-646.

Felton, R.H., & Brown, I.S. (1990). Phonological processes as predictors of specific reading skills in children at risk for reading failure. *Reading and Writing: An Interdisciplinary Journal,* 39-59.

Felton, R.H., & Wood, F.B. (1989). Cognitive deficits in reading deficits in reading disability and attention deficit disorder. *Journal of Learning Disabilities, 22,* 3-13.

Flowers, L. (1993). Brain basis for dyslexia: A summary of work in progress. *Journal of Learning Disabilities, 26*(9), 575-582.

Foorman, B.R. (1994). Phonological and orthographic processing: Separate but equal? In V.W. Berninger (Ed.), *The varieties of orthographic knowledge, I: Theoretical and developmental issues* (pp. 319-355). Dordrecht, The Netherlands: Kluwer.

Foorman, B.R., Fletcher, J., & Francis, R. (1994, August). *Review of the University of Houston Intervention Project: Objectives, progress, and problems.* Presented at the NICHD Conference on Intervention Programs for Children with Reading and Related Language Disorders, Rockville, MD.

Frederiksen, J.R., Warren, B.M., & Rosebery, A.S. (1985). A componential approach to training reading skills, Part I. Perceptual units training. *Cognition and Instruction, 2,* 91-130.

Frith, U. (1985). Beneath the surface of dyslexia. In K. Patterson, J. Marshall, & M. Coltheart (Eds.), *Surface dyslexia* (pp. 301-330). London: Erlbaum.

Galaburda, A.M., Menard, M.T., & Rosen, G.D. (1994). Evidence for aberrant auditory anatomy in developmental dyslexia. *Proceedings of the National Academy of Sciences, 91,* 8010-8013.

Gates, A., & MacGinitie, W. (1978). *Gates-MacGinitie reading tests.* New York: Teachers College Press.

German, D.J. (1992). Word-finding intervention for children and adolescents. *Topics in Language Disorders, 13*(1), 33-50.

Geschwind, N. (1972). *Selected papers on language and the brain.* Boston: Reidel.

Goodglass, H. (1980). Disorders of naming following brain injury. *American Scientist, 68,* 647-655.

Goodglass, H., & Kaplan, E. (1972). *The assessment of aphasia and related disorders.* Philadelphia, PA: Lea & Febiger.

Goswami, U., & Swan, D. (1994, April). *Confrontation naming in dyslexic and garden-variety poor readers.* Paper presented at the Society for Scientific Study of Reading, New Orleans, LA.

Gough, P.B., & Tumner, W.E. (1986). Decoding, reading, and reading disability. *Remedial and Special Education, 7,* 6-10.

Gray, W. (1967). *Gray oral reading test.* New York: Bobbs-Merrill.

Guilford, A.M., & Nawojczyk, D.C. (1988). Standardization of the Boston Naming Test at the kindergarten and elementary school levels. *Language, Speech and Hearing Services in Schools, 19,* 395-400.

Haynes, C. (1994). *Differences between name recognition and name retrieval abilities in relationship to reading performance.* Unpublished doctoral dissertation, Harvard University, Cambridge, MA.

Hurford, D.P., Johnston, M., Nepote, P., Hampton, S., Moore, S., Neal, J., Mueller, A., McGeorge, K., Huff, L., Awad, A., Tarto, C., Juliano, C., & Huffman, D. (1994). Early identification and remediation of phonological-processing deficits in first-grade children at risk for reading disabilities. *Journal of Learning Disabilities, 27*(10), 647-659.

Jansky, J., & de Hirsch, K. (1972). *Preventing reading failure.* New York: Harper & Row.

Johnson, D., & Myklebust, H. (1964). *Learning disabilities.* New York: Grune & Stratton.

Kameenui, E.J., Dixon, R.C., & Carnine, D.W. (1987). Issues in the design of vocabulary instructions. In M.G. McKeown & M. Curtis (Eds.), *The nature of vocabulary acquisition* (pp. 129-145). Hillsdale, NJ: Erlbaum.

Kamhi, A., & Catts, H. (1989). Reading disabilities: Terminology, definitions and subtyping issues. In A. Kamhi & H. Catts (Eds.), *Reading disabilities: A developmental language perspective* (pp. 35-67). Austin, TX: PRO-ED.

Kaplan, E., Goodglass, H., & Weintraub, S. (1983). *The Boston naming test.* Philadelphia, PA: Lea & Febiger.

Levy, B.A., & Hinchley, J. (1990). Individual and developmental differences in acquisition of reading skills. In T.H. Carr & B.A. Levy (Eds.), *Reading and its development: Component skills approaches.* New York: Academic Press.

Livingstone, M.S., Rosen, G.D., Drislane, F.W., & Galaburda, A.M. (1991). Physiological and anatomical evidence for a magnocellular defect in developmental dyslexia. *Neurobiology, 88,* 7943-7947.

Lovegrove, W.J., Garzia, R.P., & Nicolson, S.B. (1990). Experimental evidence of a transient system deficit in specific reading disability. *Journal of the American Optometric Association, 61,* 137-146.

Lovett, M.W., Borden, S.L., DeLuca, T., Lacerenza, L., Benson, N.J., & Brackstone, D. (1994). Treating the core deficits of developmental dyslexia: Evidence of transfer-of-learning following strategy- and phonologically-based reading training programs. *Developmental Psychology, 30,* 805-822.

McGregor, K., & Leonard, L.B. (1989). Facilitating word-finding skills .of language-impaired children. *Journal of Speech and Hearing Disorders, 54,* 141-147.

Naslund, J.C. (1990). The interrelationships among preschool predictors of reading acquisition for German children. *Reading and Writing: An Interdisciplinary Journal, 2,* 327-360

Naslund, J.C., & Schneider, W. (1991). Longitudinal effects of verbal ability, memory capacity, and phonological awareness on reading performance. *European Journal of Psychology of Education, 4,* 375-392.

Nicolson, R.I., & Fawcett, A.J. (1990). Automaticity: A new framework for dyslexia research? *Cognition, 35,* 159-182.

Nicolson, R.I., & Fawcett, A.J. (1994). Reaction times and dyslexia. *Quarterly Journal of Experimental Psychology, 47,* 29-48.

Novoa, L. (1988). *Word-retrieval process and reading acquisition and development in bilingual and monolingual children.* Unpublished doctoral dissertation, Harvard University, Cambridge, MA.

Novoa, L., & Wolf, M. (1984, October). *Word-retrieval and reading in bilingual children.* Paper presented at Boston University Language Conference, Boston, MA.

Obregón, M. (1994). *Exploring naming timing patterns by dyslexic and normal readers on the serial RAN task.* Unpublished master's thesis, Tufts University, Medford, MA.

Olson, R., Forsberg, H., & Wise, B. (1994). Genes, environment and the development of orthographic skills. In V.W. Berninger (Ed.), *The varieties of orthographic knowledge: Theoretical and developmental issues* (pp. 27-71). Dordrecht, The Netherlands: Kluwer.

Perfetti, C.A. (1985). *Reading ability.* New York: Oxford University Press.

Perfetti, C.A., Finger, E., & Hogaboam, T. (1978). Sources of vocalization latency differences between skilled and less skilled young readers. *Journal of Educational Psychology, 70,* 730-739.

Reitsma, P. (1983). Printed word learning in beginning readers. *Journal of Experimental Child Psychology, 36,* 321-339.

Scarborough, H.S. (1989). Prediction of reading disability from familial and individual differences. *Journal of Educational Psychology, 8*(1), 101-108.

Schneider, W., & Naslund, J.C. (1992). Cognitive prerequisite of reading and spelling: A longitudinal approach. In A. Demetriou, M. Shayer, & A. Efklides (Eds.), *Neo-Piagetian theories of cognitive development: Implications and applications for educators* (pp. 256-274). London: Routledge.

Segal, D., & Wolf, M. (1993). Automaticity, word retrieval, and vocabulary development in children with reading disabilities. In L. Meltzer (Ed.), *Cognitive, linguistic,
and developmental perspectives on learning disorders* (pp. 141-165). Boston: Little, Brown.

Shankweiler, D., & Liberman, I.Y. (1972). Misreading: A search for causes. In J.F.
Kavanagh & I.Y. Liberman (Eds.), *Language by ear and by eye* (pp. 293-317). Cambridge, MA: MIT Press.

Snowling, M. (1987). *Dyslexia.* Oxford: Basil Blackwell.

Snyder, L., & Downey, D. (1995). Serial rapid naming skills in children with reading
disabilities. *Annals of Dyslexia, XLV,* 31-50.

Spring, C., & Capps, C. (1974). Encoding speed, rehearsal, and probed recall of
dyslexic boys. *Journal of Educational Psychology, 66,* 780-786.

Spring, C., & Davis, J. (1988). Relations of digit naming speed with three components of reading. *Applied Psycholinguistics, 9,* 315-334.

Stanovich, K.E. (1986). 'Matthew effects' in reading: Some consequences of individual differences in acquisition of literacy. *Reading Research Quarterly, 4,* 360-407.

Stanovich, K.E. (1992). Speculations on the causes and consequences of individual
differences in early reading acquisition. In P.B. Gough, L.C. Ehri, & R. Treiman
(Eds.), *Reading acquisition* (pp. 307-342). Hillsdale, NJ: Erlbaum.

Stanovich, K.E., & Siegel, L.S. (1994). Phenotypic-performance profile of children
with reading disabilities: A regression-based test of the phonological-core vari-
able-difference model. *Journal of Educational Psychology, 86*(1), 24-53.

Swanson, L.B. (1989). *Analyzing naming speed-reading relationships in children.* Unpublished doctoral dissertation, University of Waterloo, Waterloo, Ontario, Canada.

Tallal, P., Miller, S., & Fitch, R.H. (1993). Neurobiological basis of speech: A case for
the preeminence of Temporal processing. In P. Tallal, A.M. Galaburda, R.R. Llinas,
& C. von Euler (Eds.), *Annals of the New York Academy of Sciences, Vol, 682. Temporal
information processing in the nervous system: Special reference to dyslexia and dysphasia*
(pp. 27-47). New York, NY: The New York Academy of Sciences.

Torgesen, J.K., & Wagner, R.K. (1994). *Review of the Florida State Intervention Project:
Objects, progress and problems.* Presented at the NICHD Conference on Intervention
Programs for Children with Reading and Related Language Disorders, Rockville,
MD.

Valtin, R. (1989). Dyslexia in the German language. In P.G. Aaron & R.M. Joshi
(Eds.), *Reading and writing disorders in different orthographic systems* (pp. 119-135).
Boston: Kluwer.

Vellutino, F.R., Scanlon, D.M., & Tanzman, M.S. (in press). Components of reading
ability: Issues and problems in operationalizing word identification, phonological
coding, and orthographic coding. In G.R. Lyon (Ed.), *Frames of reference for the
assessment of learning disabilities: New views on measurement issues.* Baltimore, MD: Brookes.

Wagner, R.K., & Torgesen, J.K. (1987). The nature of phonological processing and its
causal role in the acquisition of reading skills. *Psychological Bulletin, 101,* 192-212.

Wagner, R.K., Torgesen, J.K., Laughon, P.L., Simmons, K., & Rashotte, C.A. (1993). Development of young readers' phonological processing abilities. *Journal of Educational Psychology, 85*(1), 83-103.

Wagner, R.K., Torgesen, J.K., & Rashotte, C.A. (1994). The development of reading-related phonological processing abilities: New evidence of bidirectional causality from a latent variable longitudinal study. *Developmental Psychology, 30,* 73-87.

Walsh, D., Price, G., & Cunningham, M. (1988). The critical but transitory importance of letter naming. *Reading Research Quarterly, 23,* 108-122.

Wimmer, H. (1993). Characteristics of developmental dyslexia in a regular writing system. *Applied Psycholinguistics, 14,* 1-34.

Wimmer, H., & Hummer, P. (1990). How German-speaking first graders read and spell: Doubts on the importance of the logographic stage. *Applied Psycholinguistics, 11,* 349-368.

Wing, C.S. (1990). A preliminary investigation of generalization to untrained words following two treatments of children's word-finding problems. *Language, Speech, and Hearing Services in Schools, 21,* 151-156.

Wolf, M. (1982). The word-retrieval process and reading in children and aphasics. In K. Nelson (Ed.), *Children's language* (pp. 437-493). Hillsdale, NJ: Erlbaum.

Wolf, M. (1986). Rapid alternating stimulus naming in the developmental dyslexias. *Brain and Language, 27,* 360-379.

Wolf, M. (1991a). Naming speed and reading: The contribution of the cognitive neurosciences. *Reading Research Quarterly, 26*(2), 123-141.

Wolf, M. (1991b, April). *Word-wraiths: The unique contribution of the naming system to reading prediction and intervention in developmental dyslexia.* Paper presented at the Society for Research in Child Development, Seattle, WA.

Wolf, M., Bally, H., & Morris, R. (1986). Automaticity, retrieval processes, and reading: A longitudinal study in average and impaired readers. *Child Development, 57,* 988-1000.

Wolf, M., & Bowers, P. (1995). *The "Double-Deficit Hypothesis" for the developmental dyslexias.* Unpublished manuscript.

Wolf, M., & Goodglass, H. (1986). Dyslexia, dysnomia, and lexical retrieval. *Brain and Language, 28,* 154-168.

Wolf, M., & Obregón, M. (1989, April). *88 children in search of a name: A five year investigation of rate, word-retrieval, and vocabulary in reading development and dyslexia.* Paper presented at Society for Research in Child Development, Kansas City, MO.

Wolf, M., & Obregón, M. (1992). Early naming deficits, developmental dyslexia, and a specific deficit hypothesis. *Brain and Language, 42,* 219-247.

Wolf, M., Pfeil, C., Lotz, R., & Biddle, K. (1994). Towards a more universal understanding of the developmental dyslexias: The contribution of orthographic factors. In V.W. Berninger (Ed.), *The varieties of orthographic knowledge, I: Theoretical and developmental issues* (pp. 137-171). Dordrecht, The Netherlands: Kluwer.

Wolf, M., & Segal, D. (1993). *Retrieval-accuracy and Vocabulary Elaboration (R.A.V.E.): A pilot intervention program for reading disabled children.* Unpublished manuscript.

Wolf, M., & Segal, D. (1995). *Retrieval-rate, accuracy and vocabulary elaboration (R.A.V.E.) in reading-impaired children: A pilot intervention program.* Unpublished manuscript.

Wolff, P., & Melngailis, I. (1994). Family patterns of developmental dyslexia: Clinical findings. *American Journal of Medical Genetics, 122-131.*

Wolff, P., Melngailis, I., Obregón, M., & Bedrosian, M. (in press). Family patterns of developmental dyslexia, part II: Behavioral phenotypes. *American Journal of Medical Genetics.*

Wolff, P., Michel, G., & Ovrut, M. (1990a). Rate variables and automatized naming in developmental dyslexia. *Brain and Language, 39,* 556-575.

Wolff, P., Michel, G., & Ovrut, M. (1990b). The timing of syllable repetitions in developmental dyslexia. *Journal of Speech and Hearing Research, 33,* 281-289.

Wolff, P., Michel, G., Ovrut, M., & Drake, C. (1990). Rate and timing precision motor coordination in developmental dyslexia. *Developmental Psychology, 26,* 349-359.

Yap, R.L., & van der Leij, A. (1991, August). *Rate of elementary symbol processing in dyslexics.* Poster presentation at the Rodin Conference, Berne, Switzerland.

12

Trial Lessons in Reading

A Dynamic Assessment Approach

ANN MARIE LONGO, Ed.D.

Boys Town Reading Center, Father Flanagan's Boys' Home

A strong call is being made in the field of education to link assessment more closely to instruction. The search for more informative assessment approaches has resulted in a number of different approaches under the headings of performance-based (see Guthrie, Van Meter, & Mitchell, 1994), teacher-based (see Hiebert, 1991), and alternative assessment (see Winograd, 1994; Worthen, 1993).

The call for these types of assessments comes from a frustration that the traditional assessments are not informative enough to guide instruction.

> Such forms of testing [national and state tests] simply do not tell us what we need to know: namely, whether students have the capacity to use wisely what knowledge they have. This is a judgement that we can make only through tasks that require students to 'perform' in highly contextualized situations that are as faithful as possible to criterion situations. (Wiggins, 1993 p. 202)

In recent years there has been much discussion in the reading litera-

ture about testing. Questions of *how much, how often,* and most importantly, *how useful,* have been raised. Most educators agree, however,
that the most useful type of testing information is that which will
help to inform instruction (Chall & Curtis, 1990; Roswell & Chall,
1994). Trial lessons are one form of testing that does match assessment to instruction.

Trial lessons are tasks designed to test students' potential to learn
under different instructional conditions. They are a type of dynamic
assessment approach based on the assumption that the best estimate
of a student's learning ability comes from direct observation of that
student in a learning situation (Delclos, Burns, & Kulewicz, 1987).
This chapter will review such assessment techniques and give a specific example of how trial lessons may be used to assess knowledge of
word meanings. I will first give an overview of dynamic assessment
approaches in general and trial lessons in particular. I will then describe the relevant research on reading vocabulary — its importance to
reading development and how it has traditionally been tested — and
describe the procedures and the materials that can be used to administer trial lessons in vocabulary. The chapter will conclude with a discussion of the practical implications of trial lessons for both classroom instruction and diagnosis of reading difficulties.

Dynamic Assessment

Dynamic assessment is a general term that encompasses a number of
different approaches. Related terms include: *learning potential assessment* (Budoff, 1988; Feuerstein, 1979), *mediated assessment* (Bransford,
Delclos, Vye, Burns, & Hasselbring, 1987), *evaluation of the zone of
proximal development* (Vygotsky, 1930/1978), *assessment via assisted learning and transfer* (Brown & Campione, 1986), the *testing-the-limits approach* (Carlson & Weidl, 1978) and *trial lessons* (Harris & Roswell,
1953; Roswell & Natchez, 1989).

Dynamic assessment is related to Vygotsky's view of the "zone of
proximal development," the difference between a student's actual or

current development level and his or her potential development level. Vygotsky's (1930/1978) contention is that a child can perform at a more advanced level when assisted than when working alone. This difference in level of performance suggests that a learner has a range of potential rather than some fixed state of ability (Smagorinsky, 1995). Whereas static measures focus on the student's actual level of development, an interactive assessment — by providing an opportunity to learn — reveals the student's *potential* development level (Ferrara, Brown, & Campione, 1986).

Although dynamic assessment strategies are not new, they have gained more attention in recent years as a way to better identify special education students (Lidz, 1987). The expectation is that although a dynamic learning measure will be related to IQ scores, such a measure provides diagnostic information about individuals beyond that provided by intelligence or ability scores (Brown & Campione, 1986). Dynamic assessment approaches are seen as important additions to existing assessment approaches, rather than as replacements:

> The addition of dynamic assessment may serve to compensate for the inadequacies of traditional assessment approaches by extending and addressing issues that otherwise are not considered, such as improving the understanding of the learner's knowledge of task features and discerning the learner's ability to maintain and transfer what was learned. (Jitendra & Kameenui, 1993, p. 7)

Bransford et al. (1987) outline three advantages of dynamic assessment approaches: (1) they focus on the process of learning rather than just the product, (2) they address the responsiveness of the individual to instruction in a way that is not based solely on the premise that prior learning predicts future performance, and (3) they provide prescriptive information for designing potentially effective instruction.

Attempts to measure reading potential through dynamic approaches have proven valuable in gaining a better understanding of students' abilities to read words and understand passages. Cioffi and

Carney (1983) administered a word recognition test in both a static condition (students were asked to read a list of isolated words without assistance) and a dynamic condition (the examiner taught missed words). The results indicated that students were able to read at grade level during the dynamic condition, in contrast to the standard administration, where their reading level was one year below their present grade placement. On a passage-reading subtest, the examiner provided instructional support by preteaching vocabulary, discussing relevant prior knowledge and important concepts, and giving the students opportunities to say what had been learned. Again, this was contrasted with the standard administration in which the students read silently and answered questions. During the dynamic assessment condition, students read more words per minute and answered more comprehension questions correctly.

Brozo (1990) also compared static and interactive assessment using an Informal Reading Inventory (IRI). He found that students could read materials at a higher grade level in the interactive assessment condition (when appropriate instruction was provided) than in the static condition.

Trial Lessons

First described by Harris and Roswell (1953) as a way to select an approach for teaching word recognition skills, trial lessons have been recommended as an informal way to test a student's ability to learn under different instructional conditions (Chall & Curtis, 1987; Harris & Sipay, 1990; Hutson & Niles, 1974; Putnam, 1996; Roswell & Chall, 1994; Roswell & Natchez, 1989). Their focus is on the learning process.

The use of trial lessons is recommended as an integral part of the diagnostic examination of students who are having difficulty in reading, in order to determine which instructional approach will be most effective (Roswell & Chall, 1994). For example, to determine how to best teach word recognition skills, a number of trial lessons can be designed using three different approaches: visual, phonic, and visual-motor. In an informal, collaborative session, the student is taught individual words by each of the three methods. In the phonic method, for example, the teacher starts out with a blending technique, in which known words, such as *book,* are changed to phonetically similar words (e.g., *took, look,* or *hook*) by substituting different initial consonants. Several initial consonants are taught, studied, and combined with appropriate word endings. In addition to observing whether the student can learn initial sounds readily, the teacher observes how rapidly she learns, how much repetition, support, and encouragement she needs, and how much effort she puts forth. The teacher discusses which techniques seem appropriate for the student, and helps her understand her own reading problem. The student's participation serves as a powerful motivation for future learning because it focuses on what she *can do* and makes her aware of strategies that may make her a more successful reader (Roswell & Natchez, 1989; Kletzien & Bednar, 1990).

Formal individual evaluations of reading often focus on the differences between students or on the cause of the student's reading problem, rather than on what teachers can do to help the individual student who is having problems. Trial lessons used in addition to formal assessments can help to give a total picture not only of the student's present level of reading, but also of what can be done to move her to the next level.

One assessment instrument that incorporates formal assessment of reading with the more interactive approach of trial lessons is the Diagnostic Assessments of Reading with Trial Teaching Strategies test (DARTTS; Roswell & Chall, 1992). The first part of the program (Diagnostic Assessments of Reading) is a criterion-referenced test that yields mastery scores on several components of reading: word recognition, word analysis, oral reading, silent reading, word meanings, and spelling. The second part of the program (Trial Teaching Strategies) includes lessons designed to help teachers find the most appropriate methods and materials to use with students. The trial teaching strategies included in the program are for word recognition, phonics, oral reading, silent reading, written expression, and spelling.

To illustrate, the trial lessons in advanced word analysis include the rule of silent *e*. Once the teacher has established that the student knows the short vowel sounds, the teacher might say, "Now let me show you what happens when an *e* appears at the end of some words. This word is *tap*. By adding *e* at the end, the word becomes *tape*. The *e* changed the short vowel sound to a long vowel sound, making the vowel sound say its name — *a*. The *e* is not pronounced. It is silent." The teacher would then show examples of other words that follow the silent *e* rule (e.g., *mad, made; cap, cape*), asking the student to read each pair and supplying the pronunciation when needed. The student would then be asked to read the following sentences:

You made me mad.
Put on your cap and your cape.
The tub has a tube.
The note is not for you.

Again, the teacher supplies word pronunciations as needed and corrects any misreading by the student. The session proceeds at a pace that is appropriate for helping the student grasp the concept. To reinforce the concept, the teacher dictates words, then phrases and sentences, changing the short vowel sounds to long vowel sounds and then changing long vowel sounds to short ones (Roswell & Chall, 1994). (The materials for teaching the trial strategies are provided by the DARTTS test.)

Although trial lessons are often used to establish the best ways to teach students how to read words, less work has been done on their use in teaching students the meanings of words. It is to meaning vocabulary that I turn next.

Vocabulary Development

The high correlations between knowledge of word meanings, reading comprehension, and cognitive development have been well documented (Davis, 1968; Thorndike, 1974). Also, there is considerable research on the development of vocabulary knowledge with age. The greatest increases take place in the early grade levels, with the rate of growth slowing down as vocabulary changes from concrete to more abstract knowledge (see Chall, 1987b; McKeown & Curtis, 1987).

These changes in vocabulary knowledge with age have a direct bearing on reading achievement. Chall (1979, 1983) has proposed a six-stage theory that describes reading development as moving from *learning to read* (decoding, fluency) to *reading to learn* new information and perspectives. Each of the stages is defined in terms of the reading process and the knowledge it requires, as well as the language demands placed on the reader. The stage theory provides a criterion-based framework that helps us understand what the reader can and cannot do at different stages of reading development. The framework is also useful in helping to understand what the reader needs to be able to do to make progress (Chall & Curtis, 1992).

Vocabulary knowledge becomes extremely important during Stage 3 ("reading for learning the new," grades 4-8). In order to progress through this stage, students must be able to read and study textbooks and other informational texts that contain new ideas. This ability is developed via a systematic study of words and via reactions to texts through discussion, answering questions, and writing. This stage requires and gives further practice with less familiar, more abstract concepts and word meanings (Chall, 1983).

Vocabulary Instruction

Even though there is strong agreement among researchers and educators concerning the importance of vocabulary knowledge and the need to teach word meanings, there is still much debate on how best to teach it (see Baumann & Kameenui, 1991). The debate centers on the role of instruction in developing word meaning knowledge. Should vocabulary meanings be taught through direct instruction (teaching definitions), or through context (having students infer the meanings of words from the context of the sentence or passage)? Those who argue for direct instruction point out that natural contexts do not necessarily provide sufficient clues for the reader to infer word meanings (Beck, McKeown, & McCaslin, 1983). Moreover, direct instruction is a more efficient method than learning from natural context (Miller & Gildea, 1987; Stahl & Fairbanks, 1986). In contrast, some researchers argue against direct instruction, pointing out that there are too many words to be taught directly and too little instructional time for it to be an efficient means of vocabulary development (Nagy & Herman, 1987; Sternberg, 1987).

To help make decisions about which instructional technique is most efficient in developing students' word knowledge, we must first have some information about how individual students learn words. Vocabulary assessment provides some answers.

Vocabulary Assessment

Word knowledge is typically assessed through the use of a standardized multiple-choice format in which the student selects a brief definition or synonym for a target word from among several choices. Curtis (1987) analyzed the kind of word knowledge assessed by traditional reading vocabulary tests by characterizing students' knowledge about word meanings, based on stages outlined by Dale (1965). The stages range from Stage 1 (never having seen or heard the word before) to Stage 4 (having precise knowledge of the word that is not tied to one specific context). Tasks were designed to identify the level or stage of students' knowledge of a specific set of words. Students' performance on these tasks was then compared to their performance with the same words in a multiple-choice format. Curtis (1987) found that, in order to choose a correct response on a multiple-choice vocabulary measure, only surface knowledge of the word was required. In other words, traditional vocabulary tests give an indication of the *breadth* of a student's word knowledge, but not necessarily of the *depth* of that knowledge.

Multiple-choice vocabulary tests have been criticized because they do not discriminate between words that are known well and words that are minimally familiar (Anderson & Freebody, 1981; Kameenui, Dixon, & Carnine, 1987). However, as Curtis (1987) points out, multiple-choice test results do provide some useful information. They provide an estimate of the range of a student's vocabulary knowledge, and information on where the student stands in relation to his peers in school. They are also correlated with measures of reading comprehension and intelligence.

An alternative to multiple-choice vocabulary testing is a format found on many Informal Reading Inventories (IRI). The vocabulary questions on an IRI are often designed to measure a student's ability to use context clues to infer the meaning of a word or phrase found in a silent reading passage. However, an analysis of the types of vocabulary words and questions on three popular IRIs revealed that the information about students' vocabulary knowledge assessed by these measures is not always useful (Duffelmeyer, Robinson, & Squier, 1989). The target word meanings were familiar to students, and the vocabulary questions were not always informative, since most of the words were presented in contexts that did not provide enough information to infer their meaning.

Another alternative to the multiple-choice format of testing vocabulary knowledge is the word meaning subtest of the Diagnostic Assessments of Reading (DAR; Roswell & Chall, 1992). As in many intelligence tests, the student's word-meaning knowledge is tested aurally on the DAR. The examiner reads each of the target words and asks the student if he knows its meaning. This information about the student's word-meaning knowledge is useful because it is not confounded by the student's word-recognition abilities. This can then give a more accurate picture of the student's strength or weakness in vocabulary knowledge. In addition, it allows the examiner to evaluate the quality of the student's word knowledge. For example, the examiner can determine whether the student is able to give precise definitions or synonyms for most of the words at a certain grade level, or whether most of the student's responses are examples tied to a specific context.

Trial Lessons in Vocabulary

I developed trial lessons in vocabulary to test their potential for assessing students' word-meaning knowledge in an instructional situation. My hypothesis was that a better understanding of the quality of word-meaning knowledge assessed by such an approach, along with information about how students learn word meanings, would help to inform us about the kinds of vocabulary instruction that may be the most efficient. I hoped that this information would be of direct use to teachers, in that it could be used to guide remediation attempts, rather than just identifying students who are likely to experience problems.

Trial Lessons in Vocabulary were developed following the guidelines for dynamic assessment outlined earlier in this chapter — that is, they are informal and interactive, and they provide feedback to the student during assessment. Three vocabulary approaches are used in the trial lessons: learning word meaning directly (from definitions), learning from an indirect approach (teaching students to infer the meaning of a word from the context of the sentence), and learning word parts such as prefixes (also known as structural analysis).

In the *Direct* condition, the student is shown a word while it is pronounced by the instructor. He is then given the definition of the word. A sentence using that word is read to the student, and he is asked, "What does (*target word*) mean in this sentence?" For example, consider the following sentence: "Mr. Jones had an *ample* supply of pencils." The sentence in this condition does not provide the meaning of the word, but does supply a context in which to explain the word's meaning. When given a sentence like this, students are asked to paraphrase the meaning in order to demonstrate that they understand the definition (e.g., "He had more pencils than he needed").

In the *Indirect* condition, the student is shown a word while it is pronounced by the examiner. He is then read a sentence using that word and asked, "What does (*target word*) mean in this sentence?" The sentences in this condition are constructed to provide the meaning of the word. For example, consider the following sentence: "The *timid* kitten ran when the big dog came into her yard."

In the *Word Part* condition, the student is shown a base word (e.g., *judge*), while it is pronounced by the examiner, and then given the definition of the base. He is then shown a prefix and its meaning (e.g., *pre-* means "before"). The examiner then reads a sentence using a word combining the two, and the student is asked, "What does (*target word*) mean in this sentence?" For example, consider the following sentence: "I don't like to *prejudge* movies." As in the Direct condition, the sentences in this condition are constructed to supply a context in which to explain the word's meaning, rather than to provide the meaning of the word. (Instructions to students can be found in Appendix A. Sample sentences can be found in Appendix B.)

Procedures for Trial Lessons in Vocabulary

The first step in administering the vocabulary trial lessons is to establish that the words that are taught during the session are unfamiliar to the student. This can be done by putting the target words on cards and then reading the target words to the student, asking them to put the words into "yes" (I know that word) and "no" (I don't know that word) piles. The trial lesson for each of the three instructional approaches involves the same three phases:

- *Model* the procedure for the first two words.
- *Practice* the procedure on eight words, providing feedback.
- *Test* the words taught, using new sentences.

During the *Model* phase, the student is given directions on different ways to learn the meaning of a word. For example, in the Indirect method, the student is told that sometimes we can learn the meaning of a word by looking at the other words in the sentence. The student is then shown a sentence and asked what the target word means in that sentence. In the Word Part method, the student is told the meaning of the prefix and the meaning of the root word, then asked to give the meaning of the target word in the sentence. In the Direct method, the student is given the definition of the word and then asked to give the meaning of the target word in the sentence.

During the *Practice* phase, the student practices the procedures shown to her during the model phase. She receives feedback, and is given additional sample sentences when necessary. After she is shown the first sentence, the student is asked to paraphrase the sentence, giving the meaning of the target word. If she does not give the correct meaning of the word, she can then be given up to two more sample sentences.

During the *Test* phase, the student is shown each of the words that have been taught in a new sentence. The sentences are designed so that the meaning of the word cannot be deciphered from the context (e.g., "The stars were *luminous*."). The student is asked to tell the meaning of the target word. Following this, she is shown the same sentence within a multiple-choice format for assessing knowledge of the target word's meaning, as in the following example:

The stars were *luminous*.
a.   small
b.   bright
c.   far away

Results from Studies Using Trial Lessons in Vocabulary

Fifth-graders who performed below grade level in reading and who were in the low average range of intelligence (IQ scores in the 75–90 range) were participants in the first study (Longo, 1992). These students were chosen for study because they are often defined as "slow learners" because of their lack of vocabulary knowledge. Consequently, their potential for learning new vocabulary words is often underestimated (Longo, 1989).

Thirty-one students were administered the trial lessons following the procedures outlined in the previous section. Overall, the students learned an average of 13 (out of 30) words according to the recall measure (where they were asked to give the definitions of taught words). The students learned an average of 25 (out of 30) words according to the recognition measure (where they were asked to choose the correct definition from a choice of three definitions). The relative effectiveness of the different methods of instruction varied depending on the criterion selected. On the recall measure, the Word Part method produced the best results. On the recognition task, the Direct and Word Part methods produced the same (highest) number of correct responses. In terms of efficiency of learning, the Indirect method required the most trials or exposures to the words, and the Direct method required the least. The Word Part condition produced definitions that were generally less precise than those produced in either the Direct or Indirect conditions.

A second study using the Trial Lessons in Vocabulary was done with high school students (Longo, 1995). Fourteen ninth- and tenth-graders who were reading three or four years below grade level were administered the trial lessons using the same procedures used in the first study. The overall results for the high school students were similar to those for the fifth-graders. That is, they learned an average of 11 (out of 30) words as measured by the recall task (giving definitions) and they learned an average of 24 (out of 30) words as measured by the recognition task (multiple choice). However, the results for the instructional methods revealed that the high school students learned the most words in the Direct condition, as measured by both the recall and recognition measures. Also, the Direct method proved to be the most efficient, as it required the fewest trials or exposures to individual words. The Indirect method required the most trials and produced the fewest correct responses on the recognition measure. The effectiveness of the Word Part method was equal to that of the Indirect method on the recall measure.

Summary and Implications

Trial lessons are a practical, informative method of evaluating not only *what* students have learned, but also *how* they learn. Trial lessons have been used to establish the most suitable method for teaching word-recognition skills (Roswell & Natchez, 1989), and they have been recommended for use in the diagnosis of reading problems (Chall & Curtis, 1987; Roswell & Chall, 1994). And, as I have argued in this chapter, trial lessons can also be effective in establishing the best method for teaching word meanings.

Trial lessons can provide a great deal of diagnostic information. For example, the trial lessons in vocabulary provide quantitative results, measuring the number of words students can learn when taught by different instructional approaches. This information is available for both groups and individuals. The trial lessons in vocabulary also allow for qualitative analysis. Information about the level of definitions provided by students can reveal important differences in how well a student can learn word meanings when taught by different methods. In addition, analysis of incorrect responses can also be helpful. For example, it is possible to establish whether errors are related to the context of the sentence or to another target word taught to the student.

The use of trial lessons is also consistent with recommendations for classroom assessment of reading (Wolf, 1993; Zemelman, Daniels, & Hyde, 1993). Calfee and Hiebert (1991) outline the characteristics of assessment for instruction — the kind of information that is important to teachers. This includes assessment that is teacher-designed for classroom decisions, performance-based, sensitive to dynamic changes in performance, and administered when needed. The trial lessons described in this chapter meet each of those criteria.

Perhaps most importantly, the instructional component of trial lessons allows for realistic expectations for students' learning potential. Too often, students — particularly those deemed to have learning problems — are given materials on which they can be successful but that do not challenge them to learn. Using trial lessons, teachers can more accurately assess the most appropriate level of materials for specific reading goals.

In a review of studies on the effects of school and teacher factors that relate to student reading achievement, one condition that was found again and again to relate positively to reading achievement was frequent and timely assessment (Chall, 1987a):

> Assessment enables the teacher, the child, the parent, and the school to see not only what has been accomplished, but in what ways the curriculum and the instructional methods need to be changed in order to better teach the students. For example, the level of difficulty of a lesson and/or text can be matched more precisely to the student if there is frequent and timely assessment of a student's progress. Assessment also provides a clear and concrete way of showing the student what is expected. Finally, it provides teachers with a way to back up the high academic expectations with a tangible system of student accountability for achievement. (p. 22)

Appendix A: Instructions to Students

Instructions for Phase One — *Model*

Direct Condition

1. **Pronounce the word for the student.**
   "This word is *ample*."
2. **Give the definition of the word.**
   "The word *ample* means 'more than enough'."
3. **Read sentence to student.**

"Mr. Jones had an ample supply of pencils."

4. Discuss sentence.

"So in the sentence *Mr. Jones had an ample supply of pencils,* I know that Mr. Jones had more than enough pencils, he had a lot of pencils."

Indirect Condition: "Sometimes we can tell the meaning of a word in a sentence by the other words in the sentence."

1. Pronounce the word for the student.

"This word is *luminous.*"

2. Read sentence to student and cover the focus word.

"I'm going to cover up the word *luminous* in the sentence *We don't need to turn on the porch light to see because the moon is so luminous,* to see what word would fit in that sentence."

3. Discuss sentence.

"We don't need to turn on the porch light to see because the moon is so *bright.* So the word *luminous* must mean 'bright'."

Word Part Condition

"Sometimes the parts of a word help us to know what the word means."

1. Pronounce the word for the student.

"This word is *readjust.*"

2. Give the definition of the prefix and base word.

"The prefix *re-* means 'again'; *adjust* means 'to arrange, put in proper order'."

3. Read sentence to student.

"He had to readjust his umbrella."

4. Discuss sentence.

"So in the sentence *He had to readjust his umbrella,* I know that he arranged his umbrella again, he put it back the way it was."

Instructions for Phase Two — Practice

"Now see if you can tell me what each of these words means. What does (the target word) mean in this sentence?" (The student gives the meaning of the word in the sentence. If the meaning is incorrect, give the student feedback and then another exposure to the word in another sentence. Give up to three exposures to the word.)

Instructions for Phase Three — Test

"For these sentences I want you to tell me what the (target) word means in this sentence."
"This is the same sentence, only this time you have a choice. Which letter (a, b, or c) best fits the meaning of the (target) word?"

Appendix B: Sample Sentences

Direct Condition

bleak
a. The fans looked bleak after the game.
b. The man had a bleak expression on his face.
c. The yard looked bleak after the storm.
test sentence — The painting was bleak.

sapling
a. The flowers grew around the sapling.
b. The sapling was covered with snow.
c. The sapling stood out in the yard.
test sentence — He put the sapling near the house.

ravenous
a. The boy was ravenous after the race.
b. I had to hurry home because I was ravenous.

c. The man came home from work ravenous.

test sentence — Everyone came to the party ravenous.

endeavor

a. I will endeavor to climb the mountain.

b. The team will endeavor to win the game.

c. We should endeavor to do our best.

test sentence — He will endeavor to do his homework.

abruptly

a. The electricity went out abruptly.

b. The party came to an end abruptly.

c. The storm came abruptly during the night.

test sentence — The man woke up abruptly during the night.

Indirect Condition

desolate

a. The stadium became desolate when the spectators left after the game.

b. The audience left the theater and it was desolate until the next show.

c. The house remained desolate after the family moved out.

test sentence — The street was desolate last night.

massive

a. The piano was too massive to fit through the doorway.

b. The amount of snow was so massive it took four hours to plow it.

c. He had such a massive collection of books he needed two rooms to store them in.

test sentence — The elephant was massive.

coaxed

a. Even though Mary wanted to go home, she was coaxed into going to the movies with her friends.

b. Even though he had a lot of homework, Bob was coaxed into going to the ball game.

c. My mom always says, "If you don't want to do something, don't let yourself get coaxed into it."

test sentence — Marie coaxed her friend to buy the sweater.

luminous

a. We didn't need to turn on the porch light to see because the moon was so luminous.

b. The cheerleaders wore luminous costumes that shone in the dark.

c. After the rain stopped, the sun came out and the afternoon was luminous.

test sentence — The stars were luminous.

agitated

a. The noise from the television agitated the man while he tried to take a nap.

b. The talking teacher agitated the student while he took the test.

c. The fly in the soup agitated the man while he tried to eat.

test sentence — He was agitated during the meeting.

Word Part Condition

repossessed

a. The man repossessed the car.

b. The girl repossessed her seat on the bus.

c. The woman repossessed her jewelry.

test sentence — The boy repossessed his favorite toy.

reunited

a. The family reunited every summer.

b. The two countries reunited.

c. The old friends reunited.

test sentence – The classmates reunited.

dislodged

a. The antenna on top of the television was dislodged.

b. The legs of the table can be dislodged.

c. The stones on the wall were dislodged.

test sentence – After riding the bike, the wheels were dislodged.

untried

a. The salesperson said the car was untried.

b. The bicycle was untried.

c. The computer she bought is untried.

test sentence – Until today his airplane was untried.

prenatal

a. Good prenatal care is very important.

b. The doctor tested the baby's prenatal heartbeat.

c. The mother went to the doctor for a prenatal checkup.

test sentence – The mother read a book on prenatal care.

References

Anderson, R., & Freebody, P. (1981). Vocabulary knowledge. In J. Guthrie (Ed.), *Comprehension and teaching: Research reviews* (pp. 77-117). Newark, DE: IRA.

Baumann, J.F., & Kameenui, E.J. (1991). Research on vocabulary instruction: Ode to Voltaire. In J. Flood, J.M. Jensen, D. Lapp, & J.R. Squire (Eds.), *Handbook of research on teaching the English language arts* (pp. 604-627). New York: Macmillan.

Beck, I.L., McKeown, M.G., & McCaslin, E.S. (1983). Vocabulary development: All contexts are not created equal. *Elementary School Journal, 83,* 177-181.

Bransford, J.D., Delclos, V.R., Vye, N.J., Burns, M.S., & Hasselbring, T.S. (1987). State of the art and future directions. In C.S. Lidz (Ed.), *Dynamic assessment: An interactional approach to evaluating learning potential* (pp. 479-496). New York: Guilford Press.

Brown, A.L., & Campione, J.C. (1986). Psychological theory and the study of learning disabilities. *American Psychologist, 14,* 1059-1068.

Brozo, W.G. (1990). Learning how at-risk learners learn best: A case for interactive assessment. *Journal of Reading, 33,* 522-527.

Budoff, M. (1988). The validity of learning potential assessment and measures for assessing learning potential. In C.S. Lidz (Ed.), *Dynamic assessment: An interactional approach to evaluating learning potential.* New York: Guilford Press.

Calfee, R., & Hiebert, E. (1991). Classroom assessment of reading. In R. Barr, M. Kamil, P. Mosenthal, & P.D. Pearson (Eds.), *Handbook of reading research: Vol 2* (pp. 281-309). New York: Longman.

Carlson, J.S., & Wiedl, K.H. (1978). Use of testing-the-limits procedure in the assessment of intellectual capabilities in children with learning difficulties. *American Journal of Mental Deficiency, 2,* 559-564.

Chall, J.S. (1979). The great debate: Ten years later, with a modest proposal for reading stages. In L.B. Resnick & P.A. Weaver (Eds.), *Theory and practice of early reading: Vol 1* (pp. 29-55). Hillside, NJ: Erlbaum.

Chall, J.S. (1983). *Stages of reading development.* New York: McGraw-Hill.

Chall, J.S. (1987a). The importance of instruction in reading methods for all teachers. In R.F. Bowler (Ed.), *Intimacy with language: A forgotten basic in teacher education* (pp. 15-23). Baltimore, MD: Orton Dyslexia Society.

Chall, J.S. (1987b). Two vocabularies for reading: Recognition and meaning. In M.G. McKeown & M.E. Curtis (Eds.), *The nature of vocabulary acquisition* (pp. 7-17). Hillsdale, NJ: Erlbaum.

Chall, J.S., & Curtis, M.E. (1987). What clinical diagnosis tells us about children's reading. *The Reading Teacher, 40,* 784-788.

Chall, J.S., & Curtis, M.E. (1990). Diagnostic achievement testing in reading. In C.R. Reynolds & R.W. Kamphaus (Eds.), *Handbook of psychological and educational assessment of children* (pp. 535-551). New York: Guilford Press.

Chall, J.S., & Curtis, M.E. (1992). Teaching the disabled or below-average reader. In S.J. Samuels & A.E. Farstrup (Eds.), *What research has to say about reading instruction* (pp. 253-276). Newark, DE: IRA.

Cioffi, G., & Carney, J.J. (1983). Dynamic assessment of reading disabilities. *The Reading Teacher, 36,* 764-769.

Curtis, M.E. (1987). Vocabulary testing and vocabulary instruction. In M. McKeown & M.E. Curtis (Eds.), *The nature of vocabulary acquisition* (pp. 37-50). Hillsdale, NJ: Erlbaum.

Dale, E. (1965). Vocabulary measurement: Techniques and major findings. *Elementary English, 42,* 895-901; 948.

Davis, F.B. (1968). Research in comprehension in reading. *Reading Research Quarterly, 3,* 499-545.

Delclos, V.R., Burns, M.S., & Kulewicz, S.J. (1987). Effects of dynamic assessment on teachers' expectations of handicapped children. *American Educational Research Journal, 25,* 325-336.

Duffelmeyer, F.A., Robinson, S.S., & Squier, S.E. (1989). Vocabulary questions on informal reading inventories. *The Reading Teacher, 44,* 142-148.

Ferrara, R.A., Brown, A.L., & Campione, J.C. (1986). Children's learning and transfer of inductive reasoning rules: Studies of proximal development. *Child Development, 57,* 1087-1099.

Feuerstein, R. (1979). *The dynamic assessment of retarded performers: The learning potential assessment device, theory, instruments, and techniques.* Baltimore, MD: University Park Press.

Guthrie, J.T., Van Meter, P., & Mitchell, A. (1994). Performance assessments in reading and language arts. *The Reading Teacher, 48,* 266-274.

Harris, A.J., & Roswell, F. (1953). Clinical diagnosis of reading disability. *Journal of Psychology, 3,* 323-340.

Harris, A.J., & Sipay, E.R. (1990). *How to increase reading ability* (9th ed.). White Plains, NY: Longman.

Hiebert, E.H. (1991). Teacher-based assessment of literacy learning. In J. Flood, J.M. Jensen, D. Lapp, & J.R. Squire (Eds.), *Handbook of research on teaching the English language arts* (pp. 510-520). New York: Macmillan.

Hutson, B.A., & Niles, J.A. (1974). Trial teaching: The missing link. *Psychology in the Schools, 11,* 188-191.

Jitendra, A.K., & Kameenui, E.J. (1993). Dynamic assessment as a compensatory assessment approach: A description and analysis. *Remedial and Special Education, 14,* 6-18.

Kameenui, E.L., Dixon, D.W., & Carnine, R.C. (1987). Issues in the design of vocabulary instruction. In M. McKeown & M.E. Curtis (Eds.), *The nature of vocabulary acquisition* (pp. 129-145). Hillsdale, NJ: Erlbaum.

Kletzien, S.B., & Bednar, M.R. (1990). Dynamic assessment for at-risk readers. *Journal of Reading, 33,* 528-532.

Lidz, C.S. (1987). *Dynamic assessment: An interactional approach to evaluating learning potential.* New York: Guilford Press.

Longo, A.M. (1989). *Teaching reading to the below average IQ student (70-90 range).* Unpublished qualifying paper, Harvard Graduate School of Education, Cambridge, MA.

Longo, A.M. (1992). *The potential of trial lessons for determining the effectiveness of three approaches for teaching vocabulary to low average fifth graders.* Unpublished doctoral dissertation, Harvard Graduate School of Education, Cambridge, MA.

Longo, A.M. (1995). *Trial lessons in vocabulary: A dynamic assessment approach.* Paper presented at the International Reading Association Annual Convention, Anaheim, CA.

McKeown, M.G., & Curtis, M.E. (1987). *The nature of vocabulary acquisition.* Hillsdale, NJ: Erlbaum.

Miller, G.A., & Gildea, P.M. (1987). How children learn words. *Scientific American, 257,* 94-99.

Nagy, W.E., & Herman, P.A. (1987). Breadth and depth of vocabulary knowledge: Implications for acquisition and instruction. In M.G. McKeown & M.E. Curtis (Eds.), *The nature of vocabulary acquisition* (pp. 19-35). Hillsdale, NJ: Erlbaum.

Putnam, L.R. (1996). Factors affecting the choice of remedial methods. In L.R. Putnam (Ed.), *How to become a better reading teacher: Strategies for assessment and intervention* (pp. 85-98). Englewood Cliffs, NJ: Merrill.

Roswell, F., & Chall, J.S. (1992). *Diagnostic assessments of reading with trial teaching strategies (DARTTS).* Chicago: Riverside.

Roswell, F., & Chall, J.S. (1994). *Creating successful readers: A practical guide to testing and teaching at all levels.* Chicago: Riverside.

Roswell, F., & Natchez, G. (1989). *Reading disability: A human approach to evaluation and treatment of reading and writing difficulties.* New York: Basic Books.

Smagorinsky, P. (1995). The social construction of data: Methodological problems of investigating learning in the zone of proximal development. *Review of Educational Research, 3,* 191-212.

Stahl, S.A., & Fairbanks, M.M. (1986). The effects of vocabulary instruction: A model-based meta-analysis. *Review of Educational Research, 56,* 72-110.

Sternberg, R.B. (1987). Most vocabulary is learned from context. In M.G. McKeown & M.C. Curtis (Eds.), *The nature of vocabulary acquisition* (pp. 89-105). Hillsdale, NJ: Erlbaum.

Thorndike, R.L. (1974). Reading as reasoning. *Reading Research Quarterly, 9,* 137-147.

Vygotsky, L.S. (1978). *Mind in Society: The development of higher psychological processes.* (M. Cole, V. John-Steiner, S. Scribner, & E. Souberman, Eds. and Trans.). Cambridge, MA: Harvard University Press. (Original work published 1930.)

Wiggins, G. (1993). Assessment: Authenticity, context, and validity. *Phi Delta Kappan, 75,* 200-214.

Winograd, P. (1994). Developing alternative assessments: Six problems worth solving. *The Reading Teacher, 47,* 420-423.

Wolf, K. (1993). From informal to informed assessment: Recognizing the role of the classroom teacher. *Journal of Reading, 36,* 518-523.

Worthen, B. (1993). Critical issues that will determine the future of alternative assessment. *Phi Delta Kappan, 74,* 444-454.

Zemelman, S., Daniels, H., & Hyde, A. (1993). *Best practice: New standards for teaching and learning in America's schools.* Portsmouth, NH: Heinemann.

13

A Developmental Framework for the Assessment of Reading Disabilities

NANCY C. JORDAN, Ed.D.

College of Education, University of Delaware

Reading disabilities have fascinated researchers for over a century. As we approach the new millennium, professionals can draw upon an enormous research literature on why children cannot learn to read. Although it is now generally recognized that reading disabilities are associated with multiple underlying factors, different causal theories have predominated during various periods in history (Chall, 1994; Chall & Curtis, 1992). Earlier causal theories emphasized visual-per-ceptual-motor (e.g., Bender, 1957; Frostig & Maslow, 1973; Kephart, 1960; Orton, 1937) and social-emotional (e.g., Fernald, 1943) factors, whereas more recent ones have been concerned with linguistic (e.g., Vellutino, 1986) and neuropsychological (e.g., Semrud-Clikeman & Hynd, 1994) processes.

Over the years, causal theories have influenced how reading dis-abilities are assessed in schools and clinics (Chall, 1994). For example, instruments such as the Frostig Developmental Test of Visual Perception (Frostig, Leferver, & Whittlesey, 1964) and the Illinois Test of Psycholinguistic Abilities (Kirk, McCarthy, & Kirk, 1968) were commonly used to diagnose reading disabilities in the 1960s and 1970s, when sensory-modality theory (i.e., the theory that children can be classified as auditory or visual learners) was in fashion. Based on the findings, treatment programs were developed and prescribed to overcome the underlying deficits (e.g., problems in visual perception). In many cases, however, the remediation did not involve the printed word and as a result was largely ineffective; for example, children became very proficient at completing abstract visual-perceptual exercises but made few gains in reading achievement (Johnson, 1978). Not surprisingly, treatment programs based on actual reading skills, rather than those based on presumed psychological causes, have proven to be most effective for teaching children with reading disabilities (Chall & Curtis, 1992).

Although the etiologies of reading disabilities are intellectually interesting, their educational utility is limited if they are not identified in relation to the components of reading. However, many evaluations of reading disabilities (for clinical or research purposes) still reflect a search for underlying psychological factors while providing minimal analyses of reading-related behaviors. In some cases, educational assessments are guided by the particular tests that are used and the scores that are obtained from these tests, rather than by an understanding of the reading process. As a result, the linkages between test findings and instructional practices may be tenuous. The aim of this chapter is to provide a framework for assessment of reading disabilities based on an understanding of reading skills at different points in development. Such an approach has the advantage not only of being instructionally meaningful, but also of providing a window through which to view more basic psychological processes (e.g., an analysis of reading skills may uncover deficits in language, cognition, and so forth). I begin by examining the development of "normal" reading skills from early childhood — before formal instruction — through secondary school and college. I then use the developmental model as a basis for examining different types of reading difficulties, namely, those associated with decoding and comprehension. I go on to outline a skill-oriented framework for assessing reading disabilities and then use the framework to analyze some published diagnostic reading tests commonly used in research and school settings.

The Development of Reading Skills

Over the years, researchers and educators have identified different stages of reading development (e.g., Bush & Huebner, 1970; Doehring & Aulls, 1979; Evans, Evans, & Mercer, 1986; Juel, 1994). A developmental model proposed by Chall (1983) provides a particularly useful guide for assessing and diagnosing reading disabilities and is summarized here. The model views reading as a continuous process and illustrates how reading requirements change from beginning to mature reading. It should be noted that there may be overlap between the various stages identified and that individual variation is likely to occur at a given level.

Prereading

In her autobiography, *One Writer's Beginnings* (1983), Eudora Welty eloquently describes her experience with letters and words during early childhood:

> I live in gratitude to my parents for initiating me — and as early as I begged for it, without keeping me waiting — into knowledge of the word, into reading and spelling, by way of the alphabet .... My love for the alphabet, which endures, grew out of reciting it but, before that, out of seeing the letters on the page. In my own story books, before I could read them for myself, I fell in love with various winding, enchanted-looking initials drawn by Walter Crane at the heads of fairy tales. (pp. 9-10)

The *prereading stage* typically covers the years from birth to the beginning of formal reading instruction in first grade. During this period, children acquire general knowledge about letters, words, and books. Most importantly, they develop awareness of the sound structure of oral language — for example, that the beginnings and endings of some words sound the same, that some words rhyme, that words can be broken into parts, and that sounds can be blended together to form words. They also learn to recognize and name the letters of the alphabet, to write letters from dictation, and to recognize common words such as those found on street or restaurant signs. Many young children develop an interest in books and can pretend that they are reading. That is, they know to hold the book right side up, to turn the pages one at a time, and to point to pictures illustrating words and ideas. These skills often develop naturally when there are books in the home and when children observe their parents or siblings reading. Many of the early literacy abilities acquired during the prereading stage are predictive of later reading achievement (Adams, 1990; Torgeson, 1993).

Initial reading or decoding

The *decoding stage* covers the period of beginning reading instruction in school, usually occurring between the first and second grades. Children acquire word analysis skills, or in other words, the ability to associate written symbols with their corresponding sounds. They learn the alphabetic principle, develop an awareness of the purpose of letters, and become increasingly sensitive to phonological differences in words (e.g., that *cat* is not *can* or that *pin* is not *pen*). Some children develop these skills on their own, while others — especially those at risk for reading disabilities — may need more explicit instruction in phonics. Children also grow in their ability to recognize high-frequency words by sight (e.g., *the, them, that, here,* etc.). Most children at this stage are more proficient at reading aloud than they are at reading silently. It should be noted that the skills children have mastered by the end of the stage may be influenced by the type of instruction that is provided in the first and second grades. For example, children taught by a phonetic approach may have a better grasp of sound-symbol correspondences than those taught by a whole-language approach that emphasizes recognition of whole words and sentences.

Confirmation and fluency

The *confirmation and fluency stage* typically covers the second and third grades. During this period, children solidify basic decoding skills, and their reading confirms what they already know. Children gain skill in using context to identify words, as well as in applying more complex phonic rules and principles. Sight vocabulary skills become more automatic. As decoding skills are internalized, reading becomes increasingly fluent. Such fluency, in turn, allows the child to expend more cognitive energy on comprehension, which becomes more important in subsequent stages. Word-by-word reading, commonly encountered in the first and second grades, becomes indicative of reading problems if it persists to the end of third grade. By this time, most children should be able to read familiar materials smoothly, with little or no conscious effort.

Reading to learn

The *reading to learn stage* roughly covers the middle and junior high school years, grades 4 through 8. As fundamental decoding skills are mastered and automatized, reading to learn begins to take precedence over learning to read. Comprehension, vocabulary, and silent-reading skills increase dramatically during this period. Students learn to read proficiently in the content areas (e.g., science or social studies), acquiring new information and experiences from textbooks. Early in this stage, listening comprehension generally exceeds reading comprehension. By the end of the reading to learn stage, however, students can understand written language as effectively as they can understand oral language. In subsequent stages, reading comprehension usually surpasses listening comprehension (Sticht, Beck, Hauke, Kleiman, & James, 1974).

Multiple points of view

The *multiple points of view stage* usually develops during the high school years. Students acquire a flexible range of reading comprehension skills. The skills, facts, and concepts acquired in previous stages provide the basis for this stage of reading. Through formal education, students learn to work with multiple sources of print; they compare and contrast diverse points of view and identify recurring themes. They develop evaluative and critical reading skills. By the end of the twelfth grade, students are able to read analytically from a wide range of fiction and nonfiction materials.

Construction and reconstruction

The *construction and reconstruction stage* represents advanced reading and covers the college years and beyond. Reading at this stage is constructive in that readers construct knowledge for themselves and create their own "truths." It depends on higher-order thinking skills, such as the abilities to reason abstractly, to use analogies, to analyze and synthesize, and to make judgments (e.g., about what to read and in how much detail). Past knowledge about a subject and broad general knowledge provide the foundations for effective reading during the college years.

Reading Skill Difficulties

Reading problems can occur at any point along the developmental continuum described by Chall (1983). Some students have specific difficulties with decoding, while others show weaknesses only with comprehension. Still others have trouble with both decoding and comprehension. In this section, I discuss why a student might fail — or at least stumble — at different stages of development. For ease of presentation, I have collapsed the aforementioned reading stages into two general categories: (1) decoding and (2) comprehension. Decoding includes the initial reading and confirmation/fluency stages; comprehension includes the stages of reading to learn, multiple viewpoints, and construction/reconstruction.

Difficulties in decoding

When children encounter reading difficulties in the primary grades, it is usually because they are struggling with one or more aspects of decoding. Children with circumscribed and unexpected problems with word recognition and word analysis are often referred to as dyslexic. Many educators and most lay people assume that children with decoding problems cannot distinguish and orient the appearance of letters (e.g., knowing that *b* looks different from *d*). However, research suggests that the majority of children with decoding problems do not have deficiencies in visual-spatial processing (e.g., Vellutino, 1979, 1986).

The association between decoding problems and deficiencies in reading-related phonological skills has been intensely researched (e.g., Goswami & Bryant, 1990; Liberman & Shankweiler, 1986; Mann, 1994; Perfetti, 1986; Wagner, Torgeson, & Rashotte, 1994). Poor decoders often have difficulty transforming written symbols into phonological codes (e.g., remembering how the letters *b* and *d* are pronounced), segmenting words into their constituent phonemes (e.g., segmenting *pan* into three phonological segments), and blending sounds to make words (e.g., blending *b-i-n* into *bin*). Children without decoding problems often acquire these skills naturally in the prereading stage by "playing" with sounds (e.g., speaking in "Pig Latin"). Although it has been reported that explicit instruction in phonological skills leads directly to improvements in word decoding (Bradley & Bryant, 1983; Goswami & Bryant, 1990; Torgeson, Wagner, & Rashotte, 1994), the most effective interventions integrate the teaching of phonological skills with the teaching of reading (Hatcher, Hulme, & Ellis, 1994).

Phonological deficiencies also affect reading skills at the fluency and confirmation stage. With direct instruction and specialized tutoring, many children with reading disabilities master a variety of phonic patterns in isolation and move beyond the decoding stage. However, they may have residual deficits in applying and coordinating these subskills when reading meaningful, connected text. Poorly automatized word analysis and sight-word recognition skills result in slow and laborious oral reading. If students spend too much time sounding out individual words, they may not attend to the meaning of a passage (Gough & Tumner, 1986). Weaknesses in fluency and automaticity may impede reading at later stages of development. Research has shown that slow and inefficient decoding skills are strongly associated with comprehension weaknesses during the middle-school years (Curtis, 1980).

Difficulties in comprehension

Reading problems identified in middle elementary school and beyond are usually associated with comprehension difficulties. Some children perform relatively well in reading until they reach the fourth grade, when higher-order cognition and language become more important to reading development. A variety of factors can limit a student's reading comprehension. As noted above, some comprehension problems are secondary to problems in decoding or fluency. However, other comprehension problems reflect primary weaknesses with language and cognition. For example, there may be fundamental deficiencies in higher-order language processing, an inadequate prior knowledge base, and/or weak metacognitive skills. Primary comprehension problems may or may not co-exist with decoding weaknesses.

Deficiencies in higher-order language processing. As readers at the middle-school level master basic decoding skills and begin to read in the content areas, higher-order language skills become increasingly important for effective text comprehension. Students with reading-comprehension problems have been found to have concomitant weaknesses in listening comprehension (e.g., Curtis, 1980; Smiley, Oakley, Worthen, Campione, & Brown, 1977). Many of these weaknesses are related to deficiencies in general linguistic skills, such the ability to understand complex grammatical structures and knowledge of syntactic rules (e.g., Flood & Menyuk, 1983). Restrictions in range of word knowledge, or vocabulary, also contribute to text-comprehension problems, especially when students are confronted with highly specialized materials (e.g., Harris & Sipay, 1990; Roswell & Natchez, 1989). Furthermore, basic problems in verbal working memory compromise comprehension (Daneman & Carpenter, 1980; Levine, 1994; Perfetti, 1985); for example, some students lose the meaning of a text because they cannot remember the earlier portion while they are reading later sections. In addition, verbal memory problems might affect students' abilities to paraphrase or to restate a passage in their own words.

Inadequate prior knowledge. Some students with comprehension difficulties lack prior knowledge of a topic or they are unable to relate the knowledge they have during reading (Torgeson, 1985; Levine, 1994). If a student has interest in and knowledge of a topic, he or she is likely to display better comprehension of a reading selection on this topic than of a reading selection on a less familiar or less interesting topic. Thus, reading comprehension problems may be specific to a particular content area. Students with long-standing reading problems may have especially weak knowledge bases, since much conventional knowledge about the world is acquired through books. Inadequate prior knowledge makes it difficult for students to advance to higher levels of reading (e.g., reading to construct one's own knowledge).

Weaknesses in metacognition. The term *metacognition* refers to the ability to reflect on one's own thinking and to manage one's learning actions (Wixson & Lipson, 1991). Effective application of metacognitive strategies allows students to direct and organize their thinking on academic tasks (Paris, Wasik, & Van der Westhuizen, 1988). Metacognitive skills are especially important for comprehending large amounts of materials presented in content-area textbooks. Numerous studies have reported a positive relationship between levels of metacognitive ability and reading comprehension skill (e.g., Baker & Anderson, 1982; Erickson, Stahl, & Rinehart, 1985; Palincsar & Brown, 1984; Paris & Myers, 1981).

Poor comprehenders show deficiencies on a variety of metacognitive tasks. Some do not understand the purpose of reading (Baker, 1979). They perceive decoding as the primary goal of reading and do not realize that it takes effort to derive meaning from books. This attitude is especially common among children who are still struggling with the decoding and fluency stages of reading. Other students have difficulty adjusting reading strategies for different purposes (Forrest-Pressley & Walker, 1984). For example, they are not aware that sometimes it is important to read very quickly for main ideas while at other times it is important to read carefully for fine details. They approach narrative materials in much the same manner as they approach content-area texts. According to Levine (1994), these students "have trouble shifting into the right reading 'gear' at the right time" (p. 167). Comprehension monitoring is another area of difficulty (August, Flavell, & Clift, 1984; Palincsar & Brown, 1984). Some poor readers have trouble deciding how well the reading material has been understood and dealing with failures to understand. They are unable to judge when a reading selection has been studied sufficiently to take a test or they do not know what do when they have not understood a selection.

A number of intervention studies have documented the effectiveness of metacognitive strategy training within the context of reading comprehension instruction (e.g., Palinscar & Brown, 1984). However, the literature suggests that the development of metacognitive skills takes place over extended periods of time and that deficiencies in this area require intensive, long-term interventions (Derry & Murphy, 1986).

Framework for Assessing Reading Skills

As noted previously, reading involves multiple components. These components include prereading, word analysis, word recognition, oral reading, word comprehension, and passage comprehension. The relative importance of each of these components may vary according to the age or grade level of the student (Roswell & Chall, 1994). Thus, a comprehensive reading assessment should consider both the components of reading and the age or grade of the student.

Prereading

Standard measures of prereading (or readiness) skills examine a child's ability to discriminate between letters (visual discrimination) and sounds (auditory discrimination) and to recognize and identify letters. However, measures of phonological awareness should also be included in test batteries used to identify children at risk for reading problems in the prereading and initial reading stages (Torgeson, Wagner, Bryant, & Pearson, 1992). The development of phonological awareness before formal instruction portends a child's success with beginning reading in the early elementary grades (Stanovich, Cunningham, & Cramer, 1984; Torgeson et al., 1994). Moreover, it has recently been found that phonological awareness ability as assessed in kindergarten predicts word recognition skills as far ahead as 11 years later (MacDonald & Cornwall, 1995).

Mann (1993, 1994) recently developed a series of phonological awareness tasks for young children that are successful in predicting reading achievement in the early elementary grades. It has been found that such tasks are more accurate predictors of future reading ability than are IQ tests, tests of visual perception, and tests of nonverbal memory. One task, which assesses phonemic-segmentation abilities, requires children to indicate which of four pictures begins with a different sound than the others. (Children could also be asked to identify different sounds at the end or in the middle of words.) Another task requires children to reverse the phonemes in a word (e.g., "How do you say *mo* backwards?"). On a third task, children are asked to "invent" spellings for words they have not been taught through formal instruction. Inventing spelling requires both phonological awareness and knowledge of letter–sound correspondences. Children who produce the most phonetically accurate spellings in kindergarten experience the greatest success with first-grade reading. Phoneme deletion tasks (e.g., Rosner, 1979), in which the child is asked to omit a phoneme from an initial, final, or medial position when repeating a word just heard, also measure phonological awareness and are predictive of later reading achievement (Badian, 1996; MacDonald & Cornwall, 1995).

Word analysis

Word analysis tests are most relevant to the early stages of reading and provide important information about the skills of primary-school children. They also can shed light on the skills of older students with persistent decoding weaknesses. Word analysis tests measure students' knowledge of sound–symbol correspondences (the essential feature of the initial reading stage). They should assess the ability to decode single consonants and vowels, consonant blends, and consonant and vowel digraphs. These patterns may be presented in isolation or in real or nonsense words. Performance on a spelling test also provides information on students' word-analysis abilities. For example, phonetically inaccurate spellings (e.g., "bat" for *bit*) may reflect poorly established sound–symbol correspondences. In later primary school, the ability to read (and spell) polysyllabic words containing prefixes and suffixes should be evaluated.

Word recognition

Tests of word recognition measure a student's ability to read words aloud. The words are presented in isolation, usually progressing from easy to more difficult. Some students can read the words automatically, by sight, while others depend on word-analysis strategies to decode even the simplest sight words. Thus, when assessing word recognition, it is important to observe for rate of recognition as well as for decoding accuracy. Word recognition skills should be examined at higher as well as lower reading levels to rule out the possibility that comprehension problems stem from weaknesses in this area.

Oral reading

Tests of oral reading measure the ability to read connected text aloud. Students read graded selections from books. Both quantitative information (i.e., level of accuracy and reading rate) and qualitative information (i.e., expression and overall fluency) should be obtained. Oral reading tests also make it possible to examine students' use of contextual clues to aid decoding and to correct mistakes. Some children over-rely on contextual clues to compensate for their word-analysis or word-recognition difficulties (Goldsmith-Phillips, 1989; Pressley & Rankin, 1994). A comparison can be made of the ability to decode words in isolation and the ability to decode words in connected text. Performance on word-recognition tests indicates whether students possess basic decoding skills, but performance on oral reading tests shows whether they can apply and coordinate decoding skills in a meaningful context.

Word comprehension

Tests of word comprehension, or vocabulary, become increasingly important at later stages of reading development. Vocabulary skills are affected by background knowledge, overall language skills, and prior experience with books. As students approach adolescence, poor knowledge of word meanings becomes a greater reading obstacle than poor ability to decode words (Chall, 1987). Students' abilities to recognize or retrieve the definitions of words, as well as their abilities to use a passage's context to derive word meanings, should be examined. In addition to assessing general word comprehension, it is important to evaluate knowledge of specialized vocabulary in the content areas (e.g., algebra, biology, etc.). Tests of oral vocabulary are preferable to tests of reading vocabulary because the latter make it difficult to distinguish problems due to a weak knowledge of word meanings from those due to poor decoding. According to Roswell and Chall (1994), performance on oral vocabulary tests provides a reliable and efficient estimate of the student's ability to function at or above grade level in reading-related areas.

Passage comprehension

Although passage comprehension is important at all stages of reading, it deserves special attention beginning in the third or fourth grade. In the early elementary grades, students generally read narrative materials with familiar story structures. Comprehension is assessed through both oral and silent reading activities. In the middle-school years, however, children begin to read for facts and increasingly abstract concepts in science, social studies, and so forth. Silent reading should be the mode of assessment during this period. Students should read and react to authentic written materials (drawn from literature, textbooks, newspapers, etc.) of increasing lengths and levels of difficulty (Roswell & Chall, 1994).

Different methods may be used to assess passage comprehension. Multiple-choice tests require students to recognize the correct answer to a question about the passage. Short-answer tests with open-ended questions, on the other hand, require students to retrieve information. Another method of assessing comprehension of a passage is the cloze procedure, in which the student must supply a missing word from a sentence or a short passage. Tests using a cloze procedure require the ability to use semantic and syntactic clues as well as word retrieval skills. It is possible for a student to perform differently on multiple-choice, short-answer, and cloze tests.

Text summarization is a less structured method that also should be used for assessing passage comprehension. Text summarization tasks require students to store, retrieve, and organize what they have read, either orally or in writing. It is an important skill for studying, learning, and taking tests in content areas.

Different types of passage comprehension should be considered in an assessment. Literal comprehension (e.g., reading for factual details and main ideas) is stressed in the early elementary grades; more abstract skills (e.g., drawing inferences and formulating principles based on the reading material) are emphasized in later stages. In addition, an assessment should evaluate students' application of metacognitive strategies, especially during the junior and senior high school period. Metacognitive strategies can be assessed by direct observation, by interviewing the student, or by interviewing classroom teachers. Information might be obtained regarding whether students can identify the purpose of a reading assignment, whether they can distinguish essential information from nonessential information, whether they can monitor their own understanding, and so forth.

Finally, it is often useful to measure students' listening comprehension abilities, in addition to their silent reading comprehension skills. By comparing listening and reading performance, an assessment can determine whether reading comprehension problems are due to general weaknesses in language and cognition or whether they stem from weaknesses in decoding (Stanovich, 1990).

Assessment Tools

In this section, I use the developmental framework for reading assessment to analyze three standardized, individually administered test batteries that are commonly used to diagnose reading disabilities in educational and research settings. The tests are the Woodcock Reading Mastery Tests (WRMT; Woodcock, 1987), the Kaufman Tests of Educational Achievement (KTEA; Kaufman & Kaufman, 1985), and the

Wechsler Individual Achievement Test (WIAT; Psychological Corporation, 1992). The norms of each test cover a wide age range, from kindergarten or first grade through high school or adulthood. A summary of the analysis is presented in Table 13-1 (p. 250).

Woodcock Reading Mastery Tests

The WRMT uses a battery of tests to measure reading ability (kindergarten through adulthood). Prereading skills are measured by means of a letter identification test and a visual-auditory learning test. In the visual-auditory learning test, children learn a vocabulary of unfamiliar symbols (or rebuses) that represent words. They are then asked to use the rebuses to form sentences. Data pertaining to the predictive validity of the prereading tests are not presented in the WRMT manual. Thus, it is not clear whether visual-auditory learning is predictive of reading achievement. Measures of phonological awareness are not included in the WRMT battery. However, the authors refer the tester to the Goldman-Fristoe-Woodcock Auditory Skills Test Battery (Goldman, Fristoe, & Woodcock, 1974) and the Woodcock-Johnson Psycho-Educational Battery (Woodcock & Johnson, 1989) to complete a diagnostic reading readiness profile. These batteries include several tests of phonological skills, including tests of sound blending, sound analysis (phoneme isolation), and sound-symbol association.

In terms of decoding, the WRMT includes a test of word analysis and a test of word recognition. The word analysis test involves nonsense words (e.g., *bim, raff, poe*) and real words with low frequency in the English language. Directions are given for analyzing errors on different phonic patterns (e.g., vowel and consonant patterns). The word recognition test requires the student to identify isolated words of varying levels of difficulty. Both the word analysis and the word recognition tests are untimed (although students are encouraged to give responses after five seconds). The WRMT does not include a test of oral reading of connected text.

For comprehension, the WRMT includes a test of word compre-

Table 13-1: Analysis of Standardized Reading Tests

Test	Reading Components					
	Prereading	Word Analysis	Word Recognition	Oral Reading (connected text)	Word Comprehension	Passage Comprehension
WRMT (1987)	Letter identification and visual-auditory learning tests.	Word analysis test; system for analyzing errors.	Word recognition test.	None.	Reading vocabulary test; system for analyzing errors in 4 content areas.	Reading comprehension test (cloze procedure); no system for analyzing errors.
KTEA (1985)	Some letter identification items on word recognition test.	Word recognition and spelling tests; system for analyzing word analysis errors.	Word recognition test.	None.	None.	Reading comprehension test (students read short passages & answer questions); system for analyzing errors in literal vs. inferential comprehension.
WIAT (1992)	Some sound/symbol association items on word recognition test.	Word recognition and spelling tests; no system for analyzing word analysis errors.	Word recognition test.	None.	Some oral vocabulary items on the listening comprehension test.	Reading comprehension test (students read short passages & answer questions); no system for analyzing errors; listening comprehension test.

hension and a test of passage comprehension. The test of word comprehension measures reading vocabulary (as opposed to oral vocabulary). It measures the student's ability to retrieve synonyms and antonyms to stimulus words and to complete verbal analogies (e.g., "clock: time :: compass: direction"). Directions are given for evaluating word comprehension skill across four areas: general, science-math, social studies, and the humanities. The passage comprehension test is a general measure that uses a cloze procedure (e.g., "The animals are so well camouflaged by nature that it is almost impossible to spot them. It takes the trained _____ of the driver-guides to bring them into focus."). Passages are usually two to three sentences in length and are read silently. The passage comprehension test is untimed (although the student is encouraged to give a response after 30 seconds have elapsed). Thus, it is possible for a student who reads relatively slowly (but accurately) to receive the same test score as one who reads very quickly. The WRMT does not measure text summarization skills at any level, and different types of comprehension (e.g., literal vs. inferential) are not differentiated. Moreover, it does not provide structured opportunities to measure metacognitive strategies.

In sum, the WRMT is a comprehensive battery that can give a fairly good picture of performance along the reading dimensions outlined in this chapter. However, supplemental measures of reading-related phonological skills and oral reading of connected text should be used for younger students and for older students with disabilities. For older students, it is important to supplement the comprehension measures with tests that require comprehension of longer text segments (in various content areas) and that require them to summarize what they have read. Such measures provide better approximations of what students are required to do in junior and senior high school. Supplemental tests of oral vocabulary and listening comprehension would provide estimates of a student's overall verbal abilities and could help to uncover primary comprehension problems.

Kaufman Test of Educational Achievement

The KTEA is a measure of school achievement (grades 1 through 12) and includes two tests of reading ability: reading decoding and reading comprehension. The battery also includes a spelling test, which measures reading-related skills. Because the test norms begin at the first grade, prereading skills are not explicitly assessed. However, on the reading decoding test, several of the early items involve letter identification. The remaining items on the reading decoding test measure the ability to pronounce real words in isolation (untimed). A system for analyzing errors associated with word attack (e.g., vowel and consonant patterns) and whole-word recognition is provided. In addition, word analysis skills can be assessed on the spelling test, which also provides a system for analyzing errors. Oral reading of connected text is not assessed on the KTEA.

On the reading comprehension test, students read paragraphs of varying lengths, then read one or more questions about the paragraphs, and give an answer to these questions. The passages can be read either silently or aloud. The student can refer back to the passages after reading the questions, thus reducing the memory demands of the test. The test is untimed. Some of the questions require students to respond with short answers (retrieval) while others use a multiple-choice format (recognition). Items are classified according to whether they measure literal or inferential comprehension, which facilitates error analyses along these dimensions. Most of the higher-level passages involve content-area subject matter. Specific measures of word comprehension are not included on the KTEA.

In sum, the KTEA provides a general measure of reading skill in decoding and passage comprehension. The systems for analyzing errors on each of the tests appear to be very useful. However, the battery alone may have limited educational usefulness for younger children with reading disabilities (i.e., beginning first graders) and should be supplemented with measures of prereading skills. At higher levels, supplemental measures of word comprehension, reading speed, text summarization, and metacognitive strategies would provide a more detailed picture of comprehension skills and might lead to more direct implications for remediation. It seems possible that some students might perform relatively well on the KTEA reading comprehension test in spite of weak performance in junior or senior high school, where memory, speed of processing and retrieval, and integration of several pieces of text are important factors.

Wechsler Individual Achievement Test

The WIAT, another measure of school achievement (kindergarten through grade 12), includes tests of basic reading skills and reading comprehension. Reading-related skills are measured on a spelling test and a test of listening comprehension. Prereading skills (i.e., sound–symbol associations) are assessed briefly with the early items of the basic reading test. The remainder of the test measures the ability to pronounce real words (word recognition). Unlike the WRMT and the KTEA, the WIAT includes no specific provisions for analyzing word analysis skills, although this can be done informally on the basic reading test and on the spelling test. Like the WRMT and the KTEA, the WIAT does not measure automaticity or oral reading fluency.

In terms of comprehension, the WIAT measures both reading comprehension and listening comprehension. On the reading comprehension test, the student reads a short passage (either orally or silently), listens to a question about it, and then responds to the question. The student is required to retrieve answers orally (rather than recognize them in a multiple-choice format) but can refer back to the text to determine an answer. The reading comprehension test is untimed, but the examiner is instructed to allow the student about 15 seconds to respond to the oral questions. The questions tap both literal and inferential comprehension. However, the items are not classified according to these dimensions and there is no system for error analysis. Most of the higher-level passages involve content-area subject matter.

The listening comprehension test measures students' abilities to understand oral language more generally. Early items focus on the ability to identify pictures that correspond with spoken words (word comprehension), and later items focus on comprehension of orally presented passages (passage comprehension). The listening comprehension test involves a greater memory component than does the reading comprehension test, since students hear the passage only once and have no text to refer to after the question has been asked.

In sum, the WIAT provides a general measure of students' decoding and reading comprehension skills. The concerns raised about the KTEA also apply to the WIAT (e.g., limited measurement of prereading skills, no measurement of oral reading fluency and reading speed, limited measurement of reading comprehension). The listening comprehension test is a unique feature of the battery and allows the examiner to estimate a student's general language abilities. This measure could be used in conjunction with other test batteries, such as the WRMT. Performance in listening comprehension helps to differentiate problems specific to reading from those associated with primary weaknesses in language and cognition.

Conclusion

Reading involves multiple components. The relative importance of each of these components varies according to a student's age and developmental level. An assessment of reading disabilities should consider all of the components of reading while reflecting the change in skill demands from beginning to mature reading. Standardized test batteries that are designed to diagnose reading disabilities in clinical and research settings may need to be supported by developmentally appropriate measures of reading or reading-related skills. In the words of Roswell and Chall (1994):

> The value of assessing reading and related language components is
> that it helps those who teach to know where students are on the

continuum of reading development, what they have already learned, and what they still need to learn to make continued progress. An added benefit is that it can help teachers understand what it means to learn to read — for students who are having difficulty as well as for those who are making expected progress. (p. 28)

References

Adams, M.J. (1990). *Beginning to read: Thinking and learning about print.* Cambridge, MA: MIT Press.

August, D.L., Flavell, J.H., & Clift, R. (1984). Comparison of comprehension monitoring of skilled and less-skilled readers. *Reading Research Quarterly, 20,* 39-53.

Badian, N.A. (1996). Dyslexia: A validation of the concept at two age levels. *Journal of Learning Disabilities, 29*(1), 102-112.

Baker, L. (1979). Comprehension monitoring: Identifying and coping with text confusions. *Journal of Reading Behavior, 4,* 365-374.

Baker, L., & Anderson, R.I. (1982). Effects of inconsistent information on text processing: Evidence for comprehension monitoring. *Reading Research Quarterly, 17,* 281-300.

Bender, L.A. (1957). Specific reading disability as a maturational lag. *Bulletin of the Orton Society, 7,* 9-18.

Bradley, L., & Bryant, P.E. (1983). Categorizing sounds and learning to read: A causal connection. *Nature, 301,* 419-421.

Bush, C.L., & Huebner, M.H. (1970). *Strategies for reading in the elementary school.* New York: Macmillan.

Chall, J.S. (1983). *Stages of reading development.* New York: McGraw-Hill.

Chall, J.S. (1987). Two vocabularies for reading: Recognition and meaning. In M.G. McKeown & M.E. Curtis (Eds.), *The nature of vocabulary acquisition.* Hillsdale, NJ: Erlbaum.

Chall, J.S. (1994). Testing linked with teaching. In N.C. Jordan & J. Goldsmith-Phillips (Eds.), *Learning disabilities: New directions for assessment and intervention* (pp. 163-176). Boston: Allyn & Bacon.

Chall, J.S., & Curtis, M.E. (1992). Teaching the disabled or below average reader. In J. Samuels & A.E. Farstrup (Eds.), *What research has to say about reading instruction* (2nd ed., pp. 253-296). Newark, DE: International Reading Association.

Curtis, M.E. (1980). Developmental components of reading skill. *Journal of Educational Psychology, 72,* 656-669.

Daneman, M., & Carpenter, P.A. (1980). Individual differences in working memory and reading. *Journal of Verbal Learning and Verbal Behavior, 19,* 450-456.

Derry, S.J., & Murphy, D.A. (1986). Designing systems that train learning ability: From theory to practice. *Review of Educational Research, 56,* 1-39.

Doehring, B.G., & Aulls, M.W. (1979). The interactive nature of reading acquisition. *Journal of Reading Behavior, 11,* 27-40.

Erickson, L.G., Stahl, S.A., & Rinehart, S.D. (1985). Metacognitive abilities of above average and below average readers: Effects of conceptual tempo, passage level, and error type on error detection. *Journal of Reading Behavior, 17,* 235-252.

Evans, S.S., Evans, S.S., & Mercer, C.D. (1986). *Assessment for instruction.* Boston: Allyn & Bacon.

Fernald, G. (1943). *Remedial techniques in basic school subjects.* New York: McGraw-Hill.

Flood, J., & Menyuk, P. (1983). The development of metalinguistic awareness and its relation to reading achievement. *Journal of Applied Developmental Psychology, 4,* 65-80.

Forrest-Pressley, D.L., & Walker, T.G. (1984). *Metacognition, cognition, and reading.* New York: Springer-Verlag.

Frostig, M., Leferver, D., & Whittlesey, J. (1964). *The Marianne Frostig developmental test of visual perception.* Palo Alto, CA: Consulting Psychologists Press.

Frostig, M., & Maslow, P. (1973). *Learning problems in the classroom: Prevention and remediation.* New York: Grune & Stratton.

Goldman, R., Fristoe, M., & Woodcock, R. (1974). *Goldman-Fristoe-Woodcock auditory skills test battery.* Circle Pines, MN: American Guidance Service.

Goldsmith-Phillips, J. (1989). Word and context in reading development: A test of the interactive compensatory hypothesis. *Journal of Educational Psychology, 81,* 299-305.

Goswami, U.C., & Bryant, P.E. (1990). *Phonological skills and learning to read.* Hillsdale, NJ: Erlbaum.

Gough, P.B., & Tumner, W.E. (1986). Decoding, reading, and reading disability. *Remedial and Special Education, 7,* 6-10.

Harris, A.J., & Sipay, E.R. (1990). *How to increase reading ability: A guide to developmental and remedial methods.* New York: Longman.

Hatcher, P.J., Hulme, C.H., & Ellis, A.W. (1994). Ameliorating early reading failure by integrating the teaching of reading and phonological skills: The phonological linkage hypothesis. *Child Development, 65,* 41-57.

Johnson, D.J. (1978). Remedial approaches to dyslexia. In A.L. Benton & D. Pearl (Eds.), *Dyslexia: An appraisal of current knowledge* (pp. 397-421). New York: Oxford University Press.

Juel, C. (1994). Teaching phonics in the context of integrated language arts. In L.M. Morrow, J.K. Smith, & L.C. Wilkinson (Eds.), *Integrated language arts: Controversy to consensus* (pp. 133-154). Boston: Allyn & Bacon.

Kaufman, A., & Kaufman, N. (1985). *Kaufman test of educational achievement.* Circle Pines, MN: American Guidance Service.

Kephart, N. (1960). *The slow learner in the classroom.* Columbus, OH: Charles E. Merrill.

Kirk, S., McCarthy, J., & Kirk, W. (1968). *The Illinois test of psycholinguistic abilities.* Urbana, IL: University of Illinois Press.

Levine, M.D. (1994). *Educational care.* Cambridge, MA: Educators Publishing Service.

Liberman, I.Y., & Shankweiler, D. (1986). Phonology and the problems of learning to read and write. *Remedial and Special Education, 6,* 8-17.

MacDonald, G.W., & Cornwall, A. (1995). The relationship between phonological awareness and reading and spelling achievement eleven years later. *Journal of Learning Disabilities, 28*(8), 523-527.

Mann, V.A. (1993). Phoneme awareness and future reading ability. *Journal of Learning Disabilities, 25,* 259-269.

Mann, V.A. (1994). Phonological skills and the prediction of early reading problems. In N.C. Jordan & J. Goldsmith-Phillips (Eds.), *Learning disabilities: New directions for assessment and intervention* (pp. 67-84). Boston: Allyn & Bacon.

Orton, S.T. (1937). *Reading, writing, and speech problems in children.* New York: Norton.

Palincsar, A.S., & Brown, A.L. (1984). Reciprocal teaching of comprehension fostering and comprehension monitoring activities. *Cognition and Instruction, 1,* 117-175.

Paris, S.G., & Myers, M. (1981). Comprehension monitoring, memory, and study strategies of good and poor readers. *Journal of Reading Behavior, 13,* 5-22.

Paris, S.G., Wasik, B.A., & Van der Westhuizen, G. (1988). Meta-metacognition: A review of research on metacognition and reading. In J.E. Readance & R.S. Baldwin (Eds.), *Dialogues in literacy research: 37th Yearbook of the National Reading Conference* (pp. 143-166). Chicago, IL: National Reading Conference.

Perfetti, C.A. (1985). *Reading ability.* New York: Oxford University Press.

Perfetti, C.A. (1986). Continuities in reading acquisition, reading skill, and reading disability. *Remedial and Special Education, 7,* 11-21.

Pressley, M., & Rankin, J. (1994). More about whole language methods of reading instruction for students at risk for early reading failure. *Learning Disabilities Research and Practice, 9*(3), 157-168.

Psychological Corporation. (1992). *Wechsler individual achievement test.* San Antonio, TX: Harcourt Brace Jovanovich.

Rosner, J. (1979). *Helping children overcome learning disabilities.* New York: Walker.

Roswell, F.G., & Chall, J.S. (1994). *Creating successful readers: A practical guide to testing and teaching at all levels.* Chicago, IL: Riverside.

Roswell, F.G., & Natchez, G. (1989). *Reading disability: A human approach to evaluation and treatment of reading and writing difficulties.* New York: Basic Books.

Semrud-Clikeman & Hynd, G.W. (1994). Brain-behavior relationships in dyslexia. In N.C. Jordan & J. Goldsmith-Phillips (Eds.), *Learning disabilities: New directions for assessment and intervention* (pp. 43-65). Boston: Allyn & Bacon.

Smiley, S., Oakley, D., Worthen, D., Campione, J.C., & Brown, A.L. (1977). Recall of thematically relevant material by adolescent good and poor readers as a function of written versus oral presentation. *Journal of Educational Psychology, 69,* 381-387.

Stanovich, K.E. (1990). Explaining the differences between dyslexic and garden-variety poor readers: The phonological-core variable difference model. *Journal of Learning Disabilities, 21,* 590-604.

Stanovich, K.E., Cunningham, A.E., & Cramer, B.B. (1984). Assessing phonological awareness in kindergarten children: Issues of task comparability. *Journal of Experimental Child Psychology, 38,* 350-357.

Sticht, T.G., Beck, L.J., Hauke, R.N., Kleiman, G.M., & James, J.H. (1974). *Auding and reading.* Alexandria, VA: Human Resources Research Organization.

Torgeson, J.K. (1985). Memory processes in reading-disabled children. *Journal of Learning Disabilities, 18,* 350-357.

Torgeson, J.K. (1993). Variations on theory in learning disabilities. In G.R. Lyon, D.B. Gray, J.F. Kavanaugh, & N.A. Krasnegor (Eds.) *Better understanding of learning disabilities: New views from research and their implications for education and public policies* (pp. 153-170). Baltimore, MD: Brookes.

Torgeson, J.K., Wagner, R.K., Bryant, B.R., & Pearson, N. (1992). Toward development of a kindergarten group test for phonological awareness. *Journal of Research and Development in Education, 25,* 113-120.

Torgeson, J.K., Wagner, R.K., & Rashotte, C.A. (1994). Longitudinal studies of phonological processing and reading. *Journal of Learning Disabilities, 27*(5), 276-286.

Vellutino, F. (1979). *Dyslexia: Theory and research.* Cambridge, MA: MIT Press.

Vellutino, F. (1986). Dyslexia. *Scientific American, 256,* 34-41.

Wagner, R.K., Torgeson, J.K., & Rashotte, C.A. (1994). Development of reading-related phonological processing abilities: New evidence of bidirectional causality from a latent variable longitudinal study. *Developmental Psychology, 30,* 73-87.

Welty, E. (1983). *One writer's beginnings.* New York: Warner Books.

Wixson, K.K., & Lipson, M.Y. (1991). Perspectives on reading disability research. In R. Barr, M. Kamil, P. Mosenthal, & P.D. Pearson (Eds.), *Handbook of reading research* (pp. 539-570). Newark, DE: International Reading Association.

Woodcock, R. (1987). *Woodcock reading mastery tests – Revised.* Circle Plains, MN: American Guidance Service.

Woodcock, R.W., & Johnson, M.B. (1989). *Woodcock-Johnson psycho-educational battery – Revised.* Allen, TX: DLM Teaching Resources.

14

Why Today's Multicultural Basal Readers May Retard, Not Enhance, Growth in Reading

SANDRA STOTSKY, Ph.D.
Harvard Graduate School of Education

"Far too few students are reaching the proficient level of reading achievement in any grade. Average achievement is either stuck or going down." — attributed to a fourth-grade teacher on the governing board of the National Assessment of Educational Progress
("Decline Found," 1995)

As part of the effort to make American students aware of this country's many ethnic, racial, and other social groups, educational publishers have made numerous changes in the cultural content of their reading instructional series for the elementary school over the past three decades. One of the key assumptions underlying their effort is the belief that these changes will enhance the self-esteem and hence the reading achievement of low-achieving students who are members of "cultural" minorities.

Five curricular studies in the past 25 years have looked at the actual effects of multicultural literature on the self-esteem of minority students or on the attitudes of non-minority children toward minority students. Of the two published in 1969, one dealt with changes in attitudes of white elementary school children toward black children after the use of "multiethnic" readers (Litcher & Johnson, 1969), and the other looked at the effects of "black studies" on black fifth-grade students (Roth, 1969). The other three are unpublished dissertations. One (Koeller, 1975) looked at the effects of listening to excerpts from children's stories about Mexican-Americans on the "self-concepts and attitudes" of sixth-grade Mexican-American children. A second (Shirley, 1988) looked at the impact of multicultural education on the "self-concept, racial attitude, and student achievement" of black and white fifth- and sixth-graders. The third (Ramirez, 1991) looked at the effects of Hispanic children's literature on the "self-esteem of lower socioeconomic Mexican American kindergarten children." Their findings? Multicultural literature had little effect, if any, on student attitudes. Nevertheless, changes continue to be made in the cultural content of elementary readers — despite the lack of evidence to support the notion that such changes will enhance the self-esteem and reading achievement of minority children.

In fact, studies carried out by the National Assessment of Educational Progress have found a decline or stagnation in reading scores in the past decade for all students. This decline/stagnation has been attributed largely to a lack of attention to basic skills. Although a lack of attention to basic skills, especially in the early grades, may well be the major culprit accounting for the recent decline/stagnation in reading scores, an analysis I have just completed suggests that several features of today's readers may themselves be contributing to the lack of improvement in reading achievement in the past decade.[1]

This chapter is organized around three central concerns that arose

---

[1] The readers for grades 4 and 6 that I examined were in the following series: D.C. Heath (1993); Harcourt Brace (1995); Houghton Mifflin (1993); Macmillan/McGraw-Hill (1993); Silver Burdett Ginn (1993); and Scott Foresman (1995).

in the course of my analysis of the cultural content of the basal readers for grades 4 and 6 in six leading reading series:

- the use of selections that include non-English vocabulary or are in another language altogether;
- the effects of the cultural smorgasbord offered in most series on children's reading comprehension and world knowledge; and
- the nature and scope of the reading vocabulary in many readers.

I want to emphasize that this chapter provides no empirical evidence that these features actually do impede children's reading growth. Its purpose is to call attention to these features as potentially powerful negative influences on the rate of reading growth that warrant much more professional attention than they have so far received.

The Use of Non-English Vocabulary or Non-English Selections

Although basal readers are supposed to teach children how to read (and write) the English language, non-English words, phrases, and sometimes sentences (usually but not always Spanish) appear in selections throughout the readers I examined. In addition, selections are sometimes offered in both an English translation and the language in which they were originally written (almost always Spanish). Yet, as far as I can determine, the teacher guides do not spell out how such selections and the use of non-English vocabulary could help develop children's ability to read English.

The Treatment of Non-English Vocabulary

One might reasonably expect that in a textbook designed to teach students how to read English, each non-English word would be italicized and footnoted — or just footnoted — with its English meaning given at the bottom of the page on which it appears, together with an indication of its pronunciation and the language it comes from (unless the editors indicate in an introduction to the selection, or it is clear from the text itself, that all the non-English words in the selection come from that particular language). The only exceptions might be those few words whose meanings can easily be guessed from context or those words or phrases that are paraphrased immediately in English in the text, with an indication in the teacher guide of the language the word comes from if it is not clear from the rest of the text. These conventions are standard, and they are observed in many readers. However, they are not observed in others, and several problems result from the failure to follow them.

Perhaps the most serious problem is "Spanglish," the use of Spanish words, phrases, and even sentences in an English text without any graphic clue, such as italicization or quotation marks, to indicate which ones are Spanish. This problem is glaringly illustrated in a story entitled "Yagua Days" in the Scott Foresman grade 4 reader. Here is one example of the problem: "Maybe you'll even have a few yagua days. Hasta Luego. Y que gocen mucho!" (p. 65). The only advice offered to the teacher in the teacher guide is to teach children the meaning and pronunciation of some of the Spanish words (even though the relationships between some letters and their sounds are very different in Spanish and English) and to recommend use of the 36-item "Spanish word list" at the end of the piece, consisting of all the Spanish words and phrases used in the text. But non-Spanish-reading children will have to flip back and forth from the text pages to this word list to make sense of the story while reading it, hopefully guessing correctly which words and phrases are Spanish and therefore on the list. Nor, in this reader, will children find *kuchen* and *Frau* italicized and explained on the student page in a tale about the Dutch, or *sheik* and *Allah* italicized and explained on the student page in a tale about Bedouins, although the meanings of these words are all given in the teacher guide. Fortunately, in the grade 6 text, Scott Foresman provides translations or paraphrases of non-English words where they occur in the student text, in addition to either underlining or italicizing them.

One series' effort to compensate for its unwillingness to provide footnote translations for all the non-English words in its reading selections actually creates a new problem. In Macmillan's grade 4 reader, *Abuelita* (grandmother) and *Tío Jorge* (Uncle George) are used in a story without explanation on the student page, as are a number of Spanish and French words in two of its grade 6 selections. The editors apparently believe they have solved the problem by putting all non-English words in each reader in a multilingual glossary at the end of the reader, which duly indicates their meanings, their pronunciations, and the language they come from. However, one cannot help speculating on the confusion that results when children are expected or taught to use a glossary at the end of a reader to look up both English words and words from a variety of other languages. The glossary in a reader basically provides dictionary practice for children. It undoubtedly introduces chaos into their language learning if they are brought to expect a dictionary to contain words from many different languages.

Chaos also results when non-English words are merely italicized and therefore cannot be distinguished from words that have been italicized to indicate stress — a conventional use of italic text. D.C. Heath uses this technique in three selections in its grade 6 reader. Two include Spanish words, and the third includes a Japanese word, but no pronunciations or meanings are provided for any of them. Silver Burdett Ginn avoids this kind of confusion in the one story in its grade 6 reader in which non-English words are used and not italicized; almost all the Spanish words are used in the conversation of a non-English-speaking character, described as such, and by convention, conversation must be in quotation marks anyway. Moreover, footnoted translations are provided for the Spanish words or phrases that may not be easy to figure out from the rest of the dialogue or the narrated text. This is also the case with the Spanish words in the Silver

Burdett Ginn grade 4 reader, all of which are italicized, but only some of which are translated in footnotes in the student text.

Original Texts with English Translations

In the readers I studied, six original non-English texts are paired with their English translations. Two are poems, one is a play, another is an autobiographical piece, the fifth is a story, and the sixth is a selection by a "hearing-impaired" Inuit that is presented both in English and in an unidentified script — presumably, the script in which Inuit is written.

The Scott Foresman grade 4 teacher guide notes that a skill to be developed is "connect[ing] Spanish to English" (Anthology E, p. 48e). What that means is not at all clear. How is it a "skill" to connect a Romance language (Spanish) to a Germanic language (English)? The two languages do not map onto each other. Later, the editors suggest that teachers might "challenge" English-speaking students to "skim the Spanish portion first to see if they can predict what it might say in English." One wonders how many editors tried out this time-wasting practice on a language they didn't know. Students who cannot read Spanish can do almost nothing with the Spanish version (except maybe hunt for a few words that resemble English words, but that is not a wise practice to encourage with texts that have few literate words derived from Latin for students to find). And those who can read and write a second language may well find themselves faced with extra assignments as a reward for their bilingual skill; the editors suggest as one writing activity that such students write about "an event in their culture" and then "write an English translation" in order to "share their cultural events" (Anthology E, p. 50).

For a short poem given in both Spanish and English in Macmillan's grade 4 reader, the teacher guide suggests that teachers play the audiocassette so that "students can compare the rhythm and rhyme in both the English and Spanish verses" (p. 470). This is again educationally meaningless; most American children have been taught little if anything about rhythmical or rhyming patterns in poetry by grade 4. Moreover, what sensible comments can fourth-graders make in comparing the rhythms of the two languages when they do not understand the original language at all? Mercifully, the Silver Burdett Ginn editors do not ask the teacher or students to do anything at all with the original Spanish version of the six-line poem they provide with an English translation in their grade 6 reader. Nowhere in their guide could I find even a hint of a rationale for the presence of the original version. Interestingly, in the one case where it would have been possible to give children genuine cross-cultural information — the Inuit narrative in Macmillan's grade 4 reader — there is *not a single word* in the student *or* teacher text about the nature, history, or purpose of the unusual written alphabet the Inuit use.

Cultural and Intellectual Incoherence

A second major problem with these readers concerns the large amounts of ethnic American and non-American content they present. Reading one selection after another in the clusters in which they are grouped, one cannot help being struck by their cultural and historical scatter. Every 6 to 12 pages or so, the focus moves from one cultural or ethnic group to another, with the setting often shifting among continents and historical periods. How this phenomenon ultimately affects children's world knowledge and general comprehension can only be surmised at this point. But it is hard to see how continually hopping from one century to another and from one culture to another can give children a stable understanding of any cultural group or its history — particularly when there seems to be so little effort devoted to locating these cultures and their place names in a historical timeframe or geographical setting.

Nor is it clear how children can gain a meaningful understanding of the organizing themes used to group selections in each reader when there are few, if any, clear intellectual connections across the selections in these thematic units. (What makes the situation even more problematic is the distinct possibility that students are experiencing a similar phenomenon in their social studies curriculum, whether that curriculum is a problem-oriented one or a sequence of units on various cultural groups on different continents during different eras.) Although worthwhile concepts are used to organize groups of selections in the readers, most groupings in most readers do not seem to contribute anything more than very obvious and very bland generalizations.

Moreover, the choice of selections for many groups often seems to be motivated by more than just their organizing concepts. For example, two groups of selections illustrating the concepts of courage and survival in two different readers both have an unarticulated feminist twist. In D.C. Heath's grade 6 reader, a unit organized under the title "Meeting the Challenge" groups together a biography of a 12-year-old New Jersey girl who helped to open up Little League baseball to girls, a Chinese fairy tale about a widow whose youngest son must exhibit great courage in the face of many ordeals to rescue her brocade from fairies, and a piece of realistic fiction about a 12-year old girl in 1849 who uses her intelligence to survive a winter by herself in the Montana wilderness before she is rescued by a group of Indians. In Houghton Mifflin's grade 6 reader, a unit organized under the title "The Spirit of Survival" groups together an adventure story about a contemporary girl who sets out to find the wild boar living in the woods near her home, a piece of fiction set in the South in 1855 about an "African American girl who leads a group of teen-agers out of slavery" to freedom, a true story about a teen-age girl who, with her father, survives a plane crash at sea, and a short novel about a young Inuit sister and brother who face incredible challenges in bringing a killed caribou back to their starving family. It is possible that students will learn from such clusters that courage comes in different forms and that young people from a variety of cultural groups and historical periods are quite capable of meeting challenges to survival. However, this is not a remarkable generalization to help children induce. Moreover, the total exclusion of white boys from the ranks of courageous young people by the editors' choice of selections in both these clusters may implicitly qualify this generalization in children's minds.

It is not clear whether children can gain significant insights into concepts like survival and courage when these topics are not illuminated with any systematic breadth or depth and when editors seem to be guided more by ideological than by intellectual considerations. That is why I was struck by the intellectual elegance of the unit organization in the readers published in 1995 by Open Court, a series with a visible balance between ethnic American or non-American writers and "mainstream" American or British writers; as the series itself indicates, it maintains a "commitment to classic literature." The ways in which selections are related to each other and to their organizing concepts — in what the series aptly calls "learning units" — suggests what can be accomplished when editors are not rigidly bound by a social or moral agenda in their choice of selections.

For example, the selections in a unit entitled "Surviving" in its grade 4 reader are linked to each other and the unit concept as follows (as spelled out on page 12 of the teacher guide): A biographical account of Matthew Henson's expedition with Robert Peary to the North Pole shows how "one can survive in a harsh climate through the direct teachings of those familiar with the environment" (the selection is *not* an account of his victimization). A piece of fiction about a young boy's efforts to remember the teachings of an Apache farmhand in order to survive a plane crash in the Arizona desert shows how "one can survive in a harsh climate by recalling previous survival techniques learned either directly or indirectly." An excerpt from *Island of the Blue Dolphins* about an abandoned young Indian girl's efforts to survive on an island in the Pacific shows how "resourcefulness and courage can enable one to deal with extreme danger." A tall tale shows how ingenuity and a positive attitude "can turn a bad situation into a good situation." A poem by David McCord about a grasshopper shows that perseverance is necessary "in surviving a prolonged hardship." An excerpt from a story by Pearl Buck about the attitudes of Japanese villagers who survive the destruction of family, friends, and homes by a giant tidal wave shows how "time can help one heal emotionally when faced with disaster or extreme hardship." A poem by A.A. Milne suggests the value of a little solitude for coping with "everyday difficulties." An autobiographical piece by a survivor of the Holocaust shows how "poetry and music can help one express fears and hopes during a trying time." An excerpt from Anne Frank's diary shows how "writing is one way to express inner fears, helping one cope with a difficult situation." Finally, an informational article on music and slavery, together with two black spirituals, show how "music and dance can help one momentarily forget hardships and still hope for better times."

As one can see, the unit contains a variety of selections sequenced in a way that enables students to *progressively deepen* their insights into the nature of the resources human beings draw upon to survive the hardships or disasters they have encountered. Although the selections deal with the lives of many different groups of people in a variety of places, not all the stories are about children, and there is no gender or racial bias. Nor is there any anti-Western tinge to this grouping or any attempt to downplay racism as one of life's challenges. The unit encourages not the superficial generalization that all kinds of people can meet challenges to survival, but rather an insight into the resources that human beings in different places and times have drawn on to survive. Such a unit encourages the development of an intellectual and emotional depth that is not possible when the range of selections offered is restricted for purposes of moral manipulation.

In the readers in the six series I examined in detail, there are occasionally groups of selections that form culturally or cross-culturally coherent wholes. One example involves the selections in the D.C. Heath grade 6 reader that deal with civic and historical content. In addition, the Scott Foresman readers give students meaningful and coherent intellectual experiences — albeit extremely brief — in units at each grade level entitled "Author Study" or "Genre Study." In one grade 6 booklet, for example, the editors group two different fantasy selections and an essay, all by Lloyd Alexander; in another booklet, they group two different pieces of historical fiction and an essay, all by Yoshiko Uchida. For grade 4, the editors group a folk song illustrated by Glen Rounds, an essay written by him, and a tall tale he wrote and illustrated. And as an example of genre study, in grade 4, the editors group a fairy tale in play form about Cinderella, poems by three authors dealing with the Cinderella story, and a Chinese version of the fairy tale. But most of the groupings in their readers — as in most readers — are not as intellectually coherent as these, and none seem to provide the kind of opportunity for powerful learning delivered by Open Court's organizational patterns — all of which are appropriate for an instructional reader.

The Reading Vocabulary

The final and perhaps most troublesome feature of many selections in these readers is the nature of the reading vocabulary in them. In grades 4 through 6, a major goal of an instructional reader is to build up children's ability to read — and then use — literate English words (i.e., words at or above a seventh-grade reading level). It is common knowledge that English has the most extensive vocabulary of any written language in the world. Thus, any lessening of opportunities to learn vocabulary has far more serious consequences for children trying to learn to read and write English (whether or not they are native speakers) than it would have for children trying to learn any other written language in the world. One must regard with dismay, therefore, the scope and nature of the vocabulary being developed in many readers, as suggested very clearly by their glossaries.

A Useless Non-English Vocabulary of Daily Life

One specialized group of words in many of these readers gives much cause for concern about vocabulary development. These are the culturally specific words that are used in selections about various American ethnic groups or non-American cultural groups. Most are non-

English words that are not commonly used in English. Nor are they literate words; for the most part, they are part of the vocabulary of everyday life. The words may be critically important for the group that uses them, but they are almost useless for helping students develop the ability to read more mature works of literature or academic texts. For example, the Inuit words for "snowy owl" and "It's coming," the word for an Italian cheese ("mozzarella"), the Spanish words for "the check," "that one," "a kind of greeting," and "potato," the French word for "boat," the Yankton Sioux word for "otter," and the Seminole term for the Florida Everglades are not worth learning as core words in a developmental reading program for the English language. Yet these non-English words are all in Macmillan's glossaries for grades 4, 5, and 6. The energy most children have to expend just to learn literate English words is great enough without the burden of learning the meanings of non-English words with no real significance for their development as readers of English. Unfortunately, students need to learn them (at least temporarily) in order to understand what they are reading. And it doesn't matter whether these words are in the glossary or translated in footnotes on student text pages, as they are in most of the other series. They distract from the hard business at hand, which is for students to acquire a familiarity with as many literate English words as they can.

A Cultural Smorgasbord of Proper Nouns

In addition to a vocabulary for daily life from a dozen or more languages, yet another group of words in many of these readers requires a great deal of learning time but also bears little or no relationship to enhanced literacy. These are the names of people, gods, goddesses, spirits, places, kings, queens, and other rulers in the various cultures featured in the selections. Needless to say, the more cultures a reader features, the more languages the proper nouns will come from and the more varied the words (and their pronunciations) will be. For example, in the glossary for Macmillan's grade 6 reader, *Mai, Maizon,*

Paulo Mendez, and *Mongo* are four of the 18 words under *m; Quito Sueno* is one of three words under *q;* and *Eliscue, Eronni,* and *Emeke* are three of the 17 words under *e.* In its grade 5 reader, *Maidu, Felicidad Maldonado, Mercado,* and *Mis Poinsettia* are four of the 11 words under *m; Le Havre, Lupe, Lakota-oyote,* and *Lake Titicaca* are four of the eight words under *l;* and *Ojibway* and *Osage* are two of the five words under *o.* By the time children in a highly multicultural reading program finish six years of elementary school, they may have acquired an immense fund of words that are almost totally useless for comprehending mature literary and academic texts in English in the secondary school. Whether they can pronounce even half of them is anybody's guess.

Words from other languages do not necessarily have pronunciation patterns similar to those of English. Nor are their sound/letter relationships necessarily similar to those of English; this is certainly the case for many sound/letter relationships in Spanish. For this reason, the lack of a pronunciation guide for a non-English word on the page on which it first appears in the student text may also have serious consequences. The pronunciations of proper nouns in particular must be learned if the students are to discuss characters and settings. But they will not learn them if their teacher doesn't take the time to give their pronunciations and to practice them. For example, the Scott Foresman grade 4 student text does not provide students with the pronunciations of *Praia do Forte, Bedouin, Hamed, Yucaju, Tenochtitlan, Itzcoatl, Tezozomac, Papago,* or *I'itoi* (a "Great Spirit" of the Papago Indians). Nor does it give the pronunciation of *kiva* (a ceremonial chamber), *sheik,* or *macaw.* The teacher guide does tell teachers how to pronounce most of them. But one suspects that many of these non-English proper nouns will require considerable oral practice, by the teacher as well as by the students — thus turning reading lessons into pronunciation lessons for both teachers and students.

A Relative Paucity of Literate Words

The glossary at the end of an instructional reader contains only those words used in the selections "whose meanings, pronunciations, and/ or usage are unfamiliar or difficult," as one group of editors put it (Macmillan, grade 4, p. 554). These are the new words highlighted for direct instruction by the teacher before or as students read a selection. The differences among the glossaries of the grades 4 and 6 readers in the number and the difficulty levels of the words are startling and informative. Tables 14-1 and 14-2 show all the words under *i* and *v* (except proper nouns) in the glossaries of the readers for grades 4 and 6 in the six series. I chose to study the words beginning with these two letters because in the upper elementary grades and above (as a perusal of these tables will confirm) they tend to be literate English words, usually derived from Latin. Next to each word, I noted the grade level assigned the word by two vocabulary researchers, Edgar Dale and Joseph O'Rourke (Dale & O'Rourke, 1976).[2] In the 1960s and 1970s, they tested over 44,000 words and phrases to determine the lowest grade level (4, 6, 8, 10, 12, 13, or 16) at which a word could be said to be known in print by a large majority of many hundreds of students at that grade level in a representative national sample. Thus, for example, a word found to be known by a majority of students *only* at grade 8 and above would have to be considered a candidate for direct instruction if it appeared in a reading selection for students with a reading level below grade 8.

As can be seen in Tables 14-1 and 14-2, there are variations among

[2] I followed several rules in assigning a grade level to words in the glossaries. If a word in a glossary appeared in exactly that form in Dale and O'Rourke's list, it was given their assigned grade level. If it was suffixed and not listed in their work, I used the grade level assigned to the base word. If the word was given more than one meaning in the glossary, then I used the lowest grade level assigned to the various meanings of the word in their work. If the word was not listed at all in their work, I assigned it the highest grade level possible. I used the grade-level placement appearing in their supplement to the 1976 edition, published in 1979, for words that were not in the 1976 edition and for words that were retested. Although their research has some limitations in its methodology, it nevertheless gives us a good sense of a word's difficulty in relation to other words and its assigned grade level.

Table 14-1: Words under *i* and *v* in the Glossaries of the Six Grade 4 Readers and the Grade Levels Assigned in Dale and O'Rourke (1976)

D.C. Heath (1993)		Harcourt Brace (1995)		Houghton Mifflin (1993)		Macmillan (1993)		Scott Foresman (1995)		Silver Burdett Ginn (1993)	
imaginative	8	idiosyncrasy	13	idle	6	ignite	6	indicate	6	identical	6
immense	8	immediately	6	impatiently	6	immortal	8	inspire	8	illustrate	4
impact	8	immersion heater	13	impossible	4	incinerate	19	inky	12	imagination	4
indifferent	12	impatient	4	infield	4	ingot	13	inseparable	6	immigrate	6
inhabitant	8	inning	6	inform	6	intimidate	10	image	10	impertinent	10
intentionally	6	innocent	4	inning	6	investigate	6	indignant	12	impress	6
intercom	6	instinct	8	instructions	6			imperfect	6	inaccurate	6
interview	6	instructor	4	introduction	4	vigil	12	impress	12	indignant	12
		insulated	10	investigate	6	vigilante group	12	improve	12	infectious	6
veer	13	intensity	8					infection	4	initial	6
version	6	intention	6					illuminate	8	innocent	4
veterinarian	6	international	8							insane	4

Table 14-1 (continued)

D.C. Heath (1993)		Harcourt Brace (1995)		Houghton Mifflin (1993)		Macmillan (1993)		Scott Foresman (1995)		Silver Burdett Ginn (1993)	
vigil	12	interrupt	6					verse	4	inspiration	6
vision	4	interview	6					virus	8	integrate	8
vulnerable	12							veterinarian	6	intention	6
		vacation	4					violin	4	introduce	4
		vain	10							invent	4
		veterinarian	6							investment	6
		vigorously	8								
		violinist	4							vegetation	8
		volcano	4							venture	8
		volunteer	4							verse	4
										victor	6
										vigil	12

Table 14-2: Words under *i* and *v* in the Glossaries of the Six Grade 6 Readers and the Grade Levels Assigned in Dale and O'Rourke (1976)

D.C. Heath (1993)		Harcourt Brace (1995)		Houghton Mifflin (1993)		Macmillan (1993)		Scott Foresman (1995)		Silver Burdett Ginn (1993)	
6	immigrant	8	illuminate	8	ignorant	—	ill at ease	immigration	6	illusion	8
10	immobilize	15	imperious	6	ignore	8	illegitimate	incarcerate	16	imitate	6
13	impassive	10	implication	8	illusion	15	imperious	intern	10	immortal	8
12	impoverished	6	impression	6	imitate	16	inculcate	internment	12	impressionist	12
10	impressionable	8	improbable	8	immense	12	improvised	immerse	13	incredibly	6
13	improvise	6	incident	8	immunization	12	indulge	immaculate	12	infantry	6
13	incognito	16	incisive	8	impulsive	12	inferno	immune system	8	influence	6
6	ingenious	13	inconsequential	8	indestructible	6	ingenious	independence	4	ingenuity	10
8	ineligible	8	incriminate	12	indignation	8	intercept	inflammation	8	inhabitant	8
16	inhibit	12	indignantly	6	infect	10	ironic	infuriate	6	inherit	6
10	inkling	8	informal	8	inlay					inlet	4
8	intensity	8	inheritance	8	instinct	10	valiant	vault	4	inquiry	8
13	intercede	12	intact	12	instinctively	13	veer	vaporize	4	inspect	4

D.C. Heath (1993)		Harcourt Brace (1995)		Houghton Mifflin (1993)		Macmillan (1993)		Scott Foresman (1995)		Silver Burdett Ginn (1993)	
interest	8			intact	12	venison	6	version	6	inspiration	6
interlock	19	vantage	12	interpret	8	verbal	8	vindictive	13	instinct	8
		virtually	13	involuntarily	8			voyage	4	instinctive	12
vain	10	vulnerable	12					voyager	4	intention	6
valiant	10			vague	8			vulnerable	12	intricate	10
venture	8			vein	6			vague	8	invasion	4
vermin	13			veteran	6			verify	8	irresolute	13
vexation	12			vigor	8						
vie	16			virtuous	10					vain	10
viper	10									vanish	4
										verbatim	12
										vertical	8
										vibration	6
										vineyard	4
										volcano	4
										vulnerability	12

the readers for each grade level in the number of words that the editors believe have unfamiliar or difficult meanings. However, the total numbers of words may not be as meaningful as they seem, if editors place in the glossary many words which are generally known at that grade level but which they believe are still difficult enough to warrant pedagogical attention. What matters is the number of hard words per grade — that is, the number of words that are still not known at that grade level according to a measure of word difficulty. Tables 14-3 and 14-4 give summaries of the information in Tables 14-1 and 14-2, showing how many of the words under i and v in the glossaries in these 12 readers are assigned a grade level in Dale and O'Rourke's research that is higher than the grade level of the reader itself. As these tables indicate, the number of words in a glossary can mislead; a large number does not necessarily indicate that the reader includes more hard words than a reader with a shorter glossary, nor does a short glossary necessarily indicate that the reader has few hard words. But, more importantly, these tables show that at each grade level, the reader with the

Table 14-3
Summary of Grade Levels Assigned in Dale & O'Rourke (1976) for Words Beginning with i and v in the Grade 4 Glossaries

Reading Level	DCH (Grade 4)	HB (Grade 4)	HM (Grade 4)	MM (Grade 4)	SF (Grade 4)	SBG (Grade 4)
4	1	7	3	—	4	7
6	5	7	5	2	6	10
8	4	3	1	1	3	3
10	—	2	—	2	—	1
12 +	4	2	—	3	2	2
Total	14	21	9	8	15	23
Over 4	13	14	6	8	11	16

Table 14-4
Summary of Grade Levels Assigned in Dale and O'Rourke (1976) for Words Beginning with *i* and *v* in the Grade 6 Glossaries

Reading Level	DCH (Grade 6)	HB (Grade 6)	HM (Grade 6)	MM (Grade 6)	SF (Grade 6)	SBG (Grade 6)
4	—	—	—	—	5	5
6	2	2	5	2	3	8
8	4	5	12	3	4	6
10	7	1	1	2	1	3
12+	9	8	3	7	6	6
Total	22	16	21	14	19	28
Over 6	20	14	16	12	11	15

most hard words beginning with these letters has about twice as many hard words as the reader with the fewest. This finding suggests a wide variation in students' exposure to literate vocabulary, depending on the reader used for their reading instruction.

One Possible Source of Influence on Vocabulary Load

The question that leaps out from an examination of these tables is why some series seem to have fewer hard words than others. One factor may be the variation in cultural content across series. As I found in my research on these readers, the series with fewer selections about ethnic America and non-Western cultures almost consistently have larger numbers of literate words than the series with the most selections. Is difference in vocabulary load a reflection of difference in cultural content? To explore this question in greater depth, I constructed a table (Table 14-5) of all the words listed under *i* and *v* in the Open Court readers for grades 4 and 6 published in 1989. Recall that

Table 14-5
Words under *i* and *v* in Open Court's Glossaries for Grades 4 and 6, with Grade Levels Assigned by Dale and O'Rourke (1976)

Open Court (1989) Grade 4 (447 pp.)				Open Court (1989) Grade 6 (445 pp.)			
idiosyncrasy	13	various	6	ichthyosaur	12	in tow	6w
idly	6	veer	13	illuminate	8	intrepid	16
ill-naturedly	8	vent	4	illumination	8	isolated	8
illusion	8	venture	8	immense	8	invariably	12
image	4	veranda	10	implement	8	intelligibly	8
impatient	4	verbal	8	impulse	8		
impressed	6	vibrate	6	incident	6	vogue	12
impression	6	vision	4	indent	6	vague	8
indifferently	12	volunteer	4	indisputable	8	valiant	10
incubator	6			induction	10	valor	8
indaba	—			indulgently	16	vantage	12
indignantly	12			inquiringly	8	variation	8
innocent	4			inquisitive	6	vendor	12
innocently	4			inscription	8	vengeance	8
inoculate	12			insert	6	vermillion	12
inspect	4			insignificant	8	vexed	16
inspire	8			insolence	10	vigorously	8
instinct	8			insolent	10	villa	10
integrity	10			instinctive	12	virtually	13
intently	10			insure	6	virtuous	10
interest	6			intently	10	visage	12
interpret	8			intermittently	12		
intervail	—			intimately	10		

this is a series with an explicit commitment to "classic" literature. I used the 1989 series for this comparison because the number of pages in these readers was closer to the number in the other series than were the lengthier student texts in the 1995 series (there are 638 pages in its 1995 grade 4 reader and 761 pages in grade 6). The contrast between Open Court and the other reading series is revealing. To judge by the number of words in Table 14-5, Open Court includes a larger number of literate words in its readers for grades 4 and 6 than any of the other series. Table 14-6 shows that Open Court also uses more hard words than the other series.

Open Court is widely regarded as a "hard" series, i.e., it contains more difficult selections than other reading series (J.S. Chall, personal communication, November 1995; J. Squire, personal communication, October 1995). Although the exact reasons for this phenomenon are not clear, it is possible that the language used by Open Court's array of "classic" authors contributes to the difference (particularly since it also contains some of the same multicultural authors and selections

Table 14-6
Summary of the Grade Levels Assigned in Dale and O'Rourke (1976) for Words Beginning with *i* and *v* in the Open Court Glossaries for Grades 4 and 6

Reading Level	Open Court Grade 4 (1989)	Open Court Grade 6 (1989)
4	8	—
6	8	5
8	6	16
10	3	9
12+	7	13
Total	32	43
	Over 4 = 24	Over 6 = 28

found in the other series). Some of the authors in its grade 4 reader who are *not* present in the other grade 4 readers are Pearl Buck, William Blake, Henry Wadsworth Longfellow, Lewis Carroll, L. Frank Baum, Emily Dickinson, Walter de la Mare, Ogden Nash, and Rudyard Kipling, as well as several Biblical selections. The authors in its grade 6 reader who are *not* present in the other grade 6 readers include Philippa Pearce, Willa Cather, May Swenson, e.e. cummings, Mary Norton, Ernest Lawrence Thayer, Anna Sewell, J.R.R. Tolkien, E. Nesbit, Antoine de Saint-Éxupery, Mark Twain, and Alfred Lord Tennyson.[3] In addition, Open Court's grade 5 reader features works by Edgar Allen Poe and Hans Christian Andersen, writers who are totally absent from all the other series. The implication is not that ethnic authors do not use, or are not capable of using, the same vocabulary. The real question is whether editors are favoring certain kinds of selections by ethnic authors, or selections by certain kinds of ethnic authors, so that students end up reading works filled with dialogue containing few literate words, works narrated in a first-person voice rather than by a third person, and works that lack the detailed character descriptions and mood-setting passages common in nineteenth-century literature.

The differences revealed by the tables in this chapter appear to be generalizable across the total literate vocabulary for each reader. Table 7 shows the total glossary count for readers in grades 4 and 6 for the 1993 editions of the Houghton Mifflin, Macmillan, and Silver Burdett Ginn series, the 1995 edition of Open Court, and the 1987 edition of the Macmillan series. I decided to compare this earlier edition of the Macmillan reading series with its present edition and the others because it contained a large number of selections by the authors in the Open Court series who for the most part no longer appear in the other series, including the latest Macmillan series. It should be kept in

---

[3] However, Silver Burdett Ginn does include poems by Longfellow and Lewis Carroll in its grade 6 reader, and a poem by Kipling in its grade 5 reader, while D.C. Heath includes a poem by Lewis Carroll in its grade 6 reader and an excerpt from Mary Norton's work in its grade 5 reader. Macmillan also includes a poem by e.e. cummings in its grade 5 reader.

mind that over a third of the words in the glossaries in the 1993 Macmillan series are proper nouns and foreign words. As Table 14-7 indicates, the glossary count in the earlier version of the Macmillan reading series is almost identical to the glossary count in the current Open Court series, providing support for the possibility that the authors now being excluded from contemporary reading series used a more literate vocabulary than many of the authors now featured in current series.

The differences among the six leading contemporary series in the number of hard words they offer each year, as well as their differences as a group from Open Court in the number of hard words offered each year, suggest that systematic differences in vocabulary development — and, hence, in reading growth — may be taking place today, depending on the reading series used. That is because the more literate words children learn each year, the larger the vocabulary base they have with which they can learn even more literate words the next year. If the changes in cultural content over the past two decades are responsible, at least in part, for the differences in vocabulary across reading series, current reading series may well have "broadened" children's horizons at the cost of their growth as readers.

Table 14-7
Total Number of Words in the Glossaries of the Readers for Grades 4 and 6 for Selected Series

Reading Series	Houghton Mifflin (1993)	Silver Burdett Ginn (1993)	Macmillan (1993)	Macmillan (1987)	Open Court (1995)
Grade 4	168	303	141	695	690
Grade 6	291	354	282	696	559

Other Sources of Influence on Vocabulary Load

It is premature to conclude that changes in cultural content are a cause of a light vocabulary load, or that these changes are the sole cause. Many factors can influence the difficulty level of the vocabulary across a group of reading selections. Reading selections may have a low vocabulary load (as they did years ago) even when they reflect "mainstream" American culture. A high number of ethnic selections may well lead to a low vocabulary load, but a low vocabulary load may be caused by other factors as well. Certainly, the large number of poems and informational selections in the Macmillan and Houghton Mifflin readers (as a proportion of the total number of selections in grades 4 and 6) may contribute to the smaller number of literate words in their readers. Poems tend to have a simpler vocabulary than prose, and the informational selections, biographies, and essays offered in all the series at these grade levels, especially those intended to teach students how to read expository prose, tend to be written in ordinary prose. Conversely, the relatively large number of science fiction and fantasy selections in the Silver Burdett Ginn and Harcourt Brace grade 4 readers (in contrast to the other readers) and the relatively large amount of historical and civic content in D.C. Heath's grade 6 reader may be contributing to their higher numbers of literate words at these grade levels.

Another source of influence on vocabulary load is an insistence today by many university educators and curriculum directors on whole-class instruction for reading.[4] Some publishers may be choosing selections with an easier vocabulary than they might otherwise have chosen, in order to make them more "accessible" to the least able readers at each grade level — even though the laudable goal of many propo-

---

[4] See, for example, Barone (1994). In her observations of the first-grade classrooms in which the children of mothers who had taken crack or cocaine were placed, Barone was startled to discover all the teachers in the district using whole-class instruction both for class discussion of reading selections and for phonics worksheets. They did not group students for needed skill work, she believed, because the teachers thought it violated "whole language" philosophy and damaged the self-esteem of low-achieving children.

nents of whole-class instruction is to offer the lower third of a class reading selections of a higher level of difficulty than what they were offered in achievement-based groups. Some selections have explicitly been offered to facilitate "cooperative reading," either by the whole class or by pairs of students — often a "skilled" reader and a "less-skilled" reader — as recommended in the teacher guide. Selections chosen for "cooperative reading" can be of any genre: Indian oral literature, a Walt Disney biography, an informational selection on elephants, or a Gary Soto short story, as in Houghton Mifflin's grade 4 reader. In any case, they are selections that students are expected to read together as a class or with partners to "support each other's comprehension," and to judge by this grade 4 reader, they do not contain many new hard words.

Last but not least, another influence on vocabulary load may be the strength of the moralistic impulses driving the choice of selections. If the chief goal of an instructional reader today is to shape young students' attitudes and feelings on specific social issues in particular ways, then we may well find many selections chosen with less concern for the quality of their language than for their capacity to serve these ends.

Concluding Remarks

To judge by the 12 readers for grades 4 and 6 that I examined in these six leading reading series, their selections have several highly problematic features that may considerably reduce their capacity to improve students' reading ability in the English language. Readers are already too easy for large numbers of students, as several researchers have found (Chall, Conard, & Harris-Sharples, 1991), and for the most part they have been too easy for years. The problems I have detailed in this chapter contribute to this insufficiency, making it more difficult for students to achieve adequate growth in reading from year to year. Moreover, some reader series have a much smaller number of literate words than others, and these differences appear fairly consistent from grade to grade, suggesting the possibility that some students will experience even less growth in reading from grade to grade than others will.

Although the lack of cultural coherence across selections in a reader is a serious problem, the chief problem I see concerns the vocabulary of the readers — the vocabulary they contain and the vocabulary they do not contain. There are several drawbacks to much of the vocabulary that students must learn in these readers in order to understand and discuss their selections. In these readers, many words — English or non-English — appear to contribute little if anything to the development of skill in reading academic and literary works in English. Some are non-English proper nouns that are hard to pronounce and read, yet must be learned for discussion of the characters in a story. Others are words, in English as well as in other languages, that refer to daily life in other cultures and are not important for growth in reading English.

The root cause of the problems discussed above — the paucity of literate words, the limitations in vocabulary, and the conceptual limitations in some selections — seems to be the bow that the editors believe they need to make (or may indeed want to make) to non-literary and non-intellectual considerations in the choice of selections for the readers. It is not possible for even the best editors in the world to dedicate themselves to a search for selections with increasingly complex characters and themes and to focus rigorously on questions of literary merit and intellectual challenge when they must simultaneously juggle the variables of race, ethnicity, gender, and "self-esteem" — all of which take precedence today over literary considerations and the development of a strong reading vocabulary.

Perhaps none of these problems is the fundamental reason why, according to the most recent NAEP assessment, reading scores in the elementary school have failed to rise in the past few years and in some states have declined. But these results are not surprising to me in light of what I found in the readers I examined. In their zeal to boost ethnic self-esteem, provide role models for girls, promote the virtues of a multilingual population, and expand children's knowledge about other peoples and cultures, many educational publishers may be creating an instructional tool more likely to produce multiple illiteracy than growth in reading. And ironically, the damage may be greatest in the very children who need help the most.

References

Barone, D. (1994) The importance of classroom context: Literacy development of children prenatally exposed to crack/cocaine — Year two. *Research in the Teaching of English*, 28(3), 286-312.

Chall, J.S., Conard, S.S., & Harris-Sharples, S. (1991). *Should textbooks challenge students?: The case for easier or harder textbooks.* New York: Teachers College Press.

Dale, E., & O'Rourke, J. (1976). *The living word vocabulary: The words we know — A national vocabulary inventory study.* Elgin, IL: Dome Press, Inc.

Decline found in reading proficiency of high school seniors. (1995, April 28). *The New York Times,* p. A18.

Koeller, S. (1975). The effect of listening to excerpts from children's stories about Mexican-Americans on the self-concepts and attitudes of sixth-grade children (Doctoral dissertation, University of Colorado, 1975). *Dissertation Abstracts International, 36,* 7186A.

Litcher, J., & Johnson, D. (1969). Changes in attitudes towards Negroes of white elementary school students after use of multiethnic readers. *Journal of Educational Psychology, 60,* 148-152.

Ramirez, G. (1991). The effects of Hispanic children's literature on the self-esteem of lower socioeconomic Mexican American kindergarten children (Doctoral dissertation, Texas Tech University). *Dissertation Abstracts International,* 52, 2394A.

Roth, R. (1969). The effects of "black studies" on Negro fifth grade students. *The Journal of Negro Education, 38,* 435-439.

Shirley, O. (1988). *The impact of multicultural education on self-concept, racial attitude, and student achievement of black and white fifth and sixth graders.* Unpublished doctoral dissertation, University of Mississippi.

15

"True Writing and Understanding of Hard Usual English Words"

The First English-Language Dictionary

MIRIAM BALMUTH, Ph.D.
Department of Curriculum and Teaching,
Hunter College of the City University of New York

The origins and format of the first English dictionary are topics particularly appropriate for a book honoring Jeanne Chall, in view of her lifelong concern with how history, vocabulary, readability, and text difficulty affect the literacy of special child and adult populations. That first dictionary, published in 1604, was a response by Robert Cawdrey to the literacy needs of certain populations in late sixteenth-century England. While little is known about Cawdrey besides the fact that he was a grammar school teacher at one time, his *A Table Alphabeticall* was

This paper is an extension of a previous survey of English dictionaries, "Early English Dictionaries in Historical Perspective," *New Horizons,* 1984.

the start of a flood of English-language dictionaries that extends through the complex tomes of our own day.

Various kinds of word listings and compilations had existed for well over a thousand years, but there had never before been a work like Cawdrey's — the first to consist solely of English words, listed alphabetically and defined by other English words (Noyes, 1943). Interlingual dictionaries that translated words from one language to another, glossaries listing definitions for words from individual books, and listings of undefined or unalphabetized groupings of words had been compiled by various teachers and scholars throughout the ages. Cawdrey's book, rooted in a host of those varied compilations, may be seen as the result of a number of dramatic events that had occurred in the century and a half that preceded it. That is to say, by the end of the sixteenth century, the social, political, economic, and religious circumstances in the English-speaking world resulted in a need for the kind of reference tool we find so useful today — a need that had not been felt with any discernible force before then.

The *Table* was pointedly dedicated to "Ladies, Gentlewomen, or other unskillful persons." Why were women so prominently singled out; why are those "ladies" and "gentlewomen" termed *unskillful;* and who are the other "unskillful persons"? These questions can be answered by exploring the environment that led to the initial flowering of English dictionaries.

The Invention of Movable Type

We might begin in the year 1450, when Johann Gutenberg perfected a machine for moving type. The wealth of printed material that followed helped greatly in the spread of literacy throughout Europe — including England. There, in 1476, William Caxton, a worldly cloth merchant and semi-official English ambassador-at-large, came home from the continent and set up the first English printing press in Westminster Abbey.

According to Caxton, he had decided in Belgium to study printing, then an infant craft, for a pressing immediate need: He had done such a fine job translating a group of French stories about the history of Troy for Margaret, Duchess of Burgundy, that he had received a number of requests for his laboriously handwritten original; he thought that printing would be a good way to provide them (Painter, 1976). Thus, Caxton's translation, *Recuyell of the Histories of Troy (1474-71)*, was the first printed English book. With his printing press, Caxton went on to publish many other distinguished works in English, both translations and native English writings: Chaucer's *Canterbury Tales*, for example, and Thomas Malory's *Morte d'Arthur*.

To Caxton's printings were soon added a multitude of publications by contemporary and subsequent English printers of the late fifteenth and the sixteenth centuries. In pre-printing days, when each book had been individually handwritten, the choice of which book to produce was understandably determined by the stature of the works, and so prestigious Latin works had been preferred. Printing, however, was so much easier and cheaper that it now became feasible to publish not only works of significance and great intrinsic merit, but writings of lesser consequence as well.

The Rise in Status of the English Language

The English language had had particularly low status since the Norman Conquest of 1066, when French became the prestigious vernacular language in England. Gradually, as England and France separated politically, the status of the English language increased and that of French declined until French retreated altogether. The greatest status, however, remained with Latin, the international language of religion and scholarship — which were practically synonymous in Christian Europe for most of the years between the fall of Rome and the fourteenth-century Renaissance. With the Renaissance, vernacular languages such as French and Italian rose in prestige. Yet in England, which lagged behind the continent in being open to the influence of the Renaissance and its upgrading of vernacular languages, the status of English also lagged behind. In fact, writings in English remained controversial through the first half of the sixteenth century. As late as 1531, humanist scholar and lexicographer Sir Thomas Elyot advocated, in his *Boke named the Gouvernour*, that a nobleman's son should be surrounded from infancy by those who would "accustom him by little and little to speak pure and elegant Latin."

As the sixteenth century wore on, however, attitudes toward English changed, and many original English writings and translations from various other languages became increasingly available. The vocabulary used in such newly produced English-language works was set down by those who had studied under traditions still heavily influenced by the Latin scholarship of pre-printing days. These new works, therefore, included many words that had been borrowed from foreign languages and were unfamiliar to the new populations of readers of English, who had not themselves studied extensively under that scholarly tradition.

Making the vocabulary in the sermons and the books even harder for all readers was a sixteenth-century literary practice of using borrowed words from foreign languages (called *inkhorn terms*), which had infused English with an even greater number of hard words. Cawdrey alludes to such terms in his foreword "To the Reader":

> Such as by their place and calling, (but especially Preachers) as have occasion to speak publicly before the ignorant people, are to be admonished, that they never affect any strange "ynckhorne" terms, but labor to speak so as the most ignorant may well understand them ...

There were so many difficult words that in the year 1582, Richard Mulcaster — a student of language and a pre-eminent educator known as "the Father of English Pedagogy" (DeMolen, 1971) — sounded a call for an English dictionary:

It were a thing very praiseworthy in my opinion, and no less profitable than praiseworthy, if someone well learned and as laborious a man, would gather all the words which we use in our English tongue, whether natural or incorporate, out of all the professions, as well learned or not, into one dictionary, and besides the right writing, which is incident to the alphabet, would open unto us therein, both their natural force and their proper use. (p. 116)

The first clear answer to that call was *A Table Alphabeticall*, containing 2,500 words that Cawdrey defined as "hard and usual." By this he meant words that were foreign in origin but in current use in England.

Among Cawdrey's purposes, as stated on his title page, was helping his readers "more easily and better understand many hard English words, which they shall hear or read in Scriptures, Sermons, or elsewhere, and also be made to use the same aptly themselves." Those purposes were related to the circumstances produced by the Reformation — namely, the proliferation of both spoken and written English in religion, and the rise of new populations of readers of English. Such new reader populations, who emerged during the century after Caxton's first printing, were derived from several sources.

One source was the Protestant Reformation, which started and became fairly well entrenched during the sixteenth-century reign of Henry VIII and his daughter Elizabeth I. One aspect of the Reformation was the adoption of English in the place of Latin in official church services, which led to the increased importance of English. Moreover, in the interest of advancing the new religious doctrines, an enormous number of theological writings in English appeared; this quantity was made possible by the existence of printing. These added to the great variety of other books that burst forth during the first half of the sixteenth century. As a result, 54 different books were published in the year 1500; by 1557, more than 5,000 different books had been produced. They were sold at book shops and fairs, and were busily hawked by peddlers at least as early as 1521 (Davies, 1974).

The readers of those books were members of the new reading population, with the important subgroup of women, whose inclusion was another result of the Reformation. At this point, church services and congregational functions became fully open to women — some sects were soon to give women equal status. Women were now part of the general population that was served by a teeming educational establishment and that read the new theological works and other English writings (Davies, 1974).

Despite the greater acceptance and participation of women in religious matters and in general literacy, however, the grouping of women with "unskillful persons" was not unusual; others of the day less tactfully pointed out the poor quality of women's scholarship (Scragg, 1974).

At that time, even women of noble and upper-middle-class status were at a lower educational level than their social counterparts of earlier generations had been. Enlightened educators and Protestant reformers paid lip service to schooling for females. Yet what took place in practice was the :Puritan model of a family in which the father — rather than the church, with its scholarly traditions — was primarily responsible for both education and religion. In that model, women and girls were assigned clear-cut housekeeping roles. Moreover, the dissolution of the Roman Catholic convents had eliminated those sites as sources of women's scholarly attainment. At the same time, women were barred from the universities — the secular centers of higher education (Balmuth, 1988). These changes resulted in a greatly lowered level of education for all women, a situation that became visible at the end of the sixteenth century and was reflected in the female population that Cawdrey addressed.

Other groups of new readers arose as a result of the rise of international commerce and immigration. In England, the sixteenth century was an extraordinary time of busy worldwide exploration, colonial expansion, and much associated commerce. This circumstance brought about the rise of a commercial class, whose members lacked the full-time religious commitment of the scholars of the past, but were interested in secular knowledge and information. Members of that class added to the numbers of readers of English. In addition, there was much commerce and communication with foreigners to whom English was an unfamiliar tongue and who had been exposed mainly to relatively simple vocabulary. To these foreigners were added refugees who fled to England from struggles to establish the Reformation in various countries on the Continent. These groups were Protestant in religion and needed to understand the new language in which the religious teachings were communicated and in which every kind of writing was set down. Thus, Cawdrey saw among his readers a number of foreigners, to whom he refers as "right Honorable & Worshipful Strangers." Not only would these readers benefit from his definitions and the information about derivations, but, since they probably wrote as well as read the new language, they would also find useful "the true orthography, that is, the true writing of many hard English words."

Yet another audience identified by Cawdrey consisted of youngsters in school who were still expected to learn Latin. The fact that they were mentioned indicates that the goal of Latin instruction for young children expressed by Elyot (1531) and mentioned above had not been lost. Cawdrey wrote that by using the *Table*, "children may hereby be prepared for the understanding of a great number of Latin words." As a grammar school teacher, Cawdrey was clearly aware of the struggles of the young students in the classrooms of his day. Furthermore, as a school teacher — a thoughtful, imaginative one — he also understood the place of vocabulary in reading acquisition. Knowing the individual words was a way to facilitate the true goal of reading, which is underscored on the book's title page with the Latin sentence and its translation: "*Legere, et non intelligere, neglegere est.* / As good not read, as not to understand."

Also, at least as important as their understanding of hard words was their knowledge of correct spelling. Indeed, Cawdrey placed "writing" before "understanding" on his title page. By Cawdrey's day, the power of the printing press — with its multiple copies of any spelling patterns that had been decided upon by the printer — had served to regularize many spellings that in pre-printing-press times showed immense variation. However, the new borrowings, which tended to be multisyllabic and hence left ample room for misspelling, must have caused considerable concern in an age that was increasingly aware of "correctness." The foreigners who were called upon to write in English may have been especially concerned about spelling forms.

Format and Contents of *A Table Alphabeticall*

For all its historic weight, the *Table* itself is a slim, narrow volume. It starts with "Abandon, cast away, or yielde up, to leave, or forsake" and ends with "Zodiack, (f) a circle in the heaven wherein be placed the 12. signes, and in which the Sunne is mooved." A great asset is the accessible, uncluttered appearance of each page and of the volume as a whole. The strong, clear print with an overtone of Gothic black-letter script, the sensible spacings, the concise, often one-word defini-tions, and the informative yet unobtrusive derivation markings result in an appealing, engaging work.

The main body of the *Table* consists of 121 pages of lists of words and their definitions. These are preceded by a title page, two pages of dedications, and a four-page foreword, "To the Reader," in which Cawdrey discusses the purpose and structure of the book, tells the reader how to use it, and advises the reader about the use of language in gen-eral.

Cawdrey did not attempt to include all the words in the language; that goal was adopted by later lexicographers. Neither did he empha-size the frequency of words in the sense that we use today, namely, after the word count tradition of the Thorndike lists.

Cawdrey made a clear distinction between foreign and borrowed words, and it was the many borrowed words in written English that concerned him. He focused only on words that were "borrowed from the Greeke, Latine & French" and carefully indicated the original lan-guage of each. Thus, Greek-derived words were followed by "(g)," French-derived words were preceded by "(f)," and Latin-derived words were unmarked. In addition, certain words that were difficult to define succinctly were followed by "(k)," for *kind*, and their generic category, as with "abricot (k) fruit" and "azure (k) colour."

The definitions were intended to be in basic English, and Cawdrey tried to avoid synonyms or defining phrases that were themselves recent derivations. His hard words were to be found fairly frequently in formal writings, but apparently had not yet been fully absorbed into the spoken English of his time. His designations of origin were remarkably accurate, considering that the sophisticated etymological studies of later years were not available.

The words on the lists are in good alphabetical order, although in a few instances the sequence is incorrect beyond the third or fourth letter; for example, *denounce* is followed by *denominator* and *recreate* is followed by *recourse*. The alphabetic sequence itself is reflective of both the alphabet of its time and the phonics of the languages from which the hard words are derived. While the sequence is the same as ours today, Cawdrey listed no words beginning with *j, k, u, w, x,* or *y*. The letter *j* did not yet exist; that sound was written with an *i*, which was used as both a consonant and a vowel (*i*nclude, *i*ustified), in the manner of modern *y* (b*y*, *y*ellow). The letter *u* did exist, but was collapsed in the letter *v;* the *v* appeared consistently in initial positions and the *u* in medial and final positions, and both letters could represent either consonant or vowel usage (*violat, vnion, abou, subdue*). The letters *k, w, x,* and *y* did exist; they appear in earlier compilations, such as Mulcaster's *Elementarie* of 1582. Those letters, however, were not used in the three languages from which the hard words were derived and upon which the lists in the *Table* were based.

The forms of the letters in the Table varied; the lists were set in a mixture of different typefaces. The same letter might appear in the Gothic block-letter — similar to modern German writing — in one word, and in a typeface similar to modern roman type in another word. The preponderance were in Gothic block-letter, however. On the other hand, the title page, the dedication, and the Letter to the Reader excluded the Gothic block-letter altogether; they used a mix of italics and roman segments, with the roman predominating by far.

Cawdrey's Sources

I said earlier that Cawdrey's compilation had its origins in prior works. While the first known European dictionary of any kind seems to be the Homeric Lexicon, a glossary compiled by Apollonius the Sophist in the first century A.D., the roots of the English dictionary may perhaps be found in an exceedingly popular Graeco-Latin schoolbook of about 200 A.D., called *Hermeneumata psuedo-Dositheana*, which listed Greek words and their Latin equivalents (Lindsay, 1921). That interlingual listing was followed by other listings down through the centuries — with metamorphoses of the basic concept, in a range of glossaries, vocabularies, foreign-language-teaching manuals, and interlingual dictionaries — but all were translations from one language to another. For many years, the language translated was confined to Latin or (starting in the fifteenth century) Greek. In the sixteenth century, however, a large number of modern-language interlingual dictionaries appeared, stimulated to a great extent by the worldwide expansion and commerce noted earlier.

By Cawdrey's time, therefore, a variety of compilations was available. Among these, two stand out as Cawdrey's immediate sources. One, which seems to have been the primary basis of Cawdrey's book, was a section of Edmund Coote's *The English Schoole-Maister*, a language and grammar teaching manual written in 1596. Coote had also hearkened to Mulcaster's plea for an English dictionary, but only one section of *The English Schoole-Maister* was devoted to a dictionary-like listing. Coote had listed some 1,400 hard words, indicated their derivations, and given a brief definition for about two-thirds of them. Cawdrey seems to have filled out and broadened the definitions of this listing and doubled the number of entries. Most of the new entries and many definitions came from Cawdrey's other major source, a Latin-English dictionary compiled by Thomas Thomas around 1588 (Starnes & Noyes, 1946).

Cawdrey's Followers

In much the same manner as Cawdrey, the dictionary makers who followed him pulled together and enlarged upon earlier compilations. The maker of the second English dictionary, John Bullokar, based his 1616 book *An English Expositor* on both Cawdrey's book and Thomas's Latin-English dictionary, but he doubled the number of entries and indicated the field of knowledge to which technical terms belonged. Then, in 1623, Henry Cockeram borrowed heavily from Bullokar for his three-part work *The English Dictionary* (the first English language work called by that term).

After Cockeram's work, a chain of even more elaborate English dictionaries followed in orderly links down through the seventeenth century. One characteristic of that chain which must have caused bitter anguish in its time was the seventeenth-century lexicographers' tendency to "forget" their sources. That was coupled with a great deal of abuse of each other's works. There was, therefore, much recrimination and ridicule, characterized by accusations of plagiarism and vitriolic exposés of thefts and gross defects — only occasionally relieved by gracious citation of sources.

Yet these controversies and passions were a sign of the intense interest of the time in words and language, and of the growing pains of a whole new world of scholarship. They may also have been a reflection of the general turmoil that characterized the seventeenth century, which has been termed "a century of revolution" (Hill, 1961). That century began with the death of Elizabeth I in 1603, which was followed by a struggle between the newly rising, often Puritan middle classes and the autocratic nobility headed by the unpopular Stuart kings. It was the century of the British civil war and the beheading of Charles I in 1649. The establishment of the Commonwealth by Oliver Cromwell, the Restoration of the monarchy, and an ongoing war with France all added to the turbulence.

Just as the events of the century before the first English dictionary affected its rise and its form, so did the events of the seventeenth century have an effect on the eighteenth-century dictionaries. The seventeenth-century turbulence inspired a desire for order, and in addition, the rising middle classes were moved by a desire for authoritative information about correctness of behavior, including language. By the eighteenth century, the evolving English dictionary was ready to incorporate the format and features that would satisfy those desires. By then, too, the original motley collection of hard words had grown into a much more inclusive, elaborately defined compilation.

In the eighteenth century, talented lexicographers like John Kersey and Nathan Bailey both trimmed and expanded that compilation with increasingly scientific scholarship, always building on the work of their predecessors. On their work, especially Bailey's (1721), Samuel Johnson in turn built his 1755 *Dictionary of the English Language*. In response to the spirit of their age, Kersey, Bailey, and Johnson helped bring to the dictionary a high level of order and workmanship, and the people of that age responded gratefully. Enormous numbers of dictionaries were bought during the eighteenth century, and dictionaries acquired great authority, an authority that has not diminished. For most persons today, dictionaries and their makers are the final arbiters of meaning, spelling, and pronunciation.

Despite its small size and modest aims, it was the pilot work of Robert Cawdrey that generated all that followed. Moreover, in it can be found most of the elements of the modern English dictionary. As Peters points out in his introduction to the facsimile edition of the *Table*, "The format and legacy of that work persist to the present day, augmented only by amplification, pronunciation, accentuation, etymologies" (pp. v–xiv). And so, not only were the needy readers of his own day indebted to the *Table Alphabeticall* (four editions were printed in response to its popularity), but all of us, members of one "population" or another, benefit daily from the vision, assiduousness, and compassion that Robert Cawdrey embodied in his character and in his *Table*.

Afterword

Scholarship about the first English dictionary is useful in the way that all scholarship is useful — providing edification in and of itself. Because of its place in the history of English dictionaries, however, the *Table Alphabeticall* is also valuable in the way that it links past and subsequent domains of scholarship. It is like a double-sided mirror, on one side reflecting the word listings that came before and on the other previewing the dictionaries that were to follow. In accord with Chall's call for matching educational research with practice, the *Table Alphabeticall* might be incorporated in various ways into a modern classroom.

First of all, simply introducing the first dictionary as an artifact of its time and place would be useful in developing an understanding of the evolution of human endeavors. With advanced students or adults, explaining the factors that led to the setting down of the Table, as discussed in this paper, would provide concrete information about the social, cultural, and political setting of the years touched upon.

With respect to the Table as a dictionary, a teacher's awareness that the Table encapsulates most of what modern dictionaries include could lead to a comparison of the early volume with new ones. This would enable students to cut through the complex modern overlays and gain clear insight into dictionaries' basic purposes and format. Reinforcement of those concepts might entail having students compile their own "first" dictionaries by listing words that they consider to be "hard usual" English words. Working individually or in groups, they could develop simple definitions, or even devise one-letter keys to word derivations using a technique similar to Cawdrey's.

Students might also use the Table to study how the English alphabet, typography, and spelling forms have changed since Cawdrey's time. Because of the clarity and accessibility of Cawdrey's words, such study would be an excellent way to match past and current language forms. The seminal concept that the form of language changes over time would be made manifest in a clear, graphic manner.

The different typefaces that Cawdrey used could be a starting point for the study of various modern letter forms, penmanship, and calligraphy — with potential as well for an appreciation of modern-day graphic design. Choosing typefaces and graphics for students' own dictionaries could be a part of such study.

Bookmaking could also be studied, and the old-style formats of such conventions as the dedication, letter to the reader, and title page could be examined and compared to the formats of modern books. Students could prepare and design dedications, letters to readers, and title pages for hypothetical books intended for a variety of different audiences.

In fact, the idea of focusing on different audiences could be extended to compiling little dictionaries for populations other than that of the dictionary-maker himself or herself. In particular, in classes where there are students for whom English is not a first language, a parallel could be drawn with the "right Honorable & Worshipful Strangers" whom Cawdrey addressed. Modern vocabularies for "foreigners" could then be targeted to specific individuals or populations.

There is substantial potential for this first dictionary to be used by classroom teachers; indeed, such use would be highly appropriate. One of the pleasures of this examination of the *Table Alphabeticall* was becoming acquainted with the character and values of Robert Cawdrey. His was an enriched and noble soul, and that of a true teacher, profoundly gratified by helping others learn and grow. The result of that acquaintanceship is my certainty that using his little book in any way — and 400 years later! — would delight Cawdrey and fulfill his truest aspirations.

References

Bailey, N. (1721). *An universal etymological English dictionary*. London.

Balmuth, M. (1984). Early English dictionaries in historical perspective. *New Horizons, 24*, 124-132.

Balmuth, M. (1988). Female education in 16th and 17th century England. *Canadian Woman Studies/Les cahiers de la femme, 9*(3-4), 17-20.

Bullokar, J. (1616). *An English Expositor*. London.

Cawdrey, R. (1604). *A Table Alphabeticall*. London: Edmund Weaver. Facsimile edition with introduction by Robert A. Peters, Scholars' Facsimiles & Reprints, Gainesville, FL, 1966.

Cockeram, H. (1623). *The English Dictionarie*. London: H.C. Gent.

Coote, E. (1596). *The English Schoole-Maister* (1st ed.). London: Printed by the Widow Orwin, for Ralph Jackson and Robert Dextar.

Davies, W.J.F. (1974). *Teaching reading in early England*. London: Pitman.

DeMolen, R.L. (Ed.). (1971). *Richard Mulcaster's positions* (Classics in Education, No. 44). New York: Teachers College Press.

Elyot, T. (1531). *The Boke named the Gouvernour*. London.

Hill, C. (1961). *A century of revolution: 1603-1714*. New York: Norton.

Johnson, S. (1755). *A dictionary of the English language*. London: J. & P. Knapton et al. Reprinted by Times Resources/Arno Press, New York, 1980.

Lindsay, W.M. (1921). *The Corpus, Epinal, Erfurt, and Leyden Glossaries: Publications of the Philological Society VIII*. London: Oxford University Press.

Mulcaster, R. (1582). *The First Part of the Elementarie ...*, Thomas Vautroullier, London. Reproduced by Scholar Press, Menston, England, 1970.

Noyes, G.E. (1943). The first English dictionary: Cawdrey's "Table Alphabeticall." *Modern Language Notes, 58,* 600-605.

Painter, G.D. (1976). *William Caxton*. New York: Putnam.

Peters, R.A. (1976). Introduction. In Robert Cawdrey, *A Table Alphabeticall* (facsimile reproduction, pp. v-xiv). Delmar, NY: Scholars' Facsimiles & Reprints.

Scragg, D.G. (1974). *A history of English spelling*. Manchester, England: Manchester University Press. Published in the USA by Harper & Row, Barnes and Noble Import Division, New York.

Starnes, D.T., & Noyes, G.E. (1946). *The English dictionary from Cawdrey to Johnson, 1604-1755*. Chapel Hill, NC: University of North Carolina Press.

Thomas, T. (1588). *Dictionarium linguae latinate et anglicanae*.

Appendix:
Curriculum Vitae
of Jeanne S. Chall

EDUCATION

B.B.A. (cum laude) — The City College of New York, 1941.

A.M. — The Ohio State University, 1947.

Ph.D. — The Ohio State University, 1952.

A.M. (Hon.) — Harvard University, 1965.

L.H.D. (Hon.) — Lesley College, 1972.

CAREER SUMMARY

Assistant, Institute of Educational Research, Teachers College, Columbia University, 1943-1945.

Research Assistant to Research Associate and Instructor, Bureau of Educational Research, The Ohio State University, 1945-1949.

Instructor to Professor, The City College of the City University of New York, 1950-1965.

Lecturer and Reading Consultant, State University, New Paltz, New York, Summers, 1954, 1955, 1956.

Visiting Lecturer, Teachers College, Columbia University, Summers, 1958, 1960, Fall 1960, and Spring, 1961.

Visiting Associate Professor of Education, Harvard University, 1963.

Professor of Education and Director, Reading Laboratory, Graduate School of Education, Harvard University, 1965-1991.

Professor Emerita, Harvard University, 1991-present.

PROFESSIONAL ASSOCIATIONS

Fellow, American Psychological Association.

Fellow, National Conference on Research in English (President, 1965-1966).

Member, American Educational Research Association.

Member, Orton Dyslexia Society (Council of Advisors, 1988-present).

International Reading Association (Board of Directors, 1962-1965).

National Society for the Study of Education (Board of Directors, 1972-1977, 1978-1981).

ADVISORY COMMITTEES

National Reading Council, A Commission Appointed by the President and the Secretary of HEW, 1970-73.

Advisory Board and Consultant, Children's Television Workshop, 1968-present.

Commission on Reading, National Academy of Education, 1984-85, for the book *Becoming a Nation of Readers* (1985).

Secretary of Education's Elementary Education Study Group, 1985-86.

NAEP Technical Review Panel, Center for Education Statistics, U.S. Department of Education, 1987-88.

EDITORIAL BOARDS

Journal of Educational Psychology
Journal of Research and Development in Education
The Reading Journal
Reading Research Quarterly
The Harvard Education Letter

HONORS

Distinguished Alumna Award at the Centennial Celebration of Ohio State University, 1970.

Distinguished Alumna Award at the 125th Celebration of the City College of the City University of New York, 1973.

The National Reading Conference Annual Publication Award for an outstanding contribution to the field of reading education, 1975.

Honored by friends and students at CCNY, March, 1978.

Citation of Merit, International Reading Association, 1979.

Elected to the Reading Hall of Fame, 1979.

Distinguished Alumna Award from Ed Lums (Educated Alumni, Ohio State University), 1979.

The 1979 Andre Favat Award for distinguished service and contributions to the English language arts from the Massachusetts Council of Teachers of English.

Elected to the National Academy of Education, 1979.

Townsed Harris Medal from Alumni Association, The City College of New York, 1982.

American Educational Research Association Award for Distinguished Contributions to Research in Education, 1982.

American Psychological Association Edward L. Thomdike Award for Distinguished Psychological Contributions to Education, 1982.

Medal for Distinguished Service in Education, Teachers College, Columbia University, 1985.

American Education Research Association (Division B) Award for Distinguished Contributions to Curriculum Studies, 1986.

Distinguished Research Award, National Conference on Research in English, 1993.

Ohio State University Hall of Fame, 1994.

BOOKS

Readability: An Appraisal of Research and Application. Columbus, OH: The Ohio State University Press, 1958. Reprinted 1974 by Bowker Publishing Company, Ltd., Epping, Essex, England.

The Reading Crisis: Why Poor Children Fall Behind. Cambridge, MA: Harvard University Press, 1990. (With Vicki A. Jacobs and Luke E. Baldwin.)

Creating Successful Readers: A Practical Guide to Testing and Teaching at All Levels. Chicago: Riverside Publishing Company, 1994. (With Florence Roswell.)

Readability Revisited: The New Dale-Chall Readability Formula. Cambridge, MA: Brookline Books, 1995. (With Edgar Dale.)

Learning to Read: The Great Debate. New York: McGraw-Hill, 1967; Updated Edition, 1983. Fort Worth, TX: Harcourt Brace, Third Edition, 1996.

Stages of Reading Development. New York: McGraw-Hill, 1983. Fort Worth, TX: Harcourt Brace, Second Edition, 1996.

RESEARCH REPORTS

A Formula for Predicting Readability. Columbus, OH: Ohio State University Press, 1948. (With Edgar Dale.)

A Study in Depth of First Grade Reading: An Analysis of the Interactions of Proposed Methods, Teacher Implementation and Child Background. Cooperative Research Project No. 2728, U.S. Office of Education, 1966. (With Shirley C. Feldmann.)

An Analysis of Textbooks in Relation to Declining S.A.T. Scores. Prepared for the Advisory Panel on the Scholastic Aptitude Test Score Decline, jointly sponsored by the College Board and Educational Testing Service, June 1977. Princeton, NJ: College Entrance Examination Board, 1977. (With Sue Conard and Susan Harris.)

Textbooks and Challenge: An Inquiry into Textbook Difficulty, Reading Achievement, and Knowledge Acquisition. A Final Report to the Spencer Foundation, September, 1983. (With Sue Conard and Susan Harris-Sharples.)

A Report on Adult Literacy in Cambridge/Boston. Report to the President of Harvard University, May 1986. (With Elizabeth Heron and Ann Hilferty.)

TESTS

Roswell-Chall Diagnostic Reading Test of Word Analysis Skills. New York and La Jolla, CA: Essay Press, 1956, 1959, and 1978.

Roswell-Chall Auditory Blending Test. New York: Essay Press, 1962.

Diagnostic Assessments of Reading and Trial Teaching Strategies (DARTTS). Chicago: Riverside Publishing Company, 1992. (With Florence Roswell.)

SELECTED ARTICLES AND BOOK CHAPTERS

"The Encyclopedia as Educational Tool." *Teachers College Record,* 62, 415-419. February 1961.

"Estimating the Size of Vocabularies of Children and Adults: An Analysis of Methodological Issues." *The Journal of Experimental Education,* 32, 147-157. Winter 1963. (With Irving Lorge.)

"Restoring Dignity and Self-Worth to the Teacher." *Phi Delta Kappan,* 57(3), 170-174. November 1975.

"Statement of Dr. Jeanne S. Chall." *Basics Skills, 1979: Hearings Before the Subcommittee on Education, Art and Humanities of the Committee on Labor and Human Resources* (U.S. Senate, 96th Congress), pp. 366-377. Washington, DC: Government Printing Office, 1979.

"Reading." In H. Mitzel (Ed.), *Encyclopedia of Educational Research* (Vol. 3, 5th ed.), pp. 1535-1559. New York: The Free Press, 1982. (With Stephen A. Stahl.)

"Literacy: Trends and Explanations." *Educational Researcher, 12*(9), 3-8. November 1983. Reprinted in L.H. Golubchick and B. Persky (Eds.), *Urban, Social and Educational Issues* (3rd ed.). Garden City Park, NJ: Avery Publishing Group, 1988.

"The Influence of Neuroscience upon Educational Practice." In S.L. Friedman, K.A. Klivington and R.W. Peterson (Eds.), *The Brain, Cognition and Education,* pp. 287-318. Orlando, FL: Academic Press, 1986. (With Rita W. Peterson.)

"Adult Literacy: New and Enduring Problems." *Phi Delta Kappan, 69*(3), 190-196. November 1987. (With Elizabeth Heron and Ann Hilferty).

"Two Vocabularies for Reading: Recognition and Meaning." In M.G. McKeown and M.E. Curtis (Eds.), *The Nature of Vocabulary Acquisition,* pp 7-17. Hillsdale, NJ: Lawrence Erlbaum Associates, 1987.

"Learning to Read: The Great Debate 20 Years Later — A Response to 'Debunking the Great Phonics Myth.'" *Phi Delta Kappan, 70*(7), 521-538. March 1989.

"The Role of Phonics in the Teaching of Reading: A Position Paper Prepared for the Secretary of Education, Washington, DC." March 1989.

"Could the Decline Be Real? Recent Trends in Reading Instruction and Support in the U.S." In E. Haertel et al, *Report of the NAEP Technical Review Panel on the 1986 Reading Anomaly, the Accuracy of NAEP Trends, and Issues Raised by State-Level NAEP Comparisons,* pp. 61-74. Washington, DC: National Center for Education Statistics and U.S. Department of Education, 1989.

"Diagnostic Achievement Testing in Reading." In C.R. Reynolds and R. Kamphaus (Eds.), *Handbook of Psychological and Educational Assessment of Children's Intelligence and Achievement,* pp. 535-551. New York: Guilford Press, 1990. (With Mary E. Curtis.)

"Textbooks and Challenge: The Influence of Educational Research." In D.L. Elliot and A. Woodward (Eds.), *Textbooks and Schooling in the United States* (Eighty-ninth Yearbook of the National Society for the Study of Education, Part I), pp. 56-70. Chicago: University of Chicago Press, 1991. (With Sue S. Conard.)

"My Life in Reading." In D. Burleson (Ed.), *Reflections.* Bloomington, IN: Phi Delta Kappa, 1991.

"Reading and Civic Literacy: Are We Literate Enough to Meet our Civic Responsibilities?" In S. Stotsky (Ed.), *Reading and Civic Literacy: Historical and Contemporary Perspectives,* pp 39-59. New York: Teachers College Press, 1991. (With Dorothy L. Henry.)

"The New Reading Debates: Evidence from Science, Art, and Ideology." *Teachers College Record, 94*(2), 315-328. Winter 1992.

"The Reading, Writing, and Language Connection." In *Literacy and Education* (in press). Hampton Press. (With Vicki Jacobs.)

Index

About the Contributors

Marilyn Jager Adams, Ph.D., received her doctorate in Cognitive and Developmental Psychology from Brown University, and is currently a Visiting Scholar at the Harvard Graduate School of Education. In recognition of her work in beginning reading, she was given the AERA Sylvia Scribner Award for outstanding contributions to education through research. She is the author of *Beginning To Read: Thinking and Learning About Print* (MIT Press, 1990) and *Phonemic Awareness in Young Children* (Brookes, 1997). She has also developed two classroom programs: *Collections for Young Children* (Open Court, 1995) and *Odyssey: A Curriculum for Thinking* (Charlesbridge, 1986).

Miriam Balmuth, Ph.D., is Professor and Coordinator of the Graduate Reading Program at Hunter College, City University of New York. Her research and publications include histories of aspects of reading, writing, and teacher education for those for whom English is a second language. She recently completed a paper on the history of teacher education at Hunter College.

Nancy Birmingham is the Assistant Principal at the Sokolowski School, Chelsea, Massachusetts. She was previously a Title I teacher in Chelsea and spent one year in England as a Fulbright teacher.

Mary E. Curtis, Ph.D., became the founding Director of Boys Town Reading Center in 1990. Previously, she was an Associate Professor at the Harvard Graduate School of Education and Associate Director of the Harvard Reading Laboratory. She earned a Ph.D. in psychology at the University of Pittsburgh, and did postdoctoral work at the Learning Research and Development Center in Pittsburgh.

Edward Fry, Ph.D., is Professor Emeritus, Rutgers University. He currently spends his time being the publisher of Laguna Beach Educational Books in California.

Sheila Garnick is director of Title I programs in the Chelsea Public Schools, Chelsea, Massachusetts. She has been a member of the First Literacy League and specializes in the use of classroom demonstration and modeling in professional development.

Roselmina (Lee) Indrisano, Ph.D., is Professor of Education and Chairperson of the Department of Student Counselling at Boston University. She is the recipient of the University's Metcalf Award for Excellence in Teaching, and the University's Scholar-Teacher Award in 1956. Currently, she is a member of the Management Team for Boston University — Chelsea Public Schools. She is a Past President of the International Reading Association and was elected to its Hall of Fame, of which she also serves as President.

Vicki Jacobs, Ph.D., is Associate Director of the Harvard Teacher Education Program, where she lectures on education, curriculum development, secondary-school reading and writing, and teaching of English. Her background includes secondary and undergraduate teaching English and composition. She is an associate faculty member of the Bard Institute for Writing and Thinking. She is also co-author of the book *Reading Crisis: Why Poor Children Fail,* with Jeanne Chall and Luke Baldwin. She received her doctorate at Harvard Graduate School of Education.

Nancy Jordan, Ed.D., is Professor in the Department of Education Studies, University of Delaware. Her present research interests are in cognitive development and learning disabilities.

Ann Marie Longo, Ed.D., is an Associate Director of Boys Town Reading Center in Father Flanagan's Boys' Center. Her teaching experience includes elementary, secondary, and college levels. She received her doctorate from the Harvard Graduate School of Education.

Denise Keefe Maresco is a first-grade teacher at the Sokolowski School, Chelsea, Massachusetts. She worked with Nancy Birmingham to **initiate co-teaching as an approach to serving children in Title I programs within the classroom setting.**

Mateo Obregón, M.A., is presently directing a project in Technology and Education in Bogota, Colombia. He received his master's degree in Child Development from Tufts University and is working toward his doctoral degree in Cognitive Science.

Jeanne R. Paratore, Ed.D., is a professor at Boston University. Her current research interests are in family, literature, peer-led instruction and performance assessment. She recently won a three-year grant from the UtS. Department of Education to study the influence of family literacy portfolios and parent-teacher interaction.

Lillian Putnam, Ed.D., is Professor Emerita, Kean College of New Jersey, where she was Director of the Reading Clinic and taught courses in diagnosis and remediation of reading disabilities for twenty-five years. She is a former President of the New Jersey Reading Association.

Florence G. Roswell is Emeritus Professor of Education, City University of New York, where she taught graduate students and was the Director of the Reading Center. She has co-authored several books on reading and diagnosis of reading disabilities, as well as several diagnostic tests.

Wood Smethurst, Ed.D., is headmaster of the Ben Franklin Academy in Atlanta, Georgia, which he founded. His present interests include writing, research in reading, cats, roses, and expanding the school's rose garden.

James Squire, Ph.D., is a retired publisher who teaches courses in publishing at the Harvard Graduate School of Education and is a Senior Research Associate at Boston University. A former Executive Secretary of NCTE, he has been Professor of English at the University of Illinois, Director of Teacher Education at University of California, Berkeley, and a past president of NCRA and the Hall of Fame in Reading of the IRA.

Steven A. Stahl, Ph.D., did his doctoral work under Jeanne Chall at Harvard University. He is currently Professor of Reading Education at the University of Georgia. He is also a principal investigator at the National Reading Research Center in Athens, Georgia, and has authored many journal articles and chapters on issues of reading and vocabulary development.

Sandra Stotsky, Ph.D., is a Research Associate at the Harvard Graduate School of Education and at the Boston University School of Education. She directs a one-week Summer Institute on Writing, Reading and Civic Education, supported by the Lincoln and Therese Filene Fund. She currently serves as a consultant on the development of civic education curricula to Eastern European countries, and is also on the committee to develop English–Language Arts standards for Massachusetts.

Joy Turpie, Ed.D., is a teacher in the Hingham (Massachusetts) Public Schools.

Maryanne Wolf, Ed.D., is Associate Professor in the Eliot-Pearson Departrnent of Child Development of the NICHHD Center for Reading and Language Research at Tufts University. She is also a Fulbright Fellow and recipient of the Distinguished Teacher Award from the Massachusetts Psychological Association. Her research involves the study of reading and language disorders within the cognitive and neurological framework.